Mum and the Sothsegger

EARLY ENGLISH TEXT SOCIETY

Original Series, No. 199

1936 (for 1934)

that he hath graunt of his lyfe whyle god is in heuene
ffor þough men breme the borough þere þe bihine loggeth
Or elles hewe of þe heede þere he a hewe had
Or do hym al þe disease þat men deuise conne
yit wol he quikke agayne and quyte alle hise foes
And treede þürt þe gates þat ouer his toppe groued
And al þi world wede into waste tontime
And þerfore my conseil þough þe king þidre hit
And alle þe lordes of þis londe yiþ lite is my charge
ye to be at gone with trouthe and tayse hym nomore
leste he turke at þi tabart ere Aro yere been endid
Þut ye suffre his seruant to be sere wores
Among you in þe moneth leue yif ye more wol
ffoew stre you þe sothe þough ye shame thenke
ffor hit wol sauere yü month swete with ynne short after
wstenne fortune you siketh and falleth eller   whreo
And yif ye sauere on his salue and serue yrerafter
And eek writhe by his worke ye whole wol tonime
And eek chaunge his ronis of care and of sorolte
And tonime into tidelwe terme of yü lif
"   Ow is lieuer is hodre holsumly y made
And a merciable meynt of þe moste greet
And moost I haue y named 48 wrgh as I conthe
And þe condiaone declared of alle
Relier thing no yafaule ne yideris aboute
Þut he hymself is fountayn and so mote he longe
And þe gracioufist guyet goyng vypon erthe
With and wise worthir of deedes
Y kidde and y knowe and erminrig of werre
There fotw sightis þe felde ouer lieuith
And trustoth on þe tynne þe torathe shal hym helpe
A dougfitul doer in deedes of armes
And a comely knight y come of þe greetest
ffül of al vertue þat to a king longeth
Ef age and of al þing as hym best semeth
Þat hit be wel in his dares we more drede aftre
Iest þeereleos falle wytrynne fohw yees
Þut god of his goodnes þat gonneruith alle þing3
hym graunte of his grace to gorü wel þe worÿld
And to yeue þis yonurge in pees and in yest
And stable hã to stonde stille fü oure dares
Until dreed me fore sone god helpe
effe couetise of unseil þat knolweth nat hymself
f syuu and of certayn Iffeue not of iffe
Hit of profitable pensron spueth þe king ofte
ire his wate and his wit wrede wnight to þe beste

Mum and the Sothsegger

EDITED FROM THE MANUSCRIPTS
CAMB. UNIV. Ll. iv. 14
AND BRIT. MUS. ADD. 41666

BY

MABEL DAY

AND

ROBERT STEELE

LONDON:
PUBLISHED FOR THE EARLY ENGLISH TEXT SOCIETY
BY HUMPHREY MILFORD, OXFORD UNIVERSITY PRESS
AMEN HOUSE, E.C. 4

OXFORD
UNIVERSITY PRESS

Great Clarendon Street, Oxford OX2 6DP
United Kingdom

Oxford University Press is a department of the University of Oxford.
It furthers the University's objective of excellence in research, scholarship,
and education by publishing worldwide. Oxford is a registered trade mark of
Oxford University Press in the UK and in certain other countries

Published in the United States of America by Oxford University Press
198 Madison Avenue, New York, NY 10016, United States of America

British Library Cataloguing in Publication Data
Data available

Library of Congress Cataloging in Publication Data
Data available

Original Series, 199

ISBN 978-0-85-991933-3

TO

THE MEMORY OF

ISRAEL GOLLANCZ, Kt.

Director of the E.E.T.S.

1910–1930

THIS BOOK

WHICH HE HAD HOPED TO EDIT

IS DEDICATED

PREFATORY NOTE

WE have to thank the Oxford University Press for permission to use a number of Professor Skeat's notes to *Richard the Redeles* (nos. II 113, III 118, 140, 186, 249) which were not incorporated in the Early English Text Society's edition of that poem. The late Sir George Warner gave permission to use his text of Mandeville, Dr. J. P. Oakden allowed us to quote his analysis of the metre of R in his *Alliterative Poetry in Middle English*, Dr. George H. Fowler's 'Rolls from the Office of the Sheriff of Beds and Bucks 1332–84' threw much light on the legal questions involved, and Mr. W. Hancock's note on the keeping of bees supplied a corrective to the fancy of our poet. We feel under great obligations to each and all of them.

M. D.
R. S.

INTRODUCTION

IN the autumn of 1928 a west-country bookseller sent up to Messrs. Hodgson for sale a number of books, and with them a dilapidated manuscript, on which he set so small a value that he instructed the auctioneers not to return it if it proved unsaleable. Mr. S. Hodgson at once recognized its value, and Mr. Kenneth Sisam among others identified it as a poem hitherto unknown, and from its contents a part of the alliterative poem then known as *Richard the Redeles*. It was sold at Messrs. Hodgson's rooms in Chancery Lane,[1] and was purchased by the British Museum (with the aid of a grant from the Early English Text Society), where it now bears the number Additional MS. 41666.

In the condition in which it was sold, the manuscript consisted of nineteen leaves of poor vellum, enclosed in a parchment cover 11½ in. long and 8 in. broad. At one time it had been a fairly substantial volume, as the stiffening of its back showed that it had formerly been ⅞ in. thick. In the middle of the front cover the figure 8 suggests that it had probably formed part of a larger collection. On the last cover an inscription, 'The lyff off kyng Rychard the ij', in a fifteenth-century hand, was added by an early owner. There are scribbles on the other pages of the cover.

The manuscript had suffered much from damp. Large portions of the margins had fallen off through mildew, the first and last portions of the poem had been lost, together with two leaves from the middle between folios 15 and 16.

Henry Bradley[2] had long before pointed out that a fragmentary poem printed by Wright, and by Skeat under the title 'Richard the Redeles', was known to Nicholas Brigham under the title 'Mum, Sothsegger'[3]—the first words of the

---

[1] A facsimile of f. 11ᵃ was included in their sale-catalogue.

[2] He also suggested the emendation in III. 106 'cloyed' for 'cloþed', *Modern Language Review*, xii. 202.

[3] 'The rejection of the unity of authorship of the three texts of *Piers the Plowman* would of course involve the abandonment of Prof. Skeat's

English text corresponding exactly to the Latin version of them in Brigham's note.[1]

The identity of language and form between this fragment and the newly discovered poem, seems to indicate that the two fragments form part of one larger composition, and we have therefore printed the whole under one title ' Mum and the Soothsegger', taken from the marginal note to line M 205 (see facsimile). Some further considerations will be dealt with later.

Neither of these manuscripts can be accepted as immediate copies of the author's text. The first fragment (R) forms part of a miscellaneous collection of treatises, added to a latish copy of the B text of *Piers Plowman* in the Cambridge University Library Ll. iv. 14 ; the second (M) was probably copied in the second third of the fifteenth century, and annotated freely from other manuscripts of the poem.

This second fragment (M) consists of nineteen leaves measuring when perfect $10\frac{3}{4}$ in. $\times\ 7\frac{1}{2}$ in., the writing being in long lines, forty-six to a page, the script page being $7\frac{1}{2}$ in. high. It is written in a good book hand, probably by a professional scribe, and has been carefully corrected at different times and by different hands. There are a certain number of variations in the handwriting of the text, but none that cannot be attributed to the beginning of a new session of work. The ink is black and good, with the exception of that on f. 5[a], where the carbon has flaked off in part, and the ink faded. The annotations, on the other hand, whatever their date, have faded to a uniform light-brown tint, no difference being readily distinguishable.

almost universally accepted attribution of "Richard the Redeless" to Langland. An interesting fact, hitherto, so far as I know, unnoticed, is that Bale (Index, ed. Poole, p. 479) mentions the latter poem, under the title "Mum, Soth-segger!" (i.e. "Hush, truth-teller"). There can be no doubt of the identity of the piece referred to, for Bale gives a Latin translation of the first two lines. The title is certainly appropriate, and so picturesque that it may well have proceeded from the author. Unluckily, the poem appears to have been anonymous in the copy seen by Brigham ' (*Athenaeum*, Ap. 21, 1906, p. 481).

[1] ' Mum, soth segger id est Taciturnitas, verorum dictrix. Liber est Anglicus, qui incipit " Dum orans ambularem presbyteris altari astantibus, Bristollensi in vrbe ", etc. *Ex venatione Nicolai Brigan* ' (Bale's *Index*, ed. R. L. Poole, p. 479).

The study of these corrections presents some difficulties. None of them, with the possible exception of that to line M 180, is in a formal hand; they are in a 'common paper hand', and, as compared with Jenkinson's facsimiles of the scriveners' obligations, might have been written at any time in the fifteenth century or the first part of the sixteenth. One way of separating them into classes is founded on the way in which corrections are made. Quite half of them are indicated by putting a dot over the word in the text to be corrected, and another over the correction in the margin. These corrections are not all written at the same period or, if so, are not in the same hand, and we have provisionally marked them A, B, C, D. D may be in the same hand as A, but in a freer and more decided mood; and C has a great resemblance to D, but uses some different forms of his letters.

The other corrections are shown in different ways. In a few cases the passage seems to have been corrected by the original scribe, the correction being written in black ink like that of the text. This corrector we call M. These are interlinear corrections (491, 492, 824, 1356, 1621), words crossed out in black (386, 1183, 1528), and some ruled out with marginal correction, perhaps in a later hand (1, 841, 1177). A fairly large number are underlined, with a curl at the beginning marking off the words to be corrected; the correction is written in the margin, the ink is faded. This corrector we call N. They are 6, 78, 107, 116, 138, 179, 281, 283, 337, 345, 456, 610, 1044, 1425, 1437, 1572, 1651, 1721, 1741. A third method marks the spot for an insertion by a caret, the insertion being written in the margin or interlineated. This corrector we call P. A certain number of words are interlined in the text or written in the margins in at least two hands, probably of later date, which we attribute to S. One hand, S^1, is in 116, 138, 180, 377, 510, 535, 604, 623, 1179; the other, S^2, in 71, 115, 205. 454, 482, 505, 589, 1336, 1404, 1569, 1573, 1606, 1623. A few words are underlined for omission; these we put down as O. A few are corrected by the insertion of single letters (22, 384, 1042, 1044), their alteration (42, 1037, 1053) or interlineation (149, 765, 1343). These are called L. 1657 may be an Elizabethan explanation.

All of these corrections, with the exception of M, must have been made after the manuscript had left the scribe's hand. There must have been at least two subsequent correctors, and the process must have been carried on at fairly widely separated intervals. We do not feel justified in assuming that the corrections indicate with any certainty more than two other manuscripts of the poem, though the possibility of others must be reckoned with.

As there is an interval of several decades between the author's original manuscript and the one before us, the corrections may in some cases have been made from an earlier and more authentic text than our own. Our attitude towards these corrections has been conservative, e.g. only one of the many additional lines has been taken into the text (l. 1336) and comparatively few of the emendations. We have taken glosses which restored the alliteration, e.g. 106, 116, 368, 411, 456, and so on, and we have taken the gloss where the manuscript is obviously wrong, as 272, 343, 491, 589.

M is thus described:

Vellum, folio, 10¾ × 7½ in. 19 leaves. 46 long lines to a page. Blanks left for initials. Second third of fifteenth century. Collations and catchwords. Imperfect at beginning and end. Parchment binding 11½ × 8 in.

Collation in 8's.

a missing.

b 1–4 missing, 5–8 ff. 1–4.

c 1–8, ff. 5–12.

d 1–3, 4 and 5 missing ; 6–8, ff. 13–18.

e 1, f. 19 (all after 1 missing).

The collations are thus shown, c. 2. fo. (an unusual form).

The collation shows that about 1,104 lines are lost at the beginning, and all after l. 1751 at the end.

R (part of MS. Ll. iv. 14, Camb. Univ. Library) is thus described:

Paper, quarto, 11 in. × 8½ in., 160 ff., 35 long lines to a page. Initials in red. Collations and catchwords. Second third of fifteenth century.

Collation in 14's.

(1) a–h, 9 a (ff. 1–107ᵃ). The vision of Piers Plowman.

(2) h, 9 b–13 b.

 i, 1 a–7 b (ff. 107ᵇ–119ᵇ), Mum and the Sothsegger. 857 lines in all.

 i (8) (f. 120), blank.

 i (9–14), missing.

Nos. 1 and 2 are in gatherings of 14 leaves.

The remaining texts in the volume, nos. 3–9, are of a miscellaneous character and are written in gatherings of 8 leaves.

Nos. 6–9 are in a later hand.

The Piers Plowman of this manuscript follows Text B, group e, and is a copy of the Oriel MS.

SUMMARY OF M

As the scheme of our fragment is not at first sight apparent, a short summary may be of use.

The opening lines continue the poet's remarks on the authorities in Henry's household: I think that a professional truth-teller would be the most valuable of them all (99). But where is such a one to be found? No one dares to tell the truth about his people to the King or to his Council (205). I have drawn up a perfect scheme for the service of our King (231). 'You had better be silent', says Mum. 'I get on well with everybody. Do as I do.' I reply, 'You are self-seeking and allow the King to shame himself', and so we parted. I wondered at Mum's success, and set out to learn the truth about it from books (322), the Universities (327), the Seven Sciences (391), the friars (with a digression on their faults) (535), the monks (552), and the secular clergy. Mum advised me to let the clergy alone—tithes are a ticklish question (701)—'I will not, till I know more', said I. 'I can trust the clergy' (713). 'You are making a mistake', said Mum. 'The clergy have failed in their duty of exhorting princes not to quarrel' (766). 'Now you are talking sense', said I. 'Tell them of it' (774). 'I will have no more to do with you', said Mum. 'Keep out of the way of the clergy, and try the citizens and lords' (787). So I did, and found they all followed Mum. Everywhere Mum was master, so I sat down wearied, and slept for seven hours (870). In a fair country I dreamed of a gardener (954) who was killing drones from his bee-hives, and expounded the philosophy of bee-keeping (1086). I asked his advice about Mum and the truth-teller. He said, 'All the evil of the land comes from Mum' (1217). 'Where am I to find the truth-teller?' said I (1221). He described the Truth-teller's abode (1275). 'I must leave you and return whence I came', said the gardener ; 'write your book and send it to the King' (1287). On waking I reflected that dreams are sometimes true, so I set myself to my task, and here I lay open my bag (1343) full of complaints of the wrong-doing and folly of all classes : prelates, archdeacons, monks, women, spreaders of rumours (introducing the story of Jenghis Khan), jurors, suitors at law, maintainers, unlucky defendants, lords who detain the king's revenues, misers and their executors, believers in false prophecies, and of lamentation for the decline of clergy and knighthood from the ways of their forefathers.

PIERS PLOWMAN AND *MUM*

The first question that will arise in the reader's mind is the relationship between these poems. Prof. Skeat's opinion as to a common authorship is not generally received to-day, but there is undoubtedly a close connexion between the two poems. Phrases and whole lines of the earlier work are repeated in the later one. The verbal similarities between the two are, however, of varying degrees of closeness, and some consist of such common phrases that they may well be due to coincidence. Two facts emerge : (i) that almost all come from the earlier part of *Piers*, (ii) that nothing points to the C-text having influenced *Mum*, and much is against it. Only four similarities have been found in *Do Wel*, &c.—the phrase 'Poperyng on þaire palefrays', l. 1373, from A xi. 210 (not in B or C), and three from the part after the A-text comes to an end, viz. the occurrence of the rare word 'goky', the picture of the 'soleyn' sitting by himself at the feast, and the suggestion in ll. 1255 ff. of the siege of Unity by Antichrist.[1]

These may come from either B or C. Of the others, thirteen

---

[1] See Notes on ll. 830, 1255, 1582.

are found in all three texts;[1] four are found in A and C, but differ slightly in B : this is probably due to corruption in the text from which all the extant B-MSS. are derived.[2] In almost all the others, the passage is either omitted in C, or the resemblance is not so close as in the case of A or B.[3]

There is little or no sign of any imitation of matter peculiar to C; the expressions in ll. 130, 628 (see Notes on those passages) are common phrases, and are found in many other places. Two passages, ll. 1372, 1649 (see Notes), are nearer to A than to B or C ; against them we may set I. 35-48 and M 1470, where the closest connexion is with B. It is clear that no safe conclusion can be drawn from these as to whether our poet's text was of the A or B type. He was familiar with the earlier part, i.e. that covered by A ; the later he seems to have read, though he may have said of it, as he did of the bee-keeper's wisdom, ' hit is to mistike for me '.

THE AUTHOR

Apart from the facts that he was connected in some way with Bristol, that he had heard Henry's proclamation after his landing (M 147), and that he swore by the Rood of Chester, we have no personal information about our author, and we are driven to form some picture of him and his attitude to life from his work.

We may perhaps see in lines III. 212-15 a self-portrait of the author in the character of Wit :

> Well homelich yhelid in an holsum gyse,
> Not ouerelonge, but ordeyned in þe olde schappe,
> With grette browis y-bente and a berde eke,
> And y-wounde in his wedis as þe wedir axith.

At first sight there would seem to be much similarity between *Mum* and *Piers Plowman*. The writers of both are critics of the faults of the society in which they live. They

---

[1] II. 139, III. 172, III. 228 (also M 174), M 9, 17, 222 (also 1737), 366-7, 605, 874-5, 1017, 1367 (also 1666), 1369, 1577.

[2] III. 253, M 655, 703, 1646. See Prof. R. W. Chambers, *Mod. Lang. Review*, v. 26-7.

[3] P. 56, I. 35-48, III. 316, M 109 (also 1016), 876, 1289, 1456, 1649.

are emphatic on the duty of lawyers to help the poor gratis;
they bring the usual accusations against the friars, such as that
of ingratiating themselves by means of easy penances;[2] against
the bishops and higher clergy, of luxurious living;[3] against the
monks, of worldliness and avarice;[4] both have a dream-vision.
But much of this is common form, to be paralleled in almost
every writer of the time: the inspiration of the writers is
totally different. Langland is an impersonal prophet with a high
religious mission, uttering his denunciations for the most part
through the mouth of Piers. He has a divine sympathy with
the hardships of the poor, his hero is a ploughman, and poverty
is to him a holy state:

> Iesu Cryst of heuene
> In a pore mannes apparaille pursueth vs euere.[5]

Mum, on the other hand, is the outcome of a long-meditated
(P. 30) treatise on the Government of Princes, which the
author is willing to submit to the judgement of the king and
his counsellors before making it public (P. 61–2). His con-
ception of kingship is much more absolute than that expressed
in *Piers Plowman*, as we may see by comparing the contempt
the author feels for those of the commons who criticize the
king's government (M 1388 ff.) with such lines as

> Thanne come there a kyng, kny3thod hym ladde,
> Mi3t of the comunes made hym to regne,

and

> Quod Conscience to the kynge, 'but the comune wil assent,
> It is ful hard, bi myn hed, here-to to brynge it,
> Alle 3owre lige leodes to lede thus euene.'[6]

---

[1] Cp. P.P.A. Pr. 84–9, viii. 45-9, M 17-25.

[2] Cp. P.P.B. xx. 307-13, M 460-5.

[3] Cp. P.P.B. iv. 124-5, M 1370-5.

[4] Cp. P.P.B. x. 306-16, M 536-52, 1364-9. There is nothing in M
to correspond to the B-text's praise of the monastic life in B x. 300-5
and v. 169-77.

[5] B xi. 179-80.

[6] P.P.B., Pr. 112-13, iv. 182-4. Miss Chadwick (*Social Life in the Days
of Piers Plowman*, 1922, p. 40), quoting these passages, points out that the
two later versions emphasize the dependence of the king on the commons
more than the A-text.

The author himself was probably one of the lesser gentry, the service of whose body and beast was due to his liege (P. 47) even if his advice was not welcomed (III. 220). He is scandalized by the profusion of badges—which might, however, be given to the Judges (the collar of S's worn by the judges to-day is a Lancastrian badge)—and by the expense of law-suits and the illegal interference with them by the retainers of the King and the Lords. He must have had a close acquaintance with what happened at the meeting of Parliament in January 1398, and the absence of any reference to the representatives of the cities is evidence, as far as it goes, that he was a countryman.

One striking characteristic of our author is his feeling for scenery, as shown in the elaborate description of the view from the top of the hill given in ll. 876–931. Middle English poetry, as a rule, does not afford long nature-passages, and except in the case of Northern poets, confines itself to imitations of the *Roman de la Rose*. In *Piers Plowman* this traditional opening is reduced to the barest minimum; the mountain and valley and plain of the vision are only mentioned; the poet's interest is in the men on the plain. Again in B xi, where he looks from 'a mountaigne that Mydelerd hy3te' (l. 315), and there is opportunity for description, it is not taken :

I seigh floures in the fritthe and her faire coloures,
And how amonge the grene grasse grewe so many hewes,
And somme soure and some swete, selcouthe me thou3te ;
Of her kynde and her coloure to carpe it were to longe

(ll. 356–9), for he is interested in the moral, that beasts rather than men obey Reason. Observation of Nature appears in short similes, such as B xviii. 409–10,

'After sharpe shoures', quod Pees, 'moste shene is the sonne,
Is no weder warmer than after watery cloudes,'

where the parallel is drawn in the following lines,

Ne no loue leuere, ne leuer frendes,
Than after werre and wo whan Loue and Pees be maistres.[1]

[1] See also B xv. 94–100, xvii. 226–30.

But the detailed delineation of a landscape, for no ulterior reason, which we find here in the second fragment, has nothing like it in *Piers Plowman*, and is not easy to parallel anywhere in Middle English literature.

ONE POEM OR TWO?

The collation of M shows that approximately 1,104 lines are missing at its beginning, while the total length of R is 857 lines. There is, therefore, no *prima facie* objection to the assumption that R may form part of the lost beginning of M. When, however, we consider the scale on which R is planned the question presents itself: Can the maximum of 247 lines between the end of R and the beginning of M be considered sufficient for the close of the narrative about the January 1398 parliament, the banishment of Henry, his return, the deposition of Richard, the election of Henry, and the author's advice as to the constitution of his household which was, we must remember, the Civil Service of the country? Obviously not, if the poem has a narrative basis, or is arranged in historical order. If, however, we are to consider it as a treatise on the Government of Princes with illustrative examples written for the benefit of Henry, we may fill in the space between the fragments with a short conclusion dealing with the freedom of parliament and the beginning of an excursus on the choice of the great officers of State and the royal household (M 206).

Another difficulty is the division of R into *passus*, there being no trace of such a division in M. To this it may be objected that the divisions in R are not organically necessary to the plan, and that their number might be increased with as much reason for new divisions as for those existing. Moreover, a fairly satisfactory explanation of their presence is that they are due to a simple imitation of the Piers Plowman text in the same manuscript by the scribe. There is no definite authority for the division between the Prologue and the first Passus, while the other three are simply put in as marginal notes, and neither M nor his correctors have any idea of a division into Passus.

The most convincing argument for the unity of the poem is

the fact that the manuscript which Brigham saw in the sixteenth century began as R does and dealt with Mum and the Sothsegger at sufficient length to give a title to the whole. Of course what Brigham had before him might conceivably have been a codex containing more than one poem, but the evidence derived from metre, turn of phrase, use of the same text of *Piers Plowman*, and occasional use of rare words seems to show that R and M have the same author.[1] But we are still left with the difficulty that R is solely concerned with the causes of the deposition of Richard, while M leaves him altogether out of account—our manuscript was labelled on the cover 'The Lyff off Kyng Rychard the ij'.

Assuming, as we do, the identity of authorship, the second fragment shows a remarkable advance by the poet in mastery of his medium.

THE DATE OF THE POEM

It has been generally recognized that R was written after the execution of Scrope, Bushy, and Green on July 29, 1399, and the release of the Earl of Warwick in August of that year (see II. 152-4, III. 94 and the notes thereon). Since the author speaks of Richard as living, especially in P. 37-41, the date of this section of the poem may be placed before February, 1400.

For M we have only one fixed date—the execution of the friars at Tyburn (M 420). Richard, dead and publicly buried at Langley, was said to have escaped disguised as a beggar to Scotland, where he was recognized and taken under the protection of the Duke of Albany.[2] The rumour spread through England, and helped to crystallize a growing discontent.

As early as the Parliament of 1399 the Commons had begun to protest against Henry's expenditure and asked for an enactment that he should not make grants or bestow offices on any man without first taking the advice of his Council. In 1402, when the rumours began that Richard was alive in Scotland, popular feeling began to turn strongly against

---

[1] See pp. xlii–xlvi and notes on P. 45, I. 57, II. 25, III. 222-3, IV. 78, for the more striking parallelisms between the two parts.

[2] See Wyntoun, *Original Chronicle*, Bk. IX, ch. xx.

Henry; cp. *Cont. Eulog.* 389, 'Anno Domini 1402°, et anno
hujus Regis 3° populus cœpit Regem graviter ferre et Regem
Ricardum desiderare, quia dicebant quod ipse cepit bona
eorum et non solvebat. Literæ insuper venerunt ad amicos
Regis Ricardi tanquam ab eodem missæ quibus scribebatur
quod ipse viveret.' The plot was discovered through a
Franciscan friar from Aylesbury, who denounced one of his
fellows to the king for rejoicing in the news of Richard's
survival. This latter was hanged at Tyburn, together with
a secular priest who was involved in the conspiracy. A
Franciscan from Leicester then denounced ten friars and
a Master of Theology from his convent. Nine of these
were taken, together with the Prior of Laund and Sir Roger
Clarendon, an illegitimate son of the Black Prince, and
hanged at Tyburn. Since the men of London would not
convict, a jury had to be obtained from Islington and Highgate.
The fullest account of the trial is found in the *Continuatio
Eulogii* (ed. Haydon, Rolls Series, 1863, pp. 389–94); a shorter
account apparently based on it is in the *English Chronicle* (ed.
Davies, *Camden Society*, 1856, pp. 23–6). The *Chronicle*, ed.
Giles, 1848, p. 28, says that two Franciscans were beheaded
at Lancaster. See also Wylie, *History of England under
Henry IV*, I. xvi.

In the Parliament of September of this year the Commons
asked what had become of King Richard's treasure. Henry's
answer was that the Earl of Northumberland and others had
got it. The Commons pressed for an inquiry, which Henry
would not grant.

The amount of this treasure is thus given in *Lystoire de la
traison et mort du Roy Richart D'Engleterre* (ed. Williams,
1846, p. 104): 'Il fu premierement trouue en son tresoir ix°
mille nobles que valent xviii° mille escuz sans ses joyaulx, et
sans sa vaisselle qui en valoit bien autant ou plus. Et il fu
trouue on tresor du tresorier Dangleterre iii° mille escuz qui
valent cl mille nobles, sans ses joyaulx et sans sa vaiselle qui
en valoient bien autant ou plus, sans les joyaulx de la Royne
que son pere le noble Roy de France lui avoit baillie a
mariage.' The total value of the royal treasure was estimated
at the time at £700,000. The Percies, beyond their part of

this treasure, obtained the grant of the Isle of Man, the wardenship of the Marches, and subsequently many forfeited estates. The loss of this sum, which may be taken to be the working capital of the Royal administration, meant continual embarrassment to Henry for the next few years, since the theory of the constitution at the time was that the revenues of the Crown should suffice for all the ordinary expenses of the king's household, i.e. the administrative expenses of the nation.

In the Parliament of 1404 complaints were loud against the king's extravagance, particularly in his household expenses. The Commons forced him to dismiss his confessor and other members of his court, besides the queen's foreign servants, and petitioned that the household should be made up of 'persones honestes & vertuouses' (*Rot. Parl.* iii. 525). In reply to the petition of the Commons that all grants and pensions since 1367 should be resumed, the king diplomatically answered, 'And for als muche that the Comunes desiren that the Kyng shulde leve upon his owne, as gode reson asketh, and alle Estates thynken the same, the Kyng thanketh hem of here gode desire, willyng put it in execution als sone as he wel may' (*Rot. Parl.* iii. 549, cp. M 1667, 'But of his owen were þe beste').

In 1406 there were similar complaints; the Speaker declared that the household was 'meyns honurable & plus de charge q̃ ne soloit estre, & unqore y ne ad null substance des persones vaillantz & suffisantz, si bosoigne y serroit, mes de raskaile pur la greindre partie' (*Rot. Parl.* iii. 577). It will be noted that the very word 'rascaille' is used in M 210, as if in protest against this accusation. After he consented to the 'thirty-one articles' of constitutional reform drawn up by this Parliament, his financial position ceased to give him trouble, and in the Parliament of 1407 the Commons even asked that better provision should be made for the lords Thomas, John, and Humphrey, and the king thanked them for the 'grande naturesse & entiere affection' they had shown to him (*Rot. Parl.* iii. 612). He did not call another parliament till 1410. It appears therefore that this part of our poem belongs to the period 1402–6, more probably towards the latter part of it.

The story of Jenghiz Khan (M 1413–56) taken from

Mandeville is not so irrelevant as it might appear. On the resignation of Richard there was several days' delay while the method of giving a parliamentary title to Henry was debated. The situation was complicated by the fact that the title of the Earl of March as Richard's successor had already been recognized in parliament. Henry cut short the hesitations by announcing a claim to the throne by conquest, a claim which would involve a surrender of all titles and lands not re-granted by him. He was then elected on the joint grounds of succession and conquest, whereon he declared that each and all his lieges should hold their lands and possessions as they had up to then held them, with all their rights and liberties, with the exception of those who should forfeit them by law (*Rot. Parl.* iii. 416–24).

From the first months of his reign Henry had trouble with the great nobles of the realm. The earls of Kent and Huntingdon and Salisbury attempted a rising in January, 1400, and were slain, while many of their adherents were executed as traitors. Conspiracies were going on all the time in Wales and the North. Northumberland and his son Henry Hotspur had been made Wardens of the West and East Marches, but after they defeated the Scots at Homildon Hill in 1402, they quarrelled with Henry over the money due to them for the defence of the Marches, and the disposal of the prisoners taken at Homildon, and entered into communications with Glendower and Mortimer, with the object of deposing Henry in favour of the Earl of March. They were encouraged by Scrope, Archbishop of York, and Skirlaw, Bishop of Durham; but Westmorland, Northumberland's most important rival, stood aloof. At the battle of Shrewsbury, in July 1403, Henry defeated the rebels; Hotspur was killed in the fight, and Worcester and others were beheaded.

The slaughter of all the eldest sons of his nobles by Jenghiz Khan in the story, and the taking into his own hand of all their lands, is used by the author as a contrast to Henry's treatment of Northumberland. For when Henry had been put on the throne by Northumberland's help, he rewarded him and his family lavishly. Yet in 1403 they joined with Mortimer and Glendower in warfare against him. After Shrewsbury (where Hotspur was killed), Northumberland threw himself upon Henry's mercy. The king imprisoned him and took possession of his castles, but after a short time his liberty and his estates were restored to him. The result of this clemency was that Northumberland was able to organize the rebellion of 1405 (in which Henry made trouble for himself by beheading the Archbishop of York), and was a continual stirrer-up of strife until he was killed at Bramham Moor in 1408.

Jenghiz Khan may well have had a topical interest at the time this part of the poem was written. For in July, 1402, Timur (or Tamburlaine), said to be his descendant, defeated the Turks at Angora, and got all Western Asia into his hands. In the winter of 1402, an English Dominican friar, called Greenlaw, who held the title of Archbishop of Ethiopia and the East, and acted as intermediary between the courts of Europe and the Eastern potentates, came to England with letters from Timur, informing Henry of his victory over the Turks, and offering welcome and protection to English traders. In February, 1403, he returned with letters from Henry to Timur (Wylie, *History of England under Henry IV*, I. xxi).

The relevant passage from Mandeville is given in Appendix II, p. 82–3, the French text being chosen because it contains the word 'seruitute' (p. 82, l. 4), which MS. Cotton Titus C. xvi translates by 'seruage', and MS. Egerton 1982 by 'thrall'. Our poem preserves the same word in M 1422.

In M 1723–33 we find a reference to the currency of prophecies such as those of Merlin or the Monk of Bridlington. Hall's *Chronicle*, under the third year of Henry IV, tells us: 'Here I passe ouer to declare howe a certayne writer writeth that this earle of Marche, the Lorde Percy and Owen Glendor wer vnwisely made belieue by a Welch Prophecier, that king Henry was the Moldwarpe, cursed of Goddes owne mouth, and that they thre were the Dragon, the Lion and the Wolffe, whiche shoulde deuide this realme betwene them, by the deuiacion and not deuination of that mawmet Merlin.'[1]

---

[1] The prophecy in question is found in a Northern form in MS. Cott. Galba E. ix, and is printed by J. Hall in the second edition of Minot's poems. A prose version is incorporated in the *Brut of England*,

In January, 1408, Northumberland made his last attempt. Followed by a few Scotch auxiliaries, he raised the standard of rebellion at Thirsk, and at Bramham Moor they were defeated by Sir Thomas Rokeby, and Northumberland was slain. In ll. 727–42 is a mention of the part that should be played by the higher clergy in restraining the anger of princes. If this is to be referred to any particular event, and not to the general attitude of the northern clergy, we might connect it with Shrewsbury, the rising of Scrope with the Earl of Nottingham in 1405, or Bramham Moor in 1408, when Northumberland was joined by the Bishop of Bangor, the Abbot of Hailes, and the Prior of Hexham. The first two are the more probable, as by 1408 Henry's financial position was more settled than the rest of the poem suggests. It is noteworthy that in ll. 1465–8 it is said that it was the disaffection of the people which turned the Percies from their duty of defending the Marches against the Scotch, and in l. 1723 the same suggestion is made.

Taken as a whole the allusions to current affairs agree very well with our estimated date of 1403–6 for the composition of the poem.

LITERARY SOURCES

Our author shows no traces of exceptionally wide reading or of university training. Cato, from whom he quotes, is a school book for beginners in Latin, the Bible texts he uses could all be gathered from the services of the Church, and Solomon, Sydrach, and the others are part of the ordinary proverb literature current at the time. The two books he had used

E.E.T.S. 131, p. 72. The poem speaks of Henry IV as the moldwerp 'weried with Goddes mowth', who will be overcome by the combined attack of the dragon, the wolf, and the lion. When the moldwerp has died an evil death, the land will be divided in three. Latin texts are quoted in *Archaeologia* xx. 256-9; MS. Bodl. 1787 speaks of the 'talpa ore dei maledicta'. After its death the land will revert to the ass (Richard II), or, in another version, to the ass or the boar or the dragon or the lion.

With regard to the prevalence of prophecies, cp. the account of the friars' conspiracy of 1402 in the *Cont. Eulog.* p. 391, where the Master of Theology of Leicester 'confessus est se exposuisse prophetiam quæ dicitur cujusdam canonici de Bridlington, juxta imaginationem suam '.

are the *Voyages* of Mandeville and the *De Proprietatibus Rerum* of Bartholomew the Englishman. Even his knowledge of this latter book is rendered doubtful by his calling him Bartholomew the Bestiary. There is a well-known work called ' Bestiarius ', but Bartholomew is nowhere else referred to under that name. The author may have picked up his knowledge from some clerk of his acquaintance and altered it to suit his own purpose. At any rate it is ultimately from Bartholomaeus that the account of the habits of bees in ll. 976–1086 comes (see Appendix I, pp. 79–81). It is notable that our poet eliminates all references to warfare among the bees, or comparisons with the life of an army. The army sentinels (see p. 79, l. 18) become magistrates in ll. 1012–13 the king's progress in the midst of his band of knights who encircle and defend him (p. 80, l. 24) is turned in ll. 1038-9 into a country excursion to admire the face of Nature. In XII. iv Bartholomaeus tells how the bees divide themselves into parties under different kings. If they find themselves in a minority, they forsake their king and go to the king who has more bees, and if their former king pursues them, they kill him. This interesting parallel our poet makes no use of.

The killing of the drones by the bee-keeper is not mentioned by Bartholomaeus, but it is recommended by FitzHerbert in 1523 (see Note on l. 968).

We have already referred to the use of Mandeville. There are quotations in the marginal notes from St. Gregory and the Civil Law ; but they, too, are commonplaces requiring no knowledge of sources even if we accept them as supplied by the author. His Seneca is neither the Roman philosopher nor the correspondent of St. Paul, but the author of the moral sentences which were really written by Publius Syrus, in use as a school reading-book, together with the more popular *Distichs* of Cato—a third-century moralizer (see Note, p. 110). Solomon, Sidrac, and Seneca are associated in lines 304–5 and l. 1212.

By Solomon the middle ages understood all the Wisdom literature, as in *Melibeus* 2249–50, where two passages from *Ecclus.* are assigned to Jhesus Syrak and Salomon respectively.

One form of the book of 'Sydrac le philosophe' tells how 847 years after Noah, Sydrac, astronomer to the Eastern king Tractabar, was sent by him to the help of Boccus, king of Bactorye, a country bordering on India. With the assistance of a book of astronomy which was made by an angel and had belonged to Noah, Sydrac protected Boccus from his enemy, and then converted him to the Christian faith. Boccus asked him 365 questions, which begin with 'yf god was euer and euer shall be', and include such subjects as no. 243, 'How shal a man of his throte wyn a bone or a thorne'. The book was translated from French into English by Hugo of Caumpeden, and printed *c.* 1510.

THE LAW COURTS AND THEIR ABUSE

The way of the medieval litigant was hard. At the time of which we are writing every step in a lawsuit had long been settled by precedent, and any mistake in procedure was fatal to his claim. But our author makes no complaint of this; it is interference with settled procedure that is his grievance. A short account of this may be of use.

Up to the period of the Black Death, speaking roughly, the machinery of justice comprised the King's Court at Westminster and the Judges on circuit, the Sheriff as the royal executant officer, and the County Court, in which the Sheriff presided, the Hundred Courts in which he, his deputy, or an official of the grantee of the Hundred presided, and the Courts Baron and Leet, more strictly manorial. The jurisdiction of the County Court, at first criminal and civil, had long been restricted to civil cases unless under a special writ directed to the Sheriff. Usually the Sheriff's power to try lesser criminal offences was exercised through the Hundred Court when he made his Tourn. By the time of our author the jurisdiction of the County Courts had almost fallen into disuse, except for occasions when the whole County was called together for elections, &c.

The rival organization was that of Quarter Sessions, established in 1363. Justices of the Peace under various names had been appointed long before, but it is only in the later medieval period that their powers were consolidated and their jurisdiction extended. Among their powers was that of restraining abuses of Purveyance, and in the first year of Henry IV they were empowered to punish the giving of liveries or the retaining of any except household servants or men learned in the Law. The sessions, too, gradually superseded the old County Courts as the place where County business was done. At Quarter Sessions trials were carried on with a strict observance of all the rules as to procedure and pleading of criminal law.

Above them all were the King's Courts at Westminster, and by these all serious cases were heard and determined, either by the Judges sitting there, or by the Judges on circuit, the cases being heard at Westminster, *nisi prius*, i.e. unless they could be tried earlier by the circuit Judges at the assizes.

Every action in the King's courts must be started by a Writ in the King's Name obtained in the Chancery—the Original Writ. The form of this writ varied with each recognized wrong, and great care was necessary to see that the proper writ, in its settled legal form, was chosen from the considerable number in the repertory of writs. The writ was directed to the Sheriff of the County in which the suit arose, and should properly be (but was not always) under seal, as otherwise the Sheriff was under oath not to accept it. If a writ which did not disclose the cause of action were selected, the litigant was liable to be fined, and must start afresh. A puzzled plaintiff might well feel aggrieved at such a result, and put it down to the fact that he had failed to bribe the judge (III. 307).

To obtain his original writ a country litigant must either make the journey to London himself or act through an agent. It appears that a class of persons had grown up in the fourteenth century, who acted as the modern solicitors for country litigants, with perhaps agents at the County Courts or Sessions, or, on the other hand, the Sheriff and his messengers may have acted as intermediaries. The cost of a writ from the Chancery was fixed at one penny for writing and sixpence for sealing, together with a fine varying in amount with the property involved, a part of the fine going to the clerks who prepared the writ. Provision was made for the free writing of the original writ for poor persons by the Clerks in Almonry, but it will be seen that 'the writing of writtz and þe waxe eke' (25, cp. 649) would be no great boon by itself if remitted, unless the fines were abolished.

The Sheriff of the County as the King's representative was the chief officer of justice, and through his hands all the execution of justice passed. His clerk wrote and sealed acquittances and was in charge of all writs, supervising the delivery of them to the messengers and their return to the Court. The Sheriff normally appointed the Bailiffs of Hundreds, whose business it was, among other things, to serve all writs relating to their Hundreds on the persons involved, and to take pledges for their appearance in court. The Bailiff was paid by those on whose behalf he acted, but his office facilitated illegal exactions, such as extortion by illegal arrest or distraint, bribes for non-service of writs, for exemption from service on juries, and escape of guilty defendants. Other officers of justice were the constables, &c., at the command of the justices of the peace.

On receipt of the original writ from Chancery the Sheriff's duty was to hand it to the Bailiff for execution. In the case, for example, of a complaint of trespass with violence, the Bailiff would proceed to attach the defendant, taking two pledges as bailsmen for his appearance at Court on a given date. Most likely he would not appear at all, making some excuse (*essoin*), whereon a small fine would be imposed, and the case adjourned. Dr. Fowler gives cases in the late fourteenth century where one defendant has made default forty-one times and another forty-eight. There were, however, means of enforcing attendance when all excuses for default were exhausted. A Distraint could be levied on all the defendant's goods and chattels, and this failing, a writ of Caption could be issued for his arrest.

The King's Court was always able to remove any action from the County Court by a special writ, and our author complains of this (M 1590) as a frequent cause of injustice when an unimportant case is transferred into the King's Courts, and a Distraint or pledges levied on the defendant's stock. At the hearing the action, begun by a writ, is explained by a statement of claim, the Narration, and if this narration varies in the slightest degree from the writ, claiming either more or less, the plaintiff is non-suited. Evidence is then called on both sides, and the jurors selected by the sheriff give their verdict under the judge's direction. But the squires who act as jurors will not give any verdict against a great man who has wronged a poor neighbour (M 1490 ff.), and the justices are often in the pay of the great. Maintenance, backed up by perjury (not then punishable by law), seems to have been universal, and the moral support of a great lord to a litigant was often manifested by a demonstration of armed force at the trial.

Our author describes the royal justices on circuit (III. 301) who should imprison the oppressors of the poor commons ; they expect presents before the plaints are called, and all the bills of complaint which will become indictments if they pass the grand jury are thrown out and brought to naught, while any resentment may incur risk to life and limb. 'Chiders from Chester' were brought into court armed, clamouring for an immediate settlement in their client's favour (III. 328), with perjured witnesses and threats. The form of a lawsuit was often used to legalize a change in the ownership of land. A suit was brought and an amicable settlement was made—a 'final concord' between the parties. This was known as a 'fine' and the records of such settlements were preserved as 'feet of fines'. It was such a settlement that the 'Chiders from Chester' terrorized the unfortunate suitors into making.

Even if a judgement in his favour were obtained, the litigant had little hope of any speedy result. Exceptions and delays could be multiplied by the unsuccessful litigant with a skilful adviser, and our author writes unhopefully of the miracle that it would be if for one year cases could be finally settled and fines and costs paid before another action was begun (M 1607 ff.). Readers of the *Paston Letters* will remember Justice Paston's advice in 1440 to a friend as to going to law with a client of the Duke of Norfolk (i. 42) and the collection of *Select Cases before the Council* (Selden Society) throws much light on the maladministration of justice throughout the century.

PHONOLOGY.

By his own statement, the author of the poem belonged to Bristol, and the dialect of both parts appears to belong to the S.W.M. Though the orthography of M is a good deal later than that of R, and its exclusive use of the pronouns *their*, *them* places it about 1450 or later, it retains much more of the western rounding than does the earlier fragment, and indeed than any extant fifteenth-century document.

The first characteristic to note in R is the unprofessional nature of the spelling. The scribe spells as he pronounces: *who* is always *ho*; *-out* (or *-ouut*) and *-ou3t*, *-aut* (*-auut*) and *-au3t* are used indifferently. Doubled consonants are frequent, both (i) after short vowels, finally[1] and in open syllables, as *wonneth*, III. 282, *stall*, pt. 3 s., II. 164, *satte*, III. 346, and (ii) after vowels long in ME. In some cases it seems impossible that they should be a mark of shortening, and more probable that the double letter is a meaningless scribal flourish: *written*, inf., P. 31, *kuyttis*, II. 158 (cp. *kyte*, II. 178), *lyff*, P. 43, &c., *coyffes*, III. 320, *townnes*, I. 15. The other cases are as follows: *betwynne*, II. 85; *cheff*, II. 114, III. 203, *cheffeteyne*, II. 114; *mysscheff*, P. 22, &c. (cp. *cheef*, I. 88); *chesse*, pt. 2 pl., I. 88; *co(u)nceill*, I. 7, &c.; *sumdell*, P. 55; *halfdelle*, IV. 2; *fotte*, III. 108; *frelle*, P. 83; *gette*, III. 183, III. 356; *grett(e)*, passim; *grott*, P. 35; *y-hotte*, III. 228 (also *hote*); *juellis*, I. 38; *patthis*, II. 24; *repreff*, P. 56 (cp. *preifis*, P. 17); *ryffled*, I. 16; *riffleris*, III. 197; *roff*, III. 248; *rosse*, P. 13; *schappe*, III. 213, III. 236; *secrette*, P. 61; *stouttely*, I. 114; *trifflour*, III. 118; *þroff*, III. 137; *welldith*, III. 297; *wotte*, II. 94; *wytteth* (OE. wītan), I. 80.

The shortening of *ǣ* shows variety. From PG. *ai* we have *ladde*, equally with *led(dyn)*, *lafte* (also *lefte*), *lesse*, *ment*. PG. *ǣ* gives *dradde* (but cp. *dride*, n. I. 11), *lente*.

a before nasal always remains, except *ony*, passim, *monside*, III. 105.

and > *ond*, except *standith*, I. 10.

[1] Final *-e* has no syllabic value to the scribe, and is used indiscriminately, *e.g. londe*, P. 12, *rosse*, pt. 3 s., P. 13, *kynge*, P. 24. Similarly in M we have *kepte*, 1, *y-herde*, 29.

ang > *ong*, except *hangith*, III. 139, *hangid*, III. 318.

y is regularly unrounded, even in *byrthen*, II. 66, *chirche*, P. 4, *miche*, I. 21 (otherwise *mcche*). The only remains of rounding are *lustiþ*, III. 38 (otherwise *list*, and probably influenced by the noun *lust*), *kuyttis*, II. 158 (also *kyte*). *e* is found only in open syllables : *meri*, *besieth*, *besely*, *sterede* (also *stireth*) ; *werche*, *werchinge* (3 times, against *worchen* once), *ferthere*, IV. 48 (otherwise *forther*), are influenced by *werk*, *fer*. *wyr* > *wur* in *worchen*, III. 316, *yworewid*, III. 72, *wormes*, III. 20. Early ME. rounding remains in *woll*, passim, and *wuste*, I. 49, I. 64, equally with *wiste*.

French *ü* has undergone an early unrounding in *hirte*, III. 89, and has become *u(o)* in *coriouse*, III. 163. *Pore*, II. 32, was probably understood by the scribe as 'poor', cp. IV. 13. The spellings *repeute*, P. 19; *plewme*, II. 163; *constrew*, III. 35, indicate the E.M. change of *ü* to *eu* or *iu*. In M these forms are only used in words which derive from OF. *eu*, as *reule*, *deuely*, etc.

OE. *ēo* retains rounding in *leode(s)* twice (also *lede*), and *hue*, III. 50, if not a scribal error for *hen*. The French rounding is preserved in *meuve*, P. 32, but regularly *meve*. *weor* > *wur* in *wurschepe*, I. 97, *worthy*, IV. 52, *world*, III. 205 (but *werld*, III. 298 and *werkis*, P. 18, P. 87). *Burne(s)* occurs twice, and *berne* once. *eow* > *ou* in *trowe* (verb) and *trouthe*, but *eu* in *trewe* (adj.) and *trewly*.

e > *ei* before *sh* in *fleissh*, III. 16 (also *flessh*, P. 83). Luick considers it possible that this diphthong maintained itself longest in Oxfordshire (*Hist. Gram.*, § 404, also Jordan, *ME. Gram* , § 284).

i > *e* in open syllable : *lemes*, II. 156 (also *lymes*, II. 62) ; *leue(d)*, III. 25, III. 290 ; *pete*, P. 23, &c. ; *preson*, III. 271, III. 303; *preuy*, II. 192; *preuyly*, P. 71, &c. ; *reden*, I. 53 ; *wekes*, III. 165; *wete*, III. 205. *Leuere* is found regularly, corrected in the margin to *lyuerey* ; *bredd*, II. 141, &c., equally with *bridd* ; *grennes*, II. 188.

e > *i* in closed syllable before dental ; *mystirmen*, III. 335 ; *yistirday*, III. 261.

er > *ar* only in *parceit*, P. 17.

ẽ (both close and open) is written *ei* in (i) *greyues*, IV. 38;

preifs, P. 17 ; (ii) *forweyned*, I. 27 ; *heipeth*, III. 42 ; (?) *leyne*,
II. 136. This spelling is found occasionally in Wyclif, London
charters, and the Paston Letters, see Dibelius, 'John Capgrave
und die englische schriftsprache', *Anglia*, xxiii. 169–70.
Zachrisson (*Pronunciation of English Vowels, 1400–1700*,
pp. 64–5) suggests that, seeing it is found in southern manuscripts which do not use *ai*, *oi* for *ā*, *ō*, it is an analogical
spelling after the pattern of such French words as *deceive*.

Signs of the change of *ẹ̄* to *ī*, which began about 1400 (see
Luick, *Hist. Gram.*, § 480) are found in *dride*, I. 11 (also
drede, P. 7, and cp. *dradde*); *fyldis*, II. 157 (also *feldus*, III. 87).
There is no sign of the corresponding change *ọ̄ > ū*; *muste*
and *wulde*, I. 60, I. 63, arise from *ŏ* influenced by initial labial.

Consonants. *wh* and *w* are misplaced in *wyle*, P. 10, and
whare, III. 150, *where*, P. 15, II. 128, III. 254, III. 317
(also *while*, *were*). 'Who' is always *ho*, though 'whom' never
loses *w*. Initial *h* is omitted in *armen*, III. 18, and added in
hauntelere, II. 128.

The spirant (*gh, ȝ*) is often omitted after a back vowel and
before *t*, e.g. *oute*, P. 47; *wroute*, I. 43; *brouute*, II. 9; *drawte*,
III. 229; conversely it is inserted in *couȝthe*, P. 49; *abouȝte*,
I. 40, II. 102 ; *fauȝte*, II. 63, &c. After *i* there are no such
forms ; *ȝt* is often spelt *th* or *ȝth*: *riȝth*, I. 37 ; *rith*, I. 102, &c.
(there are no other spellings of this word); *myȝth*, II. 181 ;
also after *ou*, *wrouȝth*, II. 192 ; *brouȝth*, III. 85. Hence in the
scribe's language the back spirant was lost, while the front
spirant seems to have remained. This is not in agreement
with the view of Jordan (§ 196), who says that the back
spirant remained through the fourteenth century, while the
front spirant weakened in the same century, but agrees with
Wyld (*Short History of English*, 1927, § 284 (7) b, c), who
quotes much earlier examples for the former than for the latter.

ʃ and *tʃ* are confused in *schoppe*, III. 230, and *cheriche(n)*,
II. 144, III. 203. This arises from the change in pronunciation of French *ch*. *dȝ* is unvoiced in *ycharchid*, III. 230 ;
chaunchyth, III. 139. This occurs frequently in Audelay, see
Dr. Ella K. Whiting's edition (E.E.T.S. 184), p. xxxiii.

u is written for *w* in *louyd*, II. 179, III. 310.

The scribe of the second fragment is a much more consistent speller. He misplaces the spirant only in *hough* (more often *how*) and *neighebourgh*, 121, *neighborowes*, 1509, and writes *wh* for *w* in *whinge*, 154. He has a good knowledge of French spelling, as the following words show : *chief, chiere, grief, matiere, bachillier, riuyere, cornier*, &c. (note also *watiers*, 1529), *dysneth* (for 'dineth', 1573 ; *O.E.D.* has no example of this spelling), *caroigne, oygnons, cumpaigny*, &c., *compte, preynte, memoire, gloire, salaire* (cp. *sallere*, IV. 46), *glorieusely, gracieusely, amoreux*. He uses the Central French form in common words like *bourgoys*, 260, 789 (cp. *burgeis*, III. 149), *c(o)urtoys*, 442, 810, *hoires*, 1436 (cp. *heeris*, III. 100), *royaulme*, 664 (cp. *rewme*, P. 74). It is possible that *rancune*, 729, 1123, 1550, not given in *O.E.D.*, is his substitution for *rancour*, which occurs at III. 185.

Anglo-Norman *aun*, used with very rare exceptions by the scribe of R, yields in M to Central French forms when unstressed, e.g. *seruant, sergeant, mayntenance, grevance*. It is retained in stressed forms, e.g. *graunte, auncyen, chauncellerie* ; but is dropped in *chanchellier*, 13 ; *lanternes*, 1749 ; *mangier*, 560 ; *plantes*, 703, 979 ; *change*, 1305 (but regularly *chaunge*). *Mansions*, 887, 1004, is not recorded in the AN. form.

There are also many Latinized spellings : *auctor, exemple, fructe, intremitte, sceptre, subtilite, conceypt, deceipt*. From the last of these are evolved the forms *deceipuyng*, 495, *deceipuen*, 1052, *perceipues*, 719. They are not found in *O.E.D.*, and derive from French forms such as *décepuoir*, where the *p* was introduced to show that *eu* was not a diphthong.[1] They are exceedingly rare in French before the fifteenth century.

In M the doubling of consonants after ME. long vowels is very rare, and almost entirely confined to comparatives and superlatives: *clenner*, 425; *gretter*, 1072 ; *grettist*, 218 ; *pruttist*, 684 ; *swetter*, 1368 ; *wacker*, 1581 ; also *swettenes*, 1020 ; *strattely*, 1641. *Patthes*, 859, and *pressonere*, 1251, probably point to the retention of a short vowel. *Bunne* (= *boun*), 358, is an unusual form. *Reuylle*, 664, probably = *revel*. *ou* is often found where *ŭ* would be expected, both in French and

---

[1] See C. Beaulieux, *Histoire de l'orthographie française*, I. 189.

English words, e.g. (i) *gouuerne, pourpo(o)s*, passim, (ii) *a-bouue*, 354, 426; *courshidnes*, 1154; *courssid*, 1500; *mouche*, 424 (otherwise *muche*); *mourdre*, 732, 1655; *fourth*, passim. *Mourdre* and *a-bouue* are sixteenth-century spellings; no *ou* forms of *curse* are given in *O.E.D.* Some words are always written with a short vowel, as *couet(ise), funder.*

OE. *ā* is regularly written *oe* in *loeth, soeth*, probably through the influence of forms like *goeth*; also *soethly*, 290. It is shortened early in *hamward*, 1179. *Aues*, 1201, might possibly be an example of N.W.M. *ǫu > aŭ*; but is more likely a back formation from *aughte.*

The shortening of *ǣ* shows much the same variety as in R. From PG. *ai* come *clenner, delte, lad, lefte* (but *lafte*, 969), *lasse, ment, thraste, wrǫstlid, wretthe*; PG. *ǣ* gives *radde.*

a before nasal always remains, except (once) *mony*, 788, *monsyd*, 504.

and from OE. *and* is more frequent than in R: *hande*, always; *standeth*, 477, but regularly *stonde*, and even *stont*, 755; *lande* (except for l. 1466, it takes the place of *londe* from l. 1397).

ang > ong, except *sprange*, 1229; *fangeth*, 1176; *fangyng*, 1355; also *fongen*, 1350; *y-funge*, 1700, the last being generally considered a W.M. development.[1] It is, of course, impossible to tell whether the *ong* forms do not represent this pronunciation.

y is generally unrounded, but there are more *u* spellings than in R; *churche, furst, luste* are regular forms, against *chirche, frist, list* (with one exception) of R. The other examples are *curtelle*, 893; *gurde*, 563; *gurdell(z)*, 569, 1072, 1513; (?) *gurdyng*, 1160, 1654; *hure*, 22, 1197 (also *hire* twice); *dude*, 1714, but regularly *dide*. The following *r* evidently tended to preserve the rounding. *y > e* in *steriers* 1569 (but *stiren*); *sherte*, 1521; also *ferthren*, as in R. The adv. is *ferther* and *forther*. *Blethely*, 995, seems to be an example of *ȳ > ē*; cp. early ME. *blupelice. wyr > wir* regularly in *wirchen; worche(n)* occurs twice, *worke* once. *wyrwe(n)*, 979, 1075, contrasts with *yworewid*, III. 72. *wors* occurs 1581, 1628. There is no example of early ME. rounding except *wol*; we even have *wyman*, 1386.

[1] But see Dr. M. Serjeantson, R.E.S., vii. 450–2.

Rounding in words from OE. *eŏ*, ON. *jū*, OF. *ue* is also more common than in R: (i) *deupe*, 647; *feul(l)*, 113, &c. (4 times); *heulde(n)*, 280, &c. (5 times); *lude(s)*, 115, 1310; *sheutyng*, 1403; (ii) *muke(ly)*, 92, &c. (3 times); *meukest*, 1031; *mukyn*, 1516; (iii) *peuple*, passim; *moeve*, 11 times; twice *move*; *fleuble*, 856, 1042. None of these words are found unrounded. *weor* > *wur* in *worldly*, *worship*, *worthy*. *Work* and *werk* are equally common, the *o* tending to displace the *e*. *Swerde* occurs 486. *Burne* and *barne* are equally common; *churle* occurs 422. Words in *ēow* are as in R; *trowe*, *trouthe* (*treuthe*, 1266), and *trewe*, *rewe*; *ferthe*, 405, and *fourthe*, 434.

French *ü* has become *ŭ*, as in R, in *coriously*, 893 (but *curiousiste*, 1006).

e, *a + sh* are diphthongized in *freysh*, 65 (otherwise *fressh*); *daisshe*, 981; *waisshe*, 722.

The only example of *i* > *ē* in open syllable is *ledes*, 889; though the forms *soon*, 1267, *soones*, 1436 show that *u* has become *ǭ*.

e > *i* in *sigger* (regularly, otherwise, *saye*, *seye*; this is presumably the original form), *silf* (about equally with *self*), *sille*, 1521, *chirmed*, 939, all of which are S.W. or S.W.M. forms; also before dental or *ng* in *yit*, passim, *carpintier*, 1006; *indure*, 1668; *intre*, 1242; *finge*, 1198. *Gvfe*, 471, 1555, 1696, is used when alliteration requires hard *g*; otherwise *yeue*. For *pryvy*, 1055, and *pryue*, 1344, see note to II. 108.

er > *ar*, only found once in R, occurs in *barn(es)*, equally with *burne*; *harkeneth*, 21; *parfite(ly)*, 491, 538; *parfourmid*, 1722.

ē is written *ei*, in *eildren*, 1427; *feil*, 1447 (also *vele*); *seilde*, 38 (generally *silde*); all these are close *ē + l*. *o* is written *oi* in *loising*, 1177 (also *lose*). *Choise*, 445 (also *chosid*), is probably due to French influence; Levins has 'to choyse, eligere'. R has *lese*, *chese*.

ę̄ is written *ie* in *bilieue*, n., 325, &c.; *(bi)lieue*, vb., 36, &c. (5 times, against once with *e* and twice with *y*); *grieued*, 307.

ę̄ is written *i* (or *y*) much more often than in R: *hire*, vb., always; *lydene*, 1030; *lyve(d)*, 59, 1030; *nyre*, 302 (also *neer*, 866); *pryved*, 719; *silde*, 151, &c.; *sike*, *siche*, vb., 4 times, also *sechis*, 783 ; *sike*, adj., 1381 ; *wyke*, 10, 1672 (also *woke*, 120)); *wyre*, 296, 316. *Lyfe*, 384, is from *īa*, but in *C.T.*, A. 1838, Chaucer rimes it with *lief.* There are some 25 examples of *i* in all.

The change of *ǭ* to *ū* is only indicated by *proufe*, 1751, and the inverted spelling *looste*, 128.

The writing of *ea* for *ę̄*, not found in R, is used here in French words before *s* : *ease*, n. and vb., *disease, vnease, pleasith, reasonable, reason(s), treason.*

Maul-gre, 1525 (but *malgre*, 1300), shows the development of a *u*-glide before *l*. The first examples of this south of Humber are late in the fifteenth century, see Luick, *Hist. Gram.*, § 503, Anm. 1.

A striking characteristic of M is the change of *a, e, ę* (and *ā* in final syllable) to *ai, ei, oi* before *tš, dž* : (i) *caicche*, 8, 164, 588, 684, 731, 1061 ; *knowlaiche*, 380 ; *messaigier*, 1138 ; *smaicche*, 7 ; *taicches*, 93, 969 ; (ii) *alleigge*, 1493 ; *feycchen*, 1009 ; *heigges*, 881, 886, 919, 936 ; *streicchen*, 1571 ; (iii) *boicches*, 1122, 1139 ; *loigge*, n. and vb., 187, 845, 901, 1021, 1241 ; (iv) *caige*, 153 ; *couraige*, 1500 ; *herbaige*, 606 ; *visaige*, 959. These words are not spelt without *i*, except *knowlache*, 733 ; *allegen*, 1376. The *i* is not found after long vowels in open syllables, in such words as *seche, preche, teche.* When the diphthong is written, it is followed (except in final *-aige*) by a long consonant; cp. *alleigge, allegen*, above, also *caicche* and *chacheth*, 1721 ; *taicches* and *(in)tachid*, 1735, 1747. *Messaigier* and *knowlaiche* are the only exceptions; the first may be due to the influence of *messaige.* Evidence for the *ai* diphthong is found in Salesbury, 1547, who says that the diphthongal sound is heard in *domaige, heritaige, languaige, aishe, waitche* (Ellis, I. 120). Levins in 1570 has *gayge, wayge*, &c. (E.E.T.S. 27, col. 197). There is no evidence for *ei* or *oi* diphthongs, yet in the examples quoted they do not appear to denote length. See Luick, *Hist. Eng. Gram.*, § 436, and *Anglia*, xvi. 485. Meyer-Lübke, in *Hist. gramm. der französischen sprache*, i. § 102, refers to a widespread, but not Parisian, fronting of *a* in *-age*, represented by the spelling *aige* ; and Vising (*Anglo-Norman Language and Literature*, p. 32) notes this as a characteristic AN. spelling first appearing in

the second half of the fourteenth century. This probably
accounts for the spelling of the words in (iv).

Consonants. The scribe's generally correct use of *wh-*
and *-ght* has been already noted. The Southern *v* for initial *f* is
preserved in *velle*, 561 ; *vresse*, 959 (cp. *fressh*, 1280), *vantstone*,
1198 ; *viftene*, 1353 ; *vireth* (perhaps F. *virer*), 1464 ; *vele*, 1624.
It should be noted that *vresse* and *viftene* are required by the
alliteration, but *velle* and *vantstone* each follow two *f*'s, and
vele is in a non-alliterating position. The forms are not
therefore due to the scribe's desire for correct alliteration.
There are no such forms in R.

Intervocalic *f* is written in *lifes*, pl., 205, 1538 ; *wifes*, pl.,
512 ; *life-is*, g. s., 852. These forms are frequent in the fifteenth
and sixteenth centuries (Wyld, *Coll. Engl.*, p. 323). We also
find *griefed*, 1445 ; *griefen*, 1588; *gifeth*, 1696. The only such
form in R is *preifis*, P. 17.

Hard *g + i* is regularly *gui*, except *gye*, 469, *gyfe*, 471, &c.,
and *gilte* (= gilt), 569 (cp. *guill(y)*, 726, 1596). The *gi*-
forms predominate in the fifteenth century, and survive about
half-way through the sixteenth, abounding in Tyndale and
Coverdale. After this time the *gu-* spelling is common (see
Jespersen, *Mod. Eng. Gram.*, p. 23).

w and *v* (*u*) are confused in (i) *groved*, 146 ; *grovid*, 907 ;
groued, 191 ; *leued*, 12 ; (ii) *abawyd*, 293 ; *salwyn*, 847.

sh is written for voiceless *s* in *courshidnes*, 1154 ; *kisshyng*,
915 ; *manasshing*, 485 ; *rehershing*, 210, 299, 1211, (*rehercyn*,
1497, 1545). The inverted form occurs in *blussid*, 239 ;
vresse, 959 (see Wyld, *Coll. Eng.*, p. 291).

dung-wete, 739, is probably an inverted spelling, testifying
to the W.M. *ng > nk*.

Inflexions. The vowel of inflexional endings is *i* or *e* ;
e and occasionally *y* are used after *n, m, i, u*, and sometimes
also after other letters.[1] There is a tendency in R to add *s*
alone to nouns whose singular ends in *e* : *dowtes, tales, fables*,

---

[1] The further rules for inflexional *e* and *i*, noted in Pecock by
F. Schmidt, *Studies in the Language of Pecock*, Uppsala, 1900, and
Dr. Hitchcock, *Pecock's Donet*, E.E.T.S. 156, p. xxiii, do not seem to
hold for either part of this poem.

but also *castes*. Occasionally in M *i* follows minims : *ordeynid*, *y-soluid*, *parfourmid*. Final *e* may be omitted anywhere, except so far as it denotes a preceding long vowel, or added where it fulfils no function, e.g. *londe*, P. 12.   In R the forms are as follows :

Nouns: g. s. *-es*, *-is*. Str. pl. *-es*, *-is*, *-s*; occasionally the Western *-us*: *feldus*, III. 87 ; *grotus*, III. 82 ; *lustus*, P. 82, I. 30 ; *rotus*, II. 140 ; *routus*, I. 16 ; *wullus*, IV. 11.   It appears that the retention of this ending was favoured by a back vowel+dental. *Burnesse*, III. 241, and *harnesse* (for *harmesse*), I. 26, should be noted.   Mutation pl. *men*, *mys*. Weak pl. *eyren*, III. 50.   Invariable, *dere*.   Irreg. *dawis*, I. 65 (also *daies*, III. 114).   Gen. pl. *lordyns*, II. 60 (cp. *lorden*, 1356).

Pronouns: Pers. nom. *I, þou*,[1] *he, hue* (III. 50), *it, yt, we, 3e, þey, þei*.   Obj. *me, þe, him, it* (dat. *him*, P. 54, ?III. 242), *us, 3ou, hem*.

Poss. *my, bi*, (before vowel or *h myn, þin*, P. 26, P. 81, I. 83), *his, hir, her, oure, 3oure* (disj. *3ouris*, P. 65), *her(e), hir*.

The reflexive pronouns have the ordinary forms, but note *3ou-self*, I. 1.

Demonstr. adjs. *þis, þat, þo, þese*.

Rel. and interrog. pronouns: *ho, whom, what*, dat. sg. neut. *whom*, III. 65.   For *þat, þo* as rel. prs. see Glossary.

Verbs: Inf. *-e*, often *-en* for metrical reasons before vowel or *h*, e.g. P. 31, P. 35, II. 85 ; *-yn*, P. 13, II. 146.   Pr. p. *-inge, -ynge*. Pp. strong: generally *-e* ; occasionally *-(e)n, -yn, yborn, ytakyn, knowyn, vnknowen* ; *y-* is prefixed to the majority. Pp. weak : *-ed, -id, -yd, -de, -te*. When monosyllabic, final *-e* is nearly always added.   *y-* is often prefixed, generally to monosyllabic forms.

Ind. pr. *-(e), -ist(e), -eth, -yth* ; pl. *-eth*, less often *-yn, -e(n)*.

Imp. *-(e)* ; pl. *-(e), -eth, -ith*.

Pret. strong : *-(e)*, 2 s. not found ; pl. *-(e)*, less often *-en, yn*, III. 362.

---

[1] It will be noted that in Passus I the author continually varies between the sg. and pl. pronoun of address.   The rest of the poem is more consistent (except II. 118) ; Mum and the author ' thou' each other, but in the vision he uses the more respectful pronoun to the bee-keeper, except in ll. 1218-19.

Pret. weak: 2 s. not found; pl. *-id(e)*, *-ed(e)*, *-de(n)*, *-dyn* (I. 2), *-ud* (I. 52).

Subj. pl. *-(e)*, *-en*.

Conjugation of strong verbs: I. *ride*, pt. s. *rood*, pl. *reden*. *rise*, pt. s. *rosse*, pl. sb. *rise*. *(slide)*, pt. pl. *slode*. *(strike)*, pp. *striked*. *þryue*, pt. s. *þroff*. *write*, *written*, pp. *write*.

II. *chese*, pt. pl. *chesse*, pp. *chose*. *fle*, pt. pl. *flowen*. *(louke)*, pp. *yloke*. *lese*, pt. pl. *lost*.

III. *begynne*, pt. s. *gan*. *hynde*, pp. *(y)bounde*. *(drink)*, pt. s. sb. *drank*. *fynde*, pt. s. and pl. *fonde*, pp. *y-founde*. *renne*, pt. pl. *ronne*. *(wind)*, pp. *y-wounde*. *brest*, pt. s. *braste*, pl. *brast(yn)*. *fighte*, pt. pl. *fouȝten*. *helpe*, pt. sb. *helped*.

IV. *bere*, pt. pl. *bare*, *boren*, pp. *y-born*. *come*, pt. s. *cam*, pl. *cam*, *come*, pp. *y-come*. *(hele)*, pp. *y-helid*. *stele*, pt. s. *stall*, pl. *stelen*.

V. *ȝeue*, pt. pl. *ȝaf*. *(lie)*, pt. pl. *lay*. *(quethe)*, pt. s. *quod*, *se*, pt. s. and pl. *sawe*, pp. *seie*. *(sit)*, pt. pl. *satte*.

VI. *(draw)*, pt. s. *drough*, *drowe*, pl. *drowe*. *(forsake)*, pt. pl. *forsoke*. *(grave)*, pp. *ygraue*. *stonde*, pt. s. *stode*. *take*, pt. pl. *toke(n)*, pp. *ytakyn*, *ytake*.

VII. *(bete)*, pp. *bete*. *falle*, pt. *fell(e)*, pp. *fallyn*, *falle*. *(growe)*, pt. *grewe*, pp. *growe*. *hange*, *honge*, pt. *hangid*, pp. *vnhonge*. *holde*, pt. *helde*, pp. *y-holde*. *(hote)*, pp. *y-hotte*, *be-hote*. *knowe*, pt. *knewe*, pp. *knowyn*, *y-knowe*. *lete*, pt. *lete*. *rede*, pt. *reed*. *(slepe)*, pt. *slepte*. *(sowe)*, pt. *sowid*. *(throwe)*, pp. *þrowe*. *(wasshe)*, pt. *wessh*. *(waxe)*, pp. *wexe*.

Strong-weak verbs: *can*, pl. *kunne*, pt. *couȝthe*, *cowde*. *(dare)*, pt. *durst(e)*. *may*, *maiste*, pl. *mowe*, *moun*, pt. *myȝth*, *myȝte(n)*. *(mot)*, pt. *must(e)*. *(owe)*, pt. *aughte*, *ouȝte*, *oute*, *owed*. *shall*, pr. sb. *sholle*, pt. *shulde*, *shuldist*. *wotte*, pt. *wost*, *wuste*, *wyste*, inf. *witte*, *wyttyn*, *wete*. Other verbs: *woll(e)*, pt. *wolde*, *wulde* (I. 60). *do*, pt. *dede*. *be(n)*, pr. *am*, *is*, pl. *beth*, pt. *was*, *were(n)*, pp. *be(n)*.

telle has pt. *tolde*, *tellde*, the latter probably a levelling from the infinitive.

The forms in M are as follows:

Nouns: g.s. *is*, always written as a separate word; no ending in *churche*, 614; pl. *-es*, *-s*, *-z*; occasionally *-is*: *balys*. 94; *breris*, 898; *ferys*, 1341; *levis*, 368; *pe(e)ris*, 155, 1399;

peris, 904. This ending was apparently most likely to remain after *ir*. Mutation pl. *men*. Weak pl. *eyen, brethern*. Invariable, *dere, fyssh, rayndeer, roobuc, shepe, seuenyght, wyntre, yere*. Wk. g. pl. *lorden*, 1356 ; no ending in *men*, 461, 541, &c. (6 times). Dat. pl. *dawe*, 1319.

Pronouns : Pers. nom. *I, þow, he, she, hit, we, ye, þay*. Obj. *me, þe, hym, hit* (dat. *hym*, 439), *vs, you, þaym*. Poss. *my, þy* (before consonants and vowels, except *þyn tent*, 74, *þyn intent*, 380), *his* (*he-is*, 339), *hire, oure, your, þair(e), þayr(e)*. Demonst. adjs. *þis, þat, þo(o), þees*.

The outstanding difference between R and M in the forms of pronouns is that in the latter the Scandinavian *þair, þaym* have displaced the native forms. This change took place in the Midlands during the fifteenth century. The *Worcester Ordinances*[1] of 1467 have both forms, the newer predominating. In the *Little Red Book of Bristol* (ed. F. B. Bickley, 1900) the Ordinances of the Cordwainers have *hem, ham, here* in 1438 (II. 167), but *their, theim* in 1443 (II. 176). In the Composition of Joanna Halwey (1453, ibid. pp. 199–206) only the later forms are found. *Ricart's Kalendar* (ed. Toulmin Smith, *Camden Soc.*, 1872), written in Bristol, 1479, has only *theire, the(i)m*, except when quoting formulae, as the Mayor's Oath, pp. 72–4.

Verbs : Inf. *-e*, except *cusky*, 580 ; *maistrie*, 882 ; *shony*, 161 ; *wandry*, 552 ; and gerundial *seen*, 901. In ll. 273, 1098, the metre requires *-en*. Pr.p. *-ing, -yng*, except *shynant*, 1316 (which may possibly represent the N.W.M. *-ande* unvoiced, cp. *dung-wete*, p. xxxvii). Pp. strong always *-e*, except *y-doluen*, 1194, and adjectival forms, *quethyn*, 1348, *mowen*, 887, generally with *y-* prefixed (both Southern points ; the latter, in the fifteenth century, is 'chiefly confined to texts which show a more or less strongly marked Southern provincial influence ', Wyld, *Coll. Eng.* 342). *Drawen*, 1573, the scribe probably took for pr. ind. pl. Pp. weak, *-id, -ed, -de, -te*, often with *y-* prefixed.

Ind. pr. (*-e*), 2 s. *-es, -is, -ys*, (*-est*, 255), 3 s. *-eth, -ith*, pl. *-en, -e, -eth* (some 12 times).

Imp. (*-e*), pl. *-e, -eth*.

---

[1] Toulmin Smith, *English Gilds*, E.E.T.S. 40, pp. 376–409.

Pret. strong, (-*e*), 2 s. *begunne*, 781 ; pl. (-*e*), -*en* 3 times.

Pret. wk., -*id*, -*ed*, -*yd*, -*te*, -*de* ; 2 s. not found. -*n* is never added for pl., nor -*e* to dissyllabic forms.

Subj. (-*e*). -*n* is never found in pl., except *been*, 46, 1062. A mark of this fragment is to confine -*en* to the ind. pr. pl. This distinction between ind. pl. and subj. pl. is characteristic of fifteenth-century English (see Dibelius, *Anglia* xxiv. 251).

Conjugation of strong verbs : I. *abide*, pt. s. *abode, boode. rise*, pt. s. *roose.* (*smite*), pt. s. *smote.*

II. *bowe*, pt. pl. *a-bowid. choise*, pt. pl. *chosid*, pp. *y-chose.* (*louke*), pp. *looke, vnloke. lose*, vb. n. *loising*, pp. (*y*)*loste.* (*shote*), pr. p. *sheutyng.* (*shove*), pr. pl. *sheue.* (*soupe*), pp. *soope.*

III. *begynne*, pt. s. *began*, pl. *gunne.* (*drinke*), pp. *y-drunke. fynde*, pt. s. *fonde. renne*, pt. pl. *runne*, pp. *y-renne, y-runne. springe*, pt. s. *sprange, spronge. wynne*, pt. s. *wanne*, pl. *wanne*, pp. *y-wonne.* (*braide*), pt. s. *abrayed. delue*, pp. *y-doluen.*

IV. *bere*, pt. pl. *bare*, pp. *bore. come*, pt. s. and pl. *came, come*, pp. *y-come.* (*hele*), pp. (*vn*)*helid. nyme*, pp. *bynome. stele*, pp. *y-stole.*

V. *bydde*, pt. s. *bade. gete*, pt. s. *forgate. ʒeue, gife*, pt. s. *yafe, forgafe. ligge*, pt. s. *lay.* (*quethe*), pt. s. *cothe*, pp. *quethyn, y-quethe. seen*, pp. (*y-*)*seye. sitte*, pt. s. *satte*, pt. subj. *sate. speke*, pp. *spoke. treede*, pt. s. *trade*, pp. *y-troode.*

VI. *drawe*, pt. pl. *drowe*, pp. *y-drawe. stonde, stande*, pt. s. *stoode. take*, pt. s. *toke*, pl. *token*, pp. (*y-*)*take.* (*wake*), pt. s. *woke.*

VII. (*bete*), pp. *y-bete.* (*blowe*), pt. pl. *blowid. falle*, pt. *feulle*, pp. *y-falle. fonge, fange*, pt. *finge*, pp. *y-funge. growe*, pt. *groued, growed. hewe*, pp. *hewe. holde*, pt. *heulde*(*n*). (*hote*), pp. *behote, y-hoote*, pass. *hatte. knowe*, pt. *knewe*, pp. (*y-*)*knowe. le*(*e*)*pe*, pt. *lepte.* (*mowe*), pp. *mowen. re*(*e*)*de*, pt. *radde. slepe*, pt. *slepte. wexe*, pt. *woxe, waxe*, pp. *ouer-woxe.*

Strong-weak verbs : *can*, pl. *cunne*, pt. *couthe*, inf. *cunne. dar*, pt. *durste. may*, 2 s. *mays*, pl. *mowe*(*n*), pt. *might*(*e*), 2 s. *mightes. mote*, 2 s. *mos*, pt. *most*(*e*). *aues* (2 s.), pt. *ought*(*e*), *aughte*(*n*). *shal*, 2 s. *shal*, pl. *shal, shullen* (1670), pt. *shuld*, 2 s. *shuldes. wote*, pl. *wite*(*n*), pt. *wiste*(*n*), inf. *wite.*

Other verbs : *wil, wol,* 2 s. *wol, wolt,* pl. *wil, wol, wolle(n),* pt. *wolde,* 2 s. *woldes. do(o),* pt. *dide,* once *dude,* pp. *do(o), y-do* inf. *be,* pr. *am, art(e), is,* pl. *bee(n),* pt. *was, were(n),* pp. *be.*

The only difference of importance between the verbs in the two fragments is that the verbs *chese, growe, rede,* have strong preterites in R and weak in M. In ll. 146, 315, the weak form is necessary to give the favourite feminine ending, and may well be original.

METRE.

In his *Alliterative Poetry in Middle English* [1] Dr. J. P. Oakden has analysed the alliterative schemes of all the Middle English alliterative poems. The following table gives his figures for R compared with our own for ll. 1–857 of M.

Type	R	M
aa/ax	621	689
aa/xa	32	22
aa/aa	33	18
aaa/ax	21	14
aaa/xa	1	1
ax/aa	1	1
xa/aa	8	6
ax/ax	21	23
xa/xa	7	1
ax/xa	1	2
xa/ax	64	39
aa/bb	2	11
ab/ab	3	4
ab/ba	5	6
aa/xx	20	15
xx/aa	1	1
aaa/xx	4	2
xx/aaa	1	0
aab/bx	1	0
abb/ax	2	0
xx/xx	8	2

[1] Manchester University Press, 1930, see p. 194.

From these figures certain facts are clear. (1) Neither fragment is of the regular type of such poems as *Troy Book*, *Siege of Jerusalem*, the *Alexander* fragments, in which nearly all the lines are of the type *aaax*. In M, however, the standard form is becoming more common, while there is a decrease in nearly all the other types except *aabb*. (2) The next most frequent type is *xaax*, with a percentage of occurrences 7·47 and 4·55 respectively. The only non-riming poems of reasonable length in which this type is equally common are *Morte Arture* with 5·91 per cent., *Piers Plowmans Creed* with 6·82 per cent., and the late *Two Married Women* with 4·90 per cent.[1] In each of these, however, the type *axax* is equally common, whereas R and M have each about 2½ per cent. In *Piers Plowman* the figures are 2·6 and 2·32 for A, 1·9 and 1·6 for B, and 1·82 and 1·32 for C. In their difference of proportion between the two types, R and M seem to be unique. (3) The type *aaxa*, which does not belong to Old English, and is very rare or absent in Middle English poems of regular type, is found in R in 3·73 per cent. and in M in 2·57 per cent. Here again the most similar poems are *Morte Arture* with 3·13 per cent., and *Piers Plowmans Creed* with 4·35 per cent. In *Piers Plowman* the percentages are 1·58, 1·65, 1·72 respectively.

The occurrence of consecutive lines alliterating on the same sound affords a method of comparison. On pp. 155-6 Dr. Oakden gives statistics. The practice varies from that of *Morte Arture*, where in 200 lines 86 are linked, to that of *Troy Book* and *William of Palerne*, where in 100 lines only 6 or less pairs may be found. R has 43 twos and 2 threes. Over the same number of lines M has 57 twos, 5 threes, and 1 four. In *Piers Plowman* the device is very rare, isolated twos being found occasionally.

A comparison of alliterating sounds shows that in both parts *s* and *sh* alliterate freely. This agrees with *William of Palerne* and *Piers Plowman*.[2] *f* and *v* alliterate, agreeing with *Piers*

---

[1] *Joseph of Arimathea* and *Cheuelere Assigne*, in which every irregularity is common, are disregarded here.

[2] P. 14, P. 77, II. 33, etc ; M. 44, 79, 93. See Schumacher, *Studien über den Stabreim in der mittelenglischen Alliterationsdichtung*, Bonner Studien zur englischen Philologie xi, 1914, pp. 212-13.

Plowman, but not with *William of Palerne*.[1] *w* and *wh* alliterate, as in *William of Palerne, Piers Plowman*, and the *Gawain* group.[2] *h* also alliterates with a vowel or *h* mute,[3] in agreement with the same group. *k* and *qu* alliterate four times in each part.[4]

Certain peculiarities in the alliteration of words compounded with a prefix serve to distinguish ME. alliterative poems.[5] The prefix *be-*, which never alliterates in OE. verse,[6] often does so in ME. The occurrence is common in *Layamon, Piers Plowman*, and *William of Palerne*, and occasional in the *Gawain* group. It is very rare in *Troy Book, Morte Arture*, and the *Alexander* poems. From this one might infer that it belongs specially to the S.W.M., yet there is no example of it in R, and in M only *beneath* in l. 426.

In both parts, as in *Piers Plowman* and *William of Palerne*, the prefix *re-* almost always alliterates. The exceptions are *reclaim*, II. 182, and *reserve*, 658. Neither word alliterates in any other poem. Words common to the two parts are: *rehearse*, II. 98, III. 315; M 210, 299, 1211, 1497; *reproof*, P. 56, M 1545; *reprove*, III. 197, M 1715. *Rehearse* always alliterates on the prefix (with the doubtful exception of *Alexander* 329), but *reproof* and *reprove* everywhere else alliterate on the stem, i.e. in *Alexander, Troy Book, William of Palerne, Gawain, Piers Plowman* B, 11 cases in all.

Examining the metre[7] of the two fragments, we find short lines in each, but more than twice as many in M. In estimating the number of syllables in a line, it must be borne in mind that *-e* and *-en*, justified etymologically and necessary to the

---

[1] I. 35, III. 24, III. 56, &c. ; M 53, 337, 362, &c.

[2] P. 27, I. 64, II. 123, &c,; M 203, 261, 296, &c.

[3] I. 96, II. 9, II. 145, &c. ; M 51, 280, 520, &c.

[4] II. 90, II. 107, III. 176, III. 327; M 381, 399, 1011, 1092. II. 107 and 1011 depend on *quentise* and *queynte*, which may have had the form *coint-*, cp. Schumacher, p. 153.

[5] See an unpublished London thesis, *Early Middle English Word-stress investigated on the Basis of the Unrhymed Alliterative Poems*, M. Day, 1921.

[6] It can be found apparently alliterating in the later works of Ælfric, as in *De Veteri et de Novo Testamento*, ed. Grein, i. 1/21-2, 4/8, 12/42-3, &c

[7] See Luick, *Anglia* xi. 392, 553.

metre, are often scribally omitted, e.g. M 177, 'and wickid[e]
wedes', III. 29, 'ne bynde[n] him noþer'. Also, final *-e* may
be added where it has no justification, III. 25, a longe tyme
aft*er*'. Final *-z* is often equivalent to syllabic *-es*, e.g. tirantz,
632 ; princz, 728 ; clercz, 749, &c., and forms such as 'þache',
741, may have to be expanded.

Of the type (x)/x/x we have I. 110 b 'haue ben abasshyd ';
II. 54 b, III. 174 a, III. 191 b, III. 232 b, IV. 53 a ; M 102 b,
217 a, 232 b, 238 b, and 17 others in ll. 1–857.

Of the type x//x we have I. 26 b, 'ne hayle-schouris',
III. 256 b, and M 290 a.

II. 17 b, III. 25 b, III. 316 b; M 166 b, 237 b, 285 b are
probably of the type (x)/ \ /x.

A number of lines are reduced to regular scansion by
allowing for the insertion of a vowel between a consonant and
a following liquid : I. 10, 'and stablithe moste', II. 131, 'So
wyntris weder', M 107, 'while flatryng helpeth'. Some
defective lines can easily be emended, as II. 41, by replacing
'toune' by 'tounes', and M 97, 391, 765, by the addition
of 'silk ', 'so', 'of'.

When all adjustments have been made, we are left with a
residuum of 9 short lines in R, and 22 in M. Each, however,
gives nearly 50 examples of final syllabic *-e* in dissyllables.
Most of these are infinitives, e.g. P. 76, I. 21 ; M 7, 13 ;
37 cases in all. Examples are also found of wk. prets., as
P. 27, P. 79 ; M 352, 550 ; plural adjs., P. 65, I. 45 ; M 456,
840 ; fem. and wk. nouns, P. 48, I. 5, III. 3, III. 33 ; M 252,
490 ; French final *-e*, I. 8, IV. 20 ; M 136, 339, and a few
miscellaneous cases.

Final *-e* in trisyllables is rarer.[1] In R there are 13 cases,
and only 7 in M : plural adjs., P. 5, P. 20, P. 62, II. 186 ;
M 177 ; wk. prets., II. 125, II. 191, III. 4, III. 322 ; M 298,
827 ; French final *-e*, II. 104, II. 178, III. 14; M 339, 437,
676; also the miscellaneous cases II. 54, III. 370, M 499.
Medial weak *-e* in trisyllables is also more common in R with
13 cases (I. 16, I. 37, I. 45, &c.) than in M with 6 (222, 362,
417, &.).

---

[1] Luick notes that words in *-rde* are often trisyllabic in R, but never
in *Piers Plowman* (*Anglia* xi. 440-1).

The conclusion of the line with an unstressed monosyllable, nearly always a pronoun, as 'be hem', I. 93, 'loued hem', II. 107, 'among þaym', 112, 'tolde of', 140, is characteristic of both fragments. It is twice as frequent in M as in R, occasional in *Piers Plowman*, and very rare elsewhere.

MUM AND THE SOTHSEGGER

[Prologus.]

And as I passid in my preier*e* / þ*er* prestis were at messe,
   In a blessid borugh / þat Bristow is named,
In a temple of þ^e trinite / þ^e toune eue*n* amyddis,
That Cristis Chirche is cleped / amonge þe comune peple,   4
Sodeynly þ*er* sourdid / selcouþ^e þingis,
A grett wondir to wyse men / as it well my3th,
And dowtes for to deme / for drede comynge aft*er*.
So sore were þe sawis / of bothe two sidis,   8
Of Richard þat regned / so riche and so noble,
That wyle he werrid be west / on þ^e wilde Yrisshe,
Henrri was entrid / on þe est half,
Whom all þ^e londe loued / in lengþ^e and in brede,   12
And rosse w*ith* him rapely / to ri3tyn his wronge,
For he shullde hem serue / of þe same aft*er*.
Thus tales me troblid / for þey trewe where,
And amarride my mynde rith moch*e* / and my wittis eke :   16
For it passid my parceit / and my p*r*eifis also,
How so wondirffull werkis / wolde haue an ende.
But in sothe whan þey sembled / some dede repeute,
As knowyn is in cumpas / of Cristen londis,   20
That rewthe was, if reson / ne had reffo*ur*med
The myssecheff & þ^e mysserule / þat me*n* þo in endurid.
I had pete of his passion / þat prince was of Walis,
And eke our*e* crouned kynge / till Crist wol[de] no leng*er* ;   24
And as a [liage] to his [lord] / þou3 I lite hade,
All my*n* hoole herte was his / while he in helthe regnid.
And for I [wuste] not witt*er*ly / what shulde fall,
Whedir God wolde [g]eue him grace / sone to amende,   28

As I passed
through Bristol,

near Christ
Church,

strange events
arose.

It was said that,
whilst Richard
was warring in
Ireland,

Henry entered
England in the
East.

These tales
greatly troubled
me.

Some wished for
a reformation of
misrule.

I was sorry for
Richard and kept
my allegiance to
him.

Not knowing
what would
happen,

The first part of the poem has hitherto been known as Richard the Redeles.

---

16 *Cesura also after* mynde.   21 *Cesura after* was.   24 MS.
woll.   25 MS. lord to his liage.   27 MS. wost [S].   28. MS.
3eue.

To be oure gioure a[g]eyn / or graunte it anoþer,

This made me to muse / many tyme and ofte,

For to written him a writte / to wissen him better,

And to meuve him of mysserewle / his mynde to reffresshe   32

For to [preie] þe prynce / þat paradise made,

To fullfill him with feith / and fortune aboue,

And not to grucchen a grott / aȝeine Godis sonde,

But mekely to suffre / what-so him sente were.   36

And ȝif him list to loke / a leef oþer tweyne,   [*fo.* 108 *a.*]

That made is to mende him / of his myssededis,

And to kepe him in confforte / in Crist and nouȝt ellis,

I wolde be gladde þat his gost / myȝte glade be my wordis,   40

And grame if it greued him / be God þat me bouȝte !

And euery Cristen kyng / þat ony [croune] bereth,

So he were lerned on þe langage / my lyff durst I wedde,

ȝif he waite well þe wordis / and so werche þer-after,   44

[Ther nys no gouernour on þe grounde / ne sholde gye him þe better,]

For all is tresour of þe trinite / þat turneth men to gode.

And as my body & my beste / oute to be my liegis,

So rithffully be reson / my rede shuld also,   48

For to conceill, and I couȝthe / my kyng and þe lordis ;

And þer-for I [fondyd] / with all my fyue wyttis

To traueile on þis tretis / to teche men þer-after

To be war of wylffulnesse / lest wondris arise.   52

And if it happe to ȝoure honde / beholde þe book onys,

And redeth on him redely / rewis an hundrid,

And if ȝe sauere sum-dell / se it forth ouere,

For reson is no repreff / be þe rode of Chester !   56

And if ȝe fynde fables / or foly þer amonge,

Or ony fantasie yffeyned / þat no frute is in,

Lete ȝoure conceill corette it / and clerkis to-gedyr,

And amende þat ys amysse / and make it more better :   60

For ȝit it is secrette / and so it shall lenger,

Tyll wyser wittis / han waytid it ouere,

That it be lore laweffull / and lusty to here.

For witterly, my will is / þat it well liked   64

ȝou and all ȝouris / and yonge men leueste,

Marginal notes:

I had long intended to write a poem of advice to the king,

recommending him to have patience.

If my advice will do him good,

I shall rejoice at it.

There is no king upon earth but might profit by my words, if he could read English.

It is my duty to advise my lord.

So I set to work on my treatise.

If my book reaches your hand, read it.

If you find fables or folly in it, correct them.

It still remains unpublished.

I hope it may profit the young.

To be-nyme hem her noyes / þat neweth hem ofte.
For and þey mvse þeron / to þe myddwardis,
They shall fele fawtis / foure score and odde, 68
That yough[th]e weneth alwey / þat it be witt euere.
And þouȝ þat elde opyn it / oþer-while amonge,
And poure on it preuyly / and preue it well after,
And constrewe ich clause / with þe culorum, 72
It shulde not apeire hem a peere / a prynce þouȝ he were,
Ne harme noþer hurte / þe hyghest of þe rewme,
But to holde him in hele / and helpe all his frendis. [*fo.* 108 *b.*]
And if ony word write be / þat wrothe make myghte 76
My souereyne, þat suget / I shulde to be,
I put me in his power / and preie him, of grace,
To take þe entent of my trouþe / þat thouȝte non ylle,
For to wrath no wyght / be my wyll neuere, 80
As my soule be saff / from synne at myn ende.
Þe story is of non estate / þat stryuen with her lustus,
But þo þat folwyn her flessh / and here frelle þouȝtis ;
So if my conceyll be clere / I can saie no more, 84
But ho be greued in his gost / gouerne him better,
And blame not þe berne / þat þe book made,
But þe wickyd will / and þe werkis after.

[Passus Primus.]

N ow, Richard þe redeles / reweth on ȝou-self,
Þat lawelesse leddyn ȝoure lyf / and ȝoure peple boþe ;
For þoru þe wyles and wronge / and wast in ȝoure tyme,
Ȝe were lyghtlich ylyfte / from þat ȝou leef þouȝte, 4
And from ȝoure willffull werkis / ȝoure will was chaungid,
And rafte was ȝoure riott and rest / for ȝoure daieȝ weren wikkid,
Þoru ȝoure cursid conceill / ȝoure karis weren newed,
And coueitise hath crasid / ȝoure croune for euere ! 8
Of alegeaunce now lerneth / a lesson oþer tweyne
Wher-by it standith / and stablithe moste—
By dride, or be dyntis / or domes vntrewe,

Marginal notes:
If older men read it, it will not harm them
If any word makes my sovereign wroth, I pray him to believe that I mean no ill.
Let him that is grieved learn to mend his ways.
Richard, void of counsel, mourn for your errors.
Your will has been turned from good.
Radix omnium malorum cupiditas.

69 MS. youghe [S]. 70 *Two letters deleted after* þouȝ. 83 folwyn :
l *retouched.*
6-7. *Cesura mark after* riott ; *l.* 6 *ends with* daieȝ. 8 *Cesura mark
also after* croune. 11 dride : e *written above the* i.

Or by creaunce of coyne / for castes of gile,   12

By pillynge of ȝoure peple / ȝoure prynces to plese,

Or þat ȝoure wylle were wrouȝte / þouȝ wisdom it nolde ;

Or be tallage of ȝoure townnes / without ony werre,

By rewthles routus / þat ryffled euere,   16

Be preysinge of polaxis / þat no pete hadde,

Or be dette for þi dees / deme as þou fyndist,—

Or be ledinge of lawe / with loue well ytemprid.

Though þis be derklich endited / for a dull nolle,   20

Miche nede is it not / to mwse þer-on,

For as mad † as I am / þouȝ I litill kunne,

I cowde it discryue / in a fewe wordys ;   [*fo.* 109 *a.*]

For legiance without loue / litill þinge availith.   24

But graceles gostis / gylours of hem-self,

That neuere had [harmesse] / ne hayle-schouris,

But walwed in her willis / forweyned in here youthe,

Þey sawe no manere siȝth / saff solas and ese,   28

And cowde no mysse amende / whan mysscheff was vp,

But sorwed for her lustus / of lordsch[i]pe þey hadde,

And neuere for her trespas / oo tere wolde þey lete.

ȝe come to ȝoure kyngdom / er ȝe ȝoure-self knewe,   32

Crouned with a croune / þat kyng vnder heuene

Miȝte not a better / haue bouȝte, as I trowe ;

So full was it filled / with vertus stones,

With perlis of pris / to punnysshe þe wrongis,   36

With rubies rede / þe riȝth for to deme,

With gemmes and juellis / joyned to-gedir,

And pees amonge þe peple / for peyne of þi lawis.

It was full goodeliche ygraue / with gold al abouȝte ;   40

The braunchis aboue / boren grett charge ;

With diamauntis derue / y-douutid of all

That wroute ony wrake / within or withoute ;

With lewte and loue / yloke to þi peeris,   44

---

16 routus : e *written above second* u.   17 pete : *first* e *altered to* y.
22 mad : d *added over last letter,* (?) e.   26 MS. harnesse.   30 for :
or *by second hand over erasure.*   lustus : e *written above second* u.
MS. lordschpe [S].   35 vertus : ou *added after* u *above the line.*
36 pris : s *altered to* se.   42 diamauntis : *abbreviation mark over
second* a *dotted for deletion.*

And sapheris swete / þat souȝte all wrongis,

Ypouudride wyth pete / þer it be ouȝte,

And traylid wíth trouþe / / and treste al aboute ;

For ony cristen kynge / a croune well ymakyd.   48

Βut where þis croune bicome / a clerk were þat wuste ;
But so as I can / declare it I thenke,

And nempne no name ; / but þo þat nest were,

Full preuyly þey pluckud / þy power awey,   52

And reden wíth realte / ȝoure rewme þoru-oute,

And as tyrauntis, of tiliers / token what hem liste,

And paide hem on her pannes / whan her penyes lacked.

For non of ȝoure peple / durste pleyne of here wrongis,   56

For drede of ȝoure dukys / & of here double harmes.

Men myȝtten as well haue hun[t]yd / an hare wíth a   [*fo.* 109 *b.*]
    tabre

As aske ony mendis / for þat þei mysdede,

Or of ony of her men / þouȝ men wulde plete,   60

For all was felawis and felawschepe / þat ȝe wíth ferde,

And no soule persone / to punnyshe þe wrongis ;

And þat maddid þi men / as þei nede muste.

For wo, þey ne wuste / to whom for to pleyne.   64

For, as it is said / by elderne dawis,

" Þer gromes and þe goodmen / beth all eliche grette,

Woll wo beth þe wones / and all þat woneth þer-in ! "

Þey ladde ȝou wíth loue / þat ȝoure lawe dradde   68

To deme ȝoure dukys myssdedis / so derue þei were.

Thus was ȝoure croune crasid / till he was cast newe,

Þoru partninge of ȝoure powere / to ȝoure paragals.

Thus lacchide þey wíth laughinge / and lourid longe after,   72

But frist sawe þey it not / ne youre-self noþer ;

For all was wisliche ywrouȝte / as ȝoure witte demed,

And no fauutis yffounde / till fortune aperid.

But had ȝoure croune be kepte / þat comons it wiste,   76

Þer nadde morder ne mysscheff / be amonge þe grette.

Thus ȝoure cautell to þe comoune / hath combred ȝou all,

That, but if God helpe / ȝoure heruest is ynne.

Right margin glosses:

adorned with sapphires, and powdered over with pity.

Where it is now who can tell ?

Thy courtiers plucked away thy power.

Thy people dared not complain.

Men might as well have hunted a hare with a tabor, as have sought redress.

This maddened thy people.

Where the servants are equal to the master, woe be to the house !

Thus was your crown cracked.

All was well done, as you thought.

---

53 reden : *first* e *altered to* y.   58 t *in later hand ; apparently over*
a minim.   64 Cesura *mark also after* wo.   77 nadde : had
nat *written above.*   78 cautell : crafte *written above.*

Blame not your council, but yourself.

Take good heed of my words.

In your council, the men whom you chose were all too young and too low-born.

When they knew you would be led by them, they thought only of their own grievances.

They told you to set aside all your true friends.

But they only cared for themselves.

Had you done what you ought, you would have hung up the first deceiver on the gallows,

But your fondness for knaves emboldened them.

Wytteth it not ȝoure conceill / but wyte[t]h it more ȝoure-self,   80
The fortune þat fallyn is / to feitheles peple ;
And wayte well my wordis / and wrappe hem to-gedir,
And constrwe [clerlie] / þe clause in þin herte
Of maters þat I thenke / to meve for þe best   84
For kyngis and kayserist / comynge here-after.
Whane ȝe were sette in ȝoure se / as a sir aughte,
Ther carpinge comynliche / of conceill arisith,
The cheuyteyns cheef / þat ȝe chesse euere,   88
Weren all to yonge of ȝeris / to yeme swyche a rewme ;
Oþer hobbis ȝe hadden / of Hurlewaynis kynne,
Reffusynge þe reule / of realles kynde.   [*fo.* 110 a.]
And whane ȝoure conceill i-knewe / ȝe come so at ones   92
For to leue on her lore / and be led be hem,
For drede þat þey had / of demynge þer-after,
And for curinge of hem-self / cried on ȝou euere,
For to hente hele / of her owen greues,   96
More þan for wurschepe / þat þey to ȝou owed.
Þey made ȝou to leue / þat regne ȝe ne myȝte
Wïthoute busshinge adoun / of all ȝoure best frendis,
Be a fals colour / her caris to wayve,   100
And to holde hem in hele / if it happe myȝte.
For trostiþ rith treuly / and in no tale better,
All þat þey moued / or mynged in þat mater
Was to be sure of hem-self / and siris to ben y-callid ;   104
For þat was all her werchinge / in worde and in dede.
But had ȝe do duly / and as a duke oughte,
Þe frist þat ȝou formed / to þat fals dede,
He shulde haue hadde hongynge / on hie on þe forckis,   108
Þouȝ ȝoure brother y-born / had be þe same.
Than wolde oþer boynardis / haue ben abasshyd
To haue meved ȝou to ony maters / þat myssheff had ben ynne.
But for ȝe cleued to knavis / in þis cas I avowe,   112
Þat boldid þi burþes / to belde vppon sorowe,
And stirid ȝou stouttely / till ȝe stombled all.

---

80 MS. wyteh [S.]   83 MS. clergie.   85 MS. kayseceris : lordes/rulers *written above* [S].   86 sir : lorde *written above*.   89 yeme : guyde or rule *written above*.   92 *Cesura mark also after* conceill. 103 *Cesura mark also after* mynged.   113 burnes : barons *written above*.

Passus secundus.

But moche now me merueilith / and well may I in sothe,
Of ȝoure large leuerey / to leodis abouȝte,
That ȝe so goodliche [g]af / but if gile letted,
As hertis y·heedyd / and hornyd of kynde,   4
So ryff as þey ronne / ȝoure rewme þoru-oute,
That non at ȝoure nede / ȝoure name wolde nempne
In fersnesse ne in foltheed / but faste fle awayward ;
And some stode astonyed / and stared for drede,   8
For eye of þe egle / þat oure helpe brouute.
And also in sothe / þe seson was paste
For hertis yheedid / so hy and so noble
To make ony myrthe / for mowtynge þat nyghed.   12
That bawtid ȝoure bestis / of here bolde chere ;   [*fo.* 110 *b.*]
Þey seuerid and sondrid / for somere hem faylid,
And flowen in-to forest / and feldis abouȝte,
All þe hoole herde / þat helde so [to]-gedir ;   16
But ȝet þey had hornes / half ȝere after.
Now liste me to lerne / ho me lere coude,
What kynnes conceyll / þat þe kyng had,
Or meued him most / to merke his liegis,   20
Or serue hem with signes / þat swarmed so thikke
Þoru-oute his lond / in lengþe and in brede,
Þat ho·so had hobblid / þoru holtes and tounes,
Or y-passid þe patthis / þer þe prynce dwellyd,   24
[Of] hertis or hyndis / on hassellis brestis,
Or some lordis leuere / þat þe lawe stried,
He shulde haue y-mette / mo þan ynowe.
For þey acombrede þe contre / and many curse seruid,   28
And carped to þe comounes / with þe kyngys mouþe,
Or with þe lordis / þer þey belefte were,
That no renke shulde rise / reson to schewe.
Þey plucked þe plomayle / from þe pore skynnes,   32

But most I marvel seeing how many liveries you granted,

that your white harts would not stand by you in your need.

But the moulting-time of the harts was drawing nigh.

They fled, but preserved their horns.

I will consider how the king's badges became so numerous,

that every one saw more than enough of them.

They cumbered the country.

They stripped the poor people.

---

a leuerey: *first* e *altered to* y.   3 MS. ȝaf.   8 astonyed : e *in later hand ; apparently over* i.   16 to *added above* [S].   17 half : a *added above.*   18 ho : o *in different ink ; no sign of alteration.*   25 MS. Or [S].   26 leuere : *first* e *altered to* y.   28 seruid : deserved *written above.*

And schewed her signes / for men shulde drede
To axe ony mendis / for her mys-dedis.
Thus leuerez ouere-loked / ȝoure liegis ichonne;

Those that bore the White-Hart badge oppressed the poor.

For þo þat had hertis / on hie on her brestis,   36
For þe more partie / I may well avowe,
Þey bare hem þe bolder / for her gay broches,
And busshid with her brestis / and bare adoun þe pouere
Liages þat loued ȝou þe lesse / for her yuell dedis.   40

For one hart that you marked on a badge, you lost ten score of faithful hearts.

So, trouthe to telle / as toune-men said,
For on þat ȝe merkyd / ȝe myssed ten schore
Of homeliche hertis / þat þe harme hente.
Thane was it foly / in feith, as me thynketh,   44
To sette siluer in signes / þat of nouȝt serued.
I not what ȝou eylid / but if it ese were;

At your accession, all was your own.

For frist at ȝoure anoyntynge / alle were ȝoure owen,
Bothe hertis and hyndis / and helde of non oþer;   [fo. 111 a.]
No lede of ȝoure lond / but as a liege aughte,   49
Ty[l] ȝe, of ȝoure dulnesse / deseueraunce made

Omne regnum in se diuisum desolabitur; luce.
Your badges spoilt the broth, and upset the pot.
I cannot tell what induced you to do this.

Þoru ȝoure side signes / þat shente all þe browet,
And cast adoun þe crokk / þe colys amyd.   52
Ȝit am I lewde / and litill good schewe
To coueyte knowliche / of kyngis wittis,
Or wilne to witte / [what] was þe mevynge
That [ladde] ȝou to lykynge / ȝoure liegis to merke,   56
Þat loued ȝou full lelly / or leuerez beg[a]nne,
And as redy to ride / or renne at ȝoure heste
As wyghte myghte wilne / wonnynge vppon erthe,
Tyll leuerez hem lette / and lordyns wrongis,   60
As ȝoure-self fonde well / whane fortune ȝou [fayled].

When you wished to trust your limbs, they failed you.

For whan ȝe list to lene / to ȝoure owen lymes,
Þey were so feble and feynte / for fauȝte of ȝoure lawe,
And so [wankel] and wayke / wexe in þe hammes   64
Þat þey had no myghte / to amende ȝoure greues
Ne to bere byrthen / ȝoure banere to helpe.

---

35 leuerez : *first* e *altered to* y.   50 MS. Ty; l *added above* [S].
55 MS. how.   56 ladde: MS. *omits* [S].   57, 60 leuerez :
first e *altered to* y.   57 MS. begynne; a *written above* y S.   61 MS.
folwyd; fayled *written above*.   62 lene: n *touched up*. lymes: *abbreviation added over* y.   64 MS. feble.

But it longith to no liegeman / his lord to anoye
Noþer in werk ne in word / but if his witt faile.   68

Then said Rea-
son to me,
" Never dis-
please your
judge and lord.

" No, redely," quod Reson / " þat reule I alowe :
Displese not þi demer / in dede ne in wordis
But if þe liste for to lede / þi lyf in dissese.

But ȝif God haue grauntyd þe / grace for to knowe   72
Ony manere mysscheff / þat myȝtte be amendyd,

Be content to
point out what
is amiss."

Schewe þat to þi souereyne / to schelde him from harmes ;
For and he be blessid / þe better þe betydyth
In tyme for to telle him / for þi trewe herte."   76

My opinion is,
that no ' main-
tainer ' should
wear a badge, or
any livery ;

Now for to telle trouthe / þus þan me thynketh,
That no manere meyntenour / shulde merkis bere,
Ne haue lordis leuere / þe lawe to apeire,
Neiþer bragger ne boster / for no breme wordis.   80
But ho-so had kunnynge / and conscience bothe
To stonde vnstombled / and stronge in his wittis,   [fo. 111 b.]

they should be
reserved for true
and good men.

Lele in his leuynge / leuyd be his owen,
Þat no manere mede / shulde make him wrye,   84
For to trien a trouthe / be-twynne two sidis,
And lette for no lordsche[p] / þe lawe to susteyne
Whane þe pore pleyned / þat put were to wrongis,
And I were of conceill / by Crist þat me bouȝte,   88

A good judge
ought to have a
badge and a
sufficient salary.

He shuld haue a signe / and sum-what be ȝere
For to kepe his contre / in quiete and in reste.
This were a good grounde / so me God helpe !
And a trewe tente / to take and to ȝeue,   92
[For] ony lord of this londet / þat leuereȝ vsith.

God alone knows
whether the
reason for giving
badges has been
a good or bad
one !

But how the gayes han y-gon / God wotte þe sothe
Amonge myȝtffull men / alle þese many ȝeris ;
And whedir þe grou[n]de of [g]ifte / were good oþer ille,   96
Trouthe haþe determyned / þe tente to þe ende,
And reson hath rehersid / þe resceyte of all.

No doubt you
wished the

ȝit I trowe ȝoure ententé / at þe frist tyme
Was, as I wene, ȝif I well thenke / in multitude of peple,   100

79 leuere : *altered to* lyuerey.   80 breme : *first* e *altered to* y *and
nasal abbreviation added.*   83 leuynge : *nasal abbreviation over* y
expunctuated.   be : *altered to* by.   86 lordschep : p *added in later
hand* [S].   93 MS *and,* lonnde.   94 gayes : d *written above* g.
96 grounde : *nasal abbreviation over* u *expunctuated* : ȝifte.   100 *Cesura
mark also after* wene.

That ȝe were þe more myȝtier / for þe many signes
Þat ȝe and ȝoure seruauntis / abouȝte so thikke sowid ;
And þat þey were more tristi / and trewer þan oþer

To loue ȝou for þe leuere / þat legaunce stroied ;   104
Or ellis for a skylle / þat skathed ȝoure-self,
Þat comounes of contre / [in] costis abouȝte

Sholde knowe be hir quentise / þat þe kyng loued hem
For her priuy prynte / passinge anoþer.   108
ȝif þat was ȝoure purpos / it passith my wittis

To deme discrecion / of ȝoure well-doynge.
Þus were ȝe disceyued / þoru ȝoure duble hertis,
Þat neuere weren to truste / so God saue my soule !   112

But had þe good greehonde / be not agreued,
But cherischid as a cheffeteyne / and cheff of ȝoure lese,
ȝe hadde had hertis ynowe at ȝoure wille / to go and to ride.
And also in serteyne / þe soþe for to telle,   116
I wondir not hyly / þouȝ heed-dere [you] failid ;   [*fo.* 112 *a.*]
For litill on ȝoure lyf / þe list for to rewe

On rascaile þat rorid / with ribbis so lene,
For fauȝte of her fode / þat flateris stelen,   120
And euere with here wylis & wast / ofte þey hem anoyed,
Þat pouerte hem prickid / full preuyliche to pleyne,
But where, þey ne wyste / ne ho it wolde amende.

Þus ȝe derid hem vnduly / with droppis of anger,   124
And stonyed hem with stormes / þat stynted neuere,
But plucked and pulled hem / anon to þe skynnes,
Þat þe fresinge frost / freted to here hertis.

So whanne ȝoure hauntelere-dere / where all ytakyn,   128
Was non of þe rasskayle / aredy full growe
To bere ony breme heed / as a best aughte,
So wyntris wedir / hem wessh with þe snowis,
With many derke mystis / þat maddid her eyne.   132
For well mowe ȝe wyttyn / & so mowe we all,
Þat harde is þe somer / þer sonne schyneth neuere.

102 sowid : shewed *written above.*   104 leuere *altered to* lyuerey.
legaunce : e *added after* g *above line.*   106 MS. had *crossed out and*
in *written above* [S].   107 be : *altered to* by.   115 Cesura *aftre*
ynowe.   117 MS. þou.   130 breme : *first* e *altered to* y *and*
nasal abbreviation added.

ȝe fostrid and fodid / a fewe of þe best,

And leyde on hem lordschipe / a leyne vppon oþer,   136

And bereued þe raskall / þat rith wolde þei hadde,

And knewe not þᵉ caris / ne cursis þat walkyd ;

But mesure is a meri mene / þouȝ men moche yerne :

Þus [rend] be þe rotus / ȝoure raskall endurid,   140

Tyll þe blessid bredd / brodid his wyngis

To couere hem from colde / as his kynde wolde.

Rith as þe hous-hennes / vppon londe hacchen

And cherichen her chekonys / fro chele of þe wynter,   144

Ryth so þᵉ hende egle / þᵉ [heyere] of hem all,

Hasteth him in heruest / to houyn his bryddis,

And besieth him besely / to breden hem feedrin,

Tyll her fre fedris / be fulliche y-pynned,   148

Þat þey haue wynge at her wyll / to wonne vppon hille ;

For venym on þe valeye / hadde foule with hem fare,

Tyll trouthe þe triacle / telde somme her sothes.

Thus baterid þis bred / on busshes abouȝte,   152

And gaderid gomes on grene / þer as þey walkyd,   [fo. 112b.]

Þat all þe schroff and schroup / sondrid from oþer.

He mellid so þe matall / with þe hand-[melle]

That [þey] lost lemes / þᵉ leuest þat þey had.   156

Thus foulyd þis faukyn / on fyldis abouȝte,

And cauȝte of þe kuyttis / a cartffull at ones,

That rentis and robis / with raveyn euere lauȝte.

ȝit was not þᵉ fawcon / full fed at his likynge,   160

For it cam him not of kynde / kytes to loue.

Than bated he boldeliche / as a brid wolde,

To plewme on his pray / þe pol fro þe nekk ;

But þe blernyed boynard / þat his bagg stall,   164

Where purraile-is pulter / was pynnyd full ofte,

Made þe fawcon to floter / and flussh for anger

That þe boy [nadd] be bounde / þat þe bagge kepte.

But sone þer-after / in a schorte tyme,   168

You fostered a few of the best, and gave them lordships.

Deus exaudit clamorem pauperum, et iudicat causam eorum; Dauid in psalmis.

As the hens cherish their chickens, so the Eagle is busy about his brood till their wings are grown.

The Eagle caused Bushy, Green, and Scrope to lose their heads.

The Eagle tried to pull the head from the neck of his prey.

---

140 rend : MS. *omits.*   be : *altered to* by.   rotus : e *written above* u.
144 cherichen : cherissheth *written above.*   chele : colde *written above.*
145 MS. Eyere [S].   155 MS. molde.   156 þey : MS. *omits* [S].
158 kuyttis : kytes *written above.*   159 euere : *final* e *crossed out.*
lauȝte : caught *written above.*   167 MS. hadd.

As fortune folwith / ech fode till his ende,
This lorell þat [ladde] / þis loby awey
Ouere frithe and forde / for his fals dedis,
Lyghte on þe lordschepe / þat to þe brid longid,   172
And was felliche ylauȝte / and luggid full ylle,
And brouȝte to þe brydd / and his blames rehersid
Preuyly at þe parlement / amonge all þe peple.

Thus hawkyd þis egle / and houed aboue,   176
Þat, as God wolde / þat gouerneth all þingis,
Ther nas kyte ne krowe / þat kareyne hantid,
Þat he ne with his lynage / ne louyd full sone.
For wher-so þey ferde / be fryth or be wones,   180
Was non of hem all / þat him hide myȝth,

But cam with him a reclayme / fro costis abouȝte,
And fell with her fetheris / flat vppon þe erthe,
As madde of her mynde / and mercy be-souȝte.   184

Þey myȝte not aschonne / þe sorowe þey had serued,
So lymed leues / were leyde all abouȝte,
And panteris preuyliche / pight vppon þe grounde,
With grennes of good heere / þat God him-self made, [fo. 113 a.]
Þat where-so þey walkid / þey waltrid dounwardis ;   189

And euere houed þe egle / on hie on þe skyes,
And kenned clerliche / as his kynde axith,
Alle þe preuy poyntis / þat þe pies wrouȝth.   192

Passus Tercius.

Now leue we þis beu brid / till I restore,
For mater þat my mynde / is meved in now,
That whi þe hie hertis / her hele so mysside,
Þat pasture axid / rith to here pure wombis,   4
I wolle schewe as I sawe / till I se better ;
And if I walke out of þe wey / I wolle me repente.

Now herkeneth, hende men / how þat me thynkyth,
Sauynge souereynes / and sages avise,   8

170 MS. hadde [S].   171 Ouere : *final* e *crossed out.*   178 hantid : u *added after* a *above line.*   185 serued : deserved *written above.* 187 *Catch-word* with grennes of good here.   188 grennes : greyhoundes *written above.*   190 euere : *final* e *crossed out.* 8 Sauynge : *nasal abbreviation over* y *expunctuated.*

Þat þe moste myscheff / vppon molde on
Is demed þe dede / ydo aȝeins kynde.

I will apply this.

Ȝit clereth þis clause / no þinge my wittis,
With-out more mater / what it mene wolde.   12
I mene of þe hertis / [of] hautesse of ȝeris,

When harts come to be a century old,

Þat pasture prikkyth / and her preuy age,
Whan þey han hoblid on þe holte / an hundrid of ȝeris,
That þey feblen in fleissh / in felle and in bones.   16

and grow feeble, they instinctively strive to catch adders.

Her kynde is to keuere / if þey cacche myȝth
Adders þat armen / alle hende bestis;
Þoru busschis and bromes / þis beste, of his kynde,
Secheth and sercheth / þo schrewed wormes,   20
Þat steleth on þe stedis / to stynge hem to deth;
And whanne it happeth þe herte / to hente þe edder,

When the hart finds the adder, he feeds on his venom,

He putyth him to peyne / as his pray asketh,
And fedith him on þe venym / his felle to anewe,   24

renews his skin, and prolongs his life.

To leue at more lykynge / a longe tyme after.
This is [clerlie] hir kynde / coltis [not] to greue,

It is against nature for harts to attack a Horse, a Swan, or a Bear.

Ne to hurlle with haras / ne hors well atamed,
Ne to stryue with swan / þouȝ it sholle werre,   28
Ne to bayten on þe bere / ne bynde him noþer,
Ne to wilne to woo / þat were hem ny sibbe,

Propter ingratitudinem liber homo reuocatur in seruit[u]tem, ut in stimulo compunccionis, et in lege ciuili.

Ne to liste for to loke / þat her alie bledde;
This was aȝeins kynde / as clerkis me tolde;   32

[fol. 113 b.]

And þer-for þe hertis / here hele so myssid,

Thus it was that they missed their safety.

And myȝte nat passe þe poynte / of her prime age.
Now constrew ho-so kunne / I can saie no more,
But fare I wolle to þe fowle / þat I beffore tolde.   36

I praise most the partridge.

Off all billid breddis / þat þe bough spareth,
  Þe propirte of partriche / to preise me lustiþ,
Þat in þe somer seson / whan sittinge nyeth,
Þat ich foule with his fere / folwith his kynde,   40

This bird tries to hatch her eggs.

Þis brid be a bank / bildith his nest,
And heipeth his [eiren] / and hetith hem after.
And whane þe dame hath ydo / þat to þe dede longith,
And hopith for to hacche / or heruest begynne,   44

---

13 MS. þat.   25 leue: *first* e *altered to* y.   26 MS. clergie [S].
not: MS. *omits*; nat *written above line* [S].   30 *Side-note*.
MS. *seruititem*.   41 be: *altered to* by.   42 MS. heires [S].

Thane cometh þer a congion / wiþ a grey cote,

As not of his nolle / as he þe nest made,

But another partridge comes and takes her place, Anoþer proud partriche / and precyth to þe nest,

And preuylich pirith / till þe dame passe,   48

And sesith on hir [sete] / wiþ hir softe plumes,

And houeth þe eyren / þat þe hue laide,

and sits on the eggs till they are hatched. And wiþ hir corps keuereth hem / till þat þey kenne,

And fostrith and fodith / till fedris schewe,   52

And cotis of kynde / hem keuere all abouȝte.

But as sone as þey styffe / and þat þey steppe kunne,

Then comes back their own mother, and they at once desert the intruder. Þan cometh and crieth / hir owen kynde dame,

And þey folwith þe vois / at þe frist note,   56

And leueth þe lurker / þat hem er ladde,

For þe schrewe schrapid / to selde for her wombis,

Þat her lendys were lene / and leued wiþ hunger.

But þan þe dewe dame / dineth hem swythe,   60

And fostrith hem forthe / till þey fle kunne.

What does this mean? "What is þis to mene, man?" maiste þou axe,

"For it is derklich endited / for a dull panne ;

Wherffore I wilne / ȝif it þi will were,   64

Ah! Hick Heavyhead! your wits are dull! Þe partriche propurtes / by whom þat þou menest?"

A! Hicke Heuyheed! / hard is þi nolle

To cacche ony kunynge / but cautell bigynne!

Herdist þou not wiþ eeris / how þat I er tellde   68

How þe egle in þe est / entrid his owen,   [fo. 114 a.]

The Eagle in like manner came back to his own young ones, And cried and clepid / after his owen kynde briddis,

Þat weren anoyed in his nest / and norished full ille,

And well ny yworewid / wiþ a wronge leder?   72

But þe nedy nestlingis / whan þey þe note herde

and the young ones followed him. Of þe [hende] egle / þe heyer of hem all,

Þei busked fro þe busches / and breris þat hem noyed,

And burnisched her beekis / and bent to-him-wardis,   76

And folowid him fersly / to fighte for þe wrongis ;

They complained how they had been ill-used for 22 years. Þey bablid wiþ her billis / how þei bete were,

And tenyd wiþ twiggis / two and twenty ȝeris.

---

45 Thane : *nasal abbreviation over a expunctuated.*   49 MS. cete : *altered to* sete [S].   softe : o *touched up.*   59 leued : *first* e *altered to* y.   67 kunynge : *nasal abbreviation over* u *expunctuated.*   74 MS. ende : h *added above line* [S].

Thus lafte þey þe leder / þat hem wrong ladde, 80
And [tyned] no twynte / but tolled her cornes,
And gaderid þe grotus / wiþ gyle, as I trowe.

Þan folwid þey her fre fader / as good feith wolde,   *They followed their true father.*
That he hem fede shulde / and fostre forther, 84
And bringe hem out of bondage / þat þey were brouȝth inne.

Thanne sighed þe swymmers / for þe swan failid,   *So did those who lamented the fate of the Swan and the Horse.*
And folwid þis faucon / þoru feldus and tounes,
Wiþ many faire [fowle] / þouȝ þey feynte were, 88
And heuy for þe hirte / þat þe hors hadde.

ȝit þey ferkyd hem forth / as faste as þey myȝte,
To haue þe egles helpe / of harme þat þey hadde ;
For he was heed of hem all / and hieste of kynde 92
To kepe þe croune / as cronecle tellith.

He blythid þe beere / and his [bond] braste,   *The Eagle freed the Bear.*
And lete him go at large / to lepe where he wolde.

But þo all þe berlingis / brast out at ones, 96
As fayne [as] þe foule / þat flieth on þe skyes
Þat Bosse was vnbounde / and brouute to his owen.

Þey gaderid hem to-gedir / on a grette rouȝte,
To helpe þe heeris / þat had many wrongis ; 100   *The followers of the Eagle complained of Green.*
Þey gaglide forth on þe grene / for þey greued were
Þat her frendis were falle / þoru felons castis.

They mornyd for þe morthir / of manffull knyȝtis,
That many a styff storme / wiþ-stode for þe comunes ; [fo. 114 b.]
[Þey] monside þe marchall / for his myssedede, 105   *They cursed the Earl Marshal.*
Þat euell coude † his craft / whan he [cloyed] þe stede.

And euere as þey folwide / þis faucon abouȝte,
At iche mevinge fotte / venyauncet þey asked 108
On all þat assentid / to þat synffull dede,

Arere now to Richard / and reste here awhile,   *Let us return to Richard.*
For a preuy poynt / þat [passith] my wittis,
Of fauutis I fynde / þat frist dede engendre 112   *I speak of the faults that so*

---

81 MS. tymed [S].   82, 87 grotus, feldus : e *written above* u.   86 þᵉ Swan *in margin*.   88 fowle : MS. foole : fowle *written above* [S.] 89 hirte : u *written above* i.   þᵉ horse *in margin*.   94 MS. brond. The Beare *in margin*.   97 MS. was [S].   102 felons : *nasal abbreviation over* n *expunctuated*.   105 MS. þᵉ [S].   106 MS. conude, cloþed. 108 MS. venyanunce.   111 MS. persith.

much harmed
the young lords.

Cursidnesse and combraunce / amonge þe yonge lordis,
And þᵉ wikkid werchinge / þat walmed in her daies,
And ʒit woll here-after / but wisdom it lette.
That were a lord of lond / þat lawe hathe in honde,   116
Þat to lyghtliche leueth / or lewte apere,
Þᵉ tale of a trifflour / in turmentours wede,
That neuere reed good rewle / ne resons bookis !

They cared for
nothing but
dress.

For ben þey rayed arith / þey recchith no forther,   120
But studieth all in strouutynge / and stireth amys euere;

In my opinion,
fashionable men
are evil coun-
sellors,

[For I say for my-self / and schewe, as me thyn[c]hith,
That ho is riall of his ray / that light reede him folwith;]
For all his witte in his wede / ys wrappid for sothe,   124
More þan in mater to amende / þe peple þat ben mys-led.
ʒit swiche fresshe foodis / beth feet in-to chambris,
[And for her wedis so wyde / wise beth y-holde;]

respected only by
fools.
Qui mollibus
vestiuntur in
domibus re-
gum sunt : in
Euangelio.
See what comes
of these be-
guilers !

And for her dignesse endauntid / of dullisshe nollis,   128
And, if þou well waite / of no wight ellis.
Þan waite mo wayes / how þe while turneth
With g[uy]leris, joyffull / for here gery jaces;
Þey casteth hem to creaunce / þe courte for to plese,   132

They hope to be
exalted for their
finery;

And hopen to be hied / in hast, yif þey myʒthe,
Þoru swiche stif strouutynge / þat stroyeth þe rewme;
But here wey is all wronge / þer wisdom is ynned,

but they come to
a bad end.

[For] þey lepith als lygh[t]ly / at þᵉ longe goynge,   136
Out of þe domes carte / as he þat þroff neuere.
For þey kepeth no coyne / þat cometh to here hondis, [fo. 115 a.]

They exchange
their coin for
chains,

But chaunchyth it for cheynes / þat in chepe hangith,
And settith all her siluer / in [seintis] and hornes,   140
And for-doth þe coyne / and many oþer craftis,

and make money
scarce.

And makeþ þe pep[l]e for pens-lac / in pointe for to wepe;
And ʒit þey beth ytake forth / and her tale leued,
And for her newe nysete / nexte to þe lordis,   144

By Lidford law,
such men ought
to thrive ill.

(Now, be þe lawe of Lydfford / in londe [&] in water
Þilke lewde ladde / ouʒte euyll to þryue,

---

122 MS. thynthith.   122–3 *In* MS. *follow* 125.   123 *Cesura
mark also after* riall.   127 *In* MS. *follows* 131.   131 MS. gyuleris.
132 creaunce : *nasal abbreviation over* a *expunctuated.*   136 MS. But,
lyghly [S].   140 MS. se + 4 *minims* + tis [S].   142 MS. pephe [S].
145 & : ne *written over erasure* [S].

Þat hongith on his hippis / more þan he wynneth)
And douȝteth no dette / so dukis hem preise,   148
But beggith and borwith / of burgeis in tounes
Furris of foyne / and oþer felle-whare,
And not þe better of a bene / þouȝ þey boru euere.

And, but if þe slevis / slide on þe erthe,   152   Except their
Þei woll be wroth as þe wynde / and warie hem þat it   sleeves touch the
                                                                 ground, they are
   made;   very wroth.
And [but] ȝif it were elbowis / adoun to the helis
Or passinge þe knee / it was not acounted.

And if Pernell preisid / þe plytis bihynde,   156   If Pernel praises
The costis were acountid / paye whan he myȝth.   the pleats, all is
                                                                 well.
Þe leesinge so likyde / ladies and oþer
Þat þey joied of þe jette / and gyside hem þer-vnder;
And if Felice fonde ony faute † / þenne of þe makynge,   160   If Felice finds
Yt was y-sent sone / to shape of þe newe.   fault, all must be
                                                                 remade.
But now þer is a gyse / þe queyntest of all,
A wondir coriouse crafte / y-come now [of] late,   The latest fashion
That men clepith kerving / þe cloþe all to pecis,   164   is to slash the
                                                                 cloth.
Þat seuene goode sowers / sixe wekes after
Moun not sett þe seemes / ne sewe hem aȝeyn.

But þer is a pr[o]ffit in þat pride / þat I preise euere,
For þei for þe pesinge paieth / pens ten duble   168   The piecing
That þe cloþe costened / þe craft is so dere.   costs twenty
                                                                 times as much as
                                                                 the stuff.
Now if I sothe shall saie / and shonne side tales,
Þer is as moche good witte / in swyche gomes nollis,
As þou shuldist mete of a myst / fro morwe tyll euen.   172
ȝit blame I no burne / to be, as him ouȝte,   [fo. 115 b.]
In comliche cloþinge / as his statt axith;
But to ledyn her lust / all here lyff-daies   Men who think
                                                                 of nothing but
In quentise of cloþinge / for to queme sir Pride,   176   dress and new
And euere-more stroutynge / and no store kepe,   fashions ought
                                                                 not to be trusted.
And iche day a newe deuyse / it dullith my wittes
Þat ony lord of a lond / shulde leue swiche þingis,

---

154 but: MS. *omits* [S].   155 acounted : *nasal abbreviation over* u
expunctuated.   156 plytis: pleytis *written above.*   157 acountid :
nasal abbreviation over o *expunctuated.*   160 MS. ffaunte.   163 of :
MS. *omits* ; *added above line* [S].   164 kervinge of clothes *in margin.*
167 MS. a prffith ; a profett *written above* [S].

Or clepe to his conceill / swiche maner*e* cotis,   180
That loueth more her lustis / þan þᵉ lore of our*e* Lord.
And if a lord his leu*ere* / lyste for to ȝeue,

Ther may no gome for goodnesse / gette þ*er*-of but lite
For curtesie, for comlynesse / ne for his kynde herte,   184
But rather for his ranco*ur* / and rennynge ou*ere* peple,
For braggynge and for bostynge / and beringe vppon oilles,
For cursidnes of conscience / and comynge to þᵉ assises.
This makyth me*n* mysdo / more þan ouȝte ellis,   188
And to stroute and to stare / and stryue aȝeyn vertu.

So [clerlie], þᵉ cause / comsith in grette,
Of all maner*e* mysscheff / þat men here vsyn.

For wolde þey blame þᵉ burnes / þat brouȝte newe gysis,   192
And dryue out þᵉ dagges / and all þᵉ Duche cotis,
And sette hem aside / and [schorn] of hem telle,
And lete hem pleye in þᵉ porche / and presse no*n* ynner*e*,
Ne no proude peniles / wi*th* his peynte sleve ;   196
And eke repr*eue* robbers / and riffleris of peple,
Flateris and fals me*n* / þat no feith vseth,
And alle deabolik doeris / dispise hem ichone,
And coile out þᵉ knyȝtys / þat knowe well hem-self,   200
Þ*a*t were sad of her sawis / and suffre well couude,†
And had traueilid in her tyme / and temprid hem-self,
And cherliche cheriche hem / as cheff in þe halle
For to ordeyne officeris / and all oþ*er* thyngis,   204
Me*n* shuld wete in a while / þat þᵉ world wolde amende ;
So vertue wolde flowe / whan vicis were ebbid.

But now to þe mat*er* / þat I be-fore meved,   [*fo*. 116*a*.]
Of þᵉ gomes so gay / þat grace hadde affendid,   208
And how stille þat steddeffaste stode / amonge þis reccheles
          peple,
Þ*a*t had awilled his wyll / as wisdom him taughte :
For he drough him to an herne / at þe halle ende,
Well homelich yhelid / in an holsum gyse,   212
Not ou*ere*longe, but ordeyned / in þe olde schappe,
Wi*th* grette browis y-bente / and a berde eke,

And y-wounde in his wedis / as þe wedir axith ;

He wondrid in his wittis / as he [well] myȝthe,   216   wondering at the vast households.

Þat þe hie houusinge / herborowe ne myghte

Halfdell þe houshould / but hales hem helped ;

But for crafte þat he couude † caste / þenne or be-þenke,

He myȝte not wonne in þe wones / for witt þat he vsid ;   220

But, arouutyd for his ray / and rebuked ofte,

He had leue of þe lord / and of ladies alle

For his good gouernaunce / to go or he drank.

Þer was non of þe mene / þat þey ne merueilid moche   224

How he cam to þe courte / and was not y-knowe ;

But als sone as þey wiste / þat Witt was his name,   As soon as men knew that his

And þat þe kyng knewe him not / ne non of his knyȝtis,   name was Wit,

He was halowid and y-huntid / and y-hotte trusse,   228   they bade him begone !

And his dwellinge ydemed / a bowe-drawte from hem,

And ich man y-charchid / to schoppe at his croune,

ȝif he nyhed hem ony nere / þan þey had him nempned.

Þe portir with his pikis / þo put him vttere,   232

And warned him þe wickett / while þe wacche durid :

" Lete sle him ! " quod þe sleues / þat slode vppon þe erthe,   The sleeve-wearers wanted to slay him,

And alle þe berdles burnes / bayed on him euere,

And schorned him, for his slaueyn / was of þe olde schappe.   and scorned him for his old clothes.

Þus Malaperte was myȝtffull / and maister of hous,   237

And euere wandrid Wisdom / without þe ȝatis.

" By him þat wrouȝte þis world ! " / quod Wisdom in wrath,   Wit threatened them with

" But ȝif ȝe woll sumtyme / I walke in amonge ȝou,   240   punishment.

I shall forbede ȝou burnesse / þe best on þis erthe,   [*fo.* 116 *b.*]

Þat is, gouernance of gettinge / and grace þat him follwith ;

For þese two trewly / twynned ȝet neuere."

And so it fell on hem, in feith / for fauȝtis þat þey vsid,   244   Thus the foolish lords lost favour.

Þat her grace was agoo / for grucchinge chere,

For þe wrong þat þey wrouȝte / to Wisdom affore.

For tristith, als trewly / as tyllinge us helpeth,

Þat iche rewme vndir roff / of þe reyne-bowe   248   Every kingdom depends on 3 sorts of men :

Sholde stable and stonde / be þese þre degres :

---

216 MS. will : e *written above.*   219 MS. couude.   220 Wytt
was banysshed oute of the Courte *in margin.*   223 gouernaunce,
drank : *nasal abbreviation over* a *expunctuated.*   228 y-hotte : bydden
written above.

1. Counsellors   By gouerna[un]ce of grete / and of good age ;

2. Warriors.   By styffnesse and strengthe / of steeris well y-yokyd,

Þat beth myȝthffull men / of þe mydill age ;   252

3. Labourers.   And be laboreris of lond / þat lyfflode ne fayle.

Thanne wolde [right dome] reule / if reson where amongis us,

Þat ich leode lokide / what longid to his age,

And neuere for to passe more / oo poynt forþer,   256

To vsurpe þe seruice / þat to sages bilongith,

To be-come conselleris / er þey kunne rede,

In schenshepe of souereynes / and shame at þe last.

Youths of 24 years can no more advise than a cow can hop in a cage.   For it fallith as well to fodis / of xxiiij ȝeris,   260

Or yonge men of yistirday / to ȝeue good redis,

As becometh a kow / to hoppe in a cage !

It is not vnknowen / to kunnynge leodis,

That rewlers of rewmes / around all þe erthe   264

Were not yffoundid / at þe frist tyme

To leue al at likynge / and lust of þe world,

Rulers should uphold the law,   But to laboure on þe lawe / as lewde men on plowes,

And to merke meyntenourȝ / with maces ichonne,   268

And to strie strouters / þat sterede aȝeine rithis,

And alle þe myssedoers / þat þey myȝte fynde,

and imprison wrong-doers,   To put hem in preson / a peere þouȝ he were ;

And [not] to rewle as reremys / and rest on þe daies,   272

And spende of þe spicerie / more þan it nedid,

not waste money in wine and dances.   Bothe wexe and wyn / in wast all abouȝte,

With deyntes y-doublid / and daunsinge to pipis,

In myrthe with moppis / myrrours of synne.   276

Rejoice in season.   Ȝit forbede I no burne / to be blithe sum while ;

But all þinge hath tyme / for to tempre glees :   [*fo.* 117 *a.*]

For caste all þe countis † / þat þe kyng holdith,

And loke how þese lordis / loggen hem-self,   280

no*ta.* no*ta.* no*ta.* Do not sit up late.   And euere shall þou fynde / as fer as þou walkiste,

[Þat] wisdom and ouere-wacche / wonneth fer asundre ;

But whane þe gouernaunce goth þus / with þo þe hous gie shulde,

250 MS. gouernanmce.   *Side-note : the numbers* 1, 2, 3 *are added in the margin.*   254 right dome : MS. *omits* [S]. *Agaynste yonnge Counsaylours in margin in late hand.*   260 *Cesura after* well.   272 not : MS. *omits* [S].   278 *two letters erased before* glees.   279 MS. counntis.   282 MS. What [S].   *Over watchynge in margin.*

And letith lyghte of þᵉ lawe / and lesse of þᵉ peple, 284   Despising of the law will not long thrive.
And herkeneth all to hono*ur* / and to ese eke,
And þat ich wyght *with* his witt / waite on him eu*e*re,
To do hem reuerence aright / þou3 þe rigge brest,
Þis warmnesse in welth / *with* wy vppon erthe 288
My3te not longe dure / as docto*ur*3 us tellith.

For ho-so þus leued / his lyff to þe ende,   For evil-doers to come to no mishap would be a wonder indeed !
Eu*e*re wrappid in welle / and *with* no wo mette,
My3te seie þat he sawe / þat seie was neu*e*re, 292
Þat heuene-[3ate] were vnhonge / out of þe hookis,
And were boun at his bidding / 3if it be my3te.

But clerkis kne[w] I no*n* 3ete / þat so couude rede   Clerks find it so in no books.
In bokis y-bounde / þou3 3e brou3te alle 296
Þat ony wy welldith / wonnynge vppon erthe ;
For in well and in woo / þᵉ werld eu*e*re turneth.

3it þer is kew-kaw / þou3 he come late,
A new þing þat noyeth / nedy me*n* and oþer, 300
Wha*n*ne realles remeveth / and ridith þoru tounes,
And carieth ou*e*re contre / þer comunes dwelleth,
To preson þᵉ pillo*ur*3 / þat oue*re* þe pore renneth ;
For þat were euene in her weye / if þey well ride 304
But 3it þer is a foule fau3te / þat I fynde ofte :   Another grievance is that great men will not do justice unless they are given presents.
Þey prien aff*ter* presentis / or pleyntis ben yclepid,
And abateth all þᵉ billis / of þo þat nou3th bringith ;
And ho-so grucche or grone / a3eins her grette willes, 308
May lese her lyff lyghtly / and no lesse weddis.

Thus is þe lawe louyd / þoru my3hty lordis willys,   Thus is the law brought low through maintenance.
Þat meyneteyne myssdoers / more þan oþer peple.
For mayntenance many day / well more is þᵉ reuthe ! 312
Hath y-had mo men / at mete and at melis
Þan ony cristen kynge / þat 3e knewe eu*e*re ; [*fo.* 117 *b.*]
For, as reson and rith / rehersid to me ones,
Tho ben me*n* of þis molde / þat most harme worchen. 316
For chyders of Chest*er* / where chose many daies   Chiders from Chester were

---

288 wy : man *written above.* 290 leued : eu *altered to* yv. 293
3ate : MS. *omits.* 295 MS. kne [S]. 297 wy : man *written above.*
299 kew kaw *in margin.* 306 Takynge of present*es in margin.*
312 maynte*n*ance : *nasal abbreviation over second* a *expunctuated* ;
mayntenance *in margin in late hand.*

brought into
Court to force a
result.

To ben of conceill for causis / þat in þᵉ court hangid,

And pledid pipoudris / alle manᵉre pleyntis.

Þey cared for no coyffes / þat men of court vsyn,   320

But meved many maters / þat man neuᵉr thouȝte,

And feyned falshed / till þey a fyne had,

And knewe no manᵉre cause / as comunes tolde.

Þei had non oþᵉr signe / to schewe þᵉ lawe   324

They wore head-
pieces instead of
coifs.

But a preuy pallette / her pannes to kepe,

To hille here lewde heed / in stede of an houe.

They pleaded
chiefly with axes
and swords.

Þey constrewed quarellis / to quenche þᵉ peple,

And pletid *with* pollaxis / and poyntis of swerdis,   328

And at þe dome-ȝeuynge / drowe out þᵉ bladis,

And lente men leuᵉre / of her longe battis.

Þey lacked alle vertues / þat a juge shulde haue ;

For, er a tale were ytolde / þey wolde trie þᵉ harmes,   332

*Wit*houte ony answere / but ho his lyf hatid.

Whoever com-
plained of them
to the king
was threatened
with death.

And ho-so pleyned to þe prince / þat pees shulde kepe,

Of þese mystirmen / medlers of wrongis,

He was lygh[t]liche ylauȝte / and y-luggyd of many,   336

And y-mummyd on þe mouthe / and manaced to þe deth.

They leid on þi leigis, Ric*h*ard / lasshis ynow,

And drede neuᵉre a dele / þᵉ dome of þe lawe.

No one dared to
rebuke them.

Þer nas rial of þᵉ rewme / þat hem durste rebuke,   340

Ne juge ne justice / þat jewis durste hem deme

For oute þat þei toke / or trespassid to þᵉ peple.

This was a wondir world / ho-so well lokyd,

Upstarts sur-
passed lords in
power.

Þat gromes ouᵉre-grewe / so many grette maistris ;   344

For þis was þᵉ rewle in þis rewme / while þey here regnyd.

Þouȝ I satte seuenenyght / and slepte full selde,

[I miȝte not reche redili / to rekene þe nombre]

More wrongs
happened than I
can tell of.

Of many mo wrongis / þan I write couude ;   348

For selde were þᵉ ser[gi]auntis / souȝte for to plete,

Or ony prentise of courte / preied of his wittis,   [*fo.* 118 *a.*]

Þᵉ while þᵉ degonys domes / weren so endauntid.

But the Lord
of Heaven saw
these men's mis-
deeds.

Tille oure *sire* in his see / aboue þe vij^{ne} sterris,   352

Sawe þe many mysscheuys / þat þese men dede,

---

330 leuᵉre : *first* e *altered to* y, *and* y *added.*   336 MS. lyghliche :
t *added above line* [S].   347 *a line omitted, supplied by Skeat.*   349 MS.
serigauntis [S].

And no mendis ymade / but menteyne[d] eue*r*e
Of him þat was hiest / y-holde for to kepe
His liegis in lawe / and so her loue gette.   356

He sente for his seruantis / þat sembled many,
Of baronys and baccheleris / wi*th* many briȝth helmes,
Wi*th* þe comunes [of] contres / þey cam all at ones ;
And as a duke douȝty / in dedis of armes,   360
In full reall aray / he rood vppon hem eue*r*e,
Tyll Degon and Dobyn / þat me*n*nys doris brastyn,
And were y-dubbid of a duke / for her while domes,
† Awakyd [fro] wecchis / and wast þat þey vsid,   364
And for her breme blastis / buffettis henten.
Þan gan it to calme / and clere all abouȝte,
Þat iche ma*n* myȝte / ho-so mynde hadde,
Se, be þe sonne / þat so briȝte schewed,   368
Þe mone at þe mydday / meve, and þe sterris,
Folwinge felou*n*s / for her false dedis,
Devourou*r*s of vetaile / þat fouȝten er þei paide.

in royal array He rode against them,

till they received severe buffets.

Then came a peaceful and clear calm.

He assembled His servants, barons, bachelors, and commons;

Passus quartus.

For where was eue*r*e ony cristen kynge / þat ȝe eue*r*e knewe,
Þat helde swiche an household / be þe halfdelle
As Richard in þis rewme / þoru myserule of oþer,
Þat alle his fynys for fauȝtis / ne his fee-fermes,   4
Ne for-feyturis fele / þat felle in his daies,
Ne þe nownagis / þat newed him eue*r*e,
As Marche and Moubray † / and many mo oþer,
Ne alle þe issues of court / þat to þe kyng longid,   8
Ne sellynge, þat sowkid / siluer rith faste,
Ne alle þe prophete of þe lond / þat þe prince owed,
Whane þe cou*n*tis were caste / wi*th* þe custu*m* of wullus,
Myȝte not areche / ne his rent noþer,   12
To paie þe pore peple / þat his puruyou*r*s toke,
Wi*th*oute preier*e* at a parleme*n*t / a poundage biside, [*fo.* 118 *b.*]
And a fifteneth / and a dyme eke,
And wi*th* all þe custu*m* of þe cloþe / þat cometh to fayres ? 16

Whose household was ever larger than Richard's ?

Not all his fines, forfeitures,

law-fees,

and custom of wools,

could repay the poor for his exactions.

354 MS. menteyne it [S].   355 for *added above line by scribe.*
359 MS. þe [S].   364 MS. And awakyd for [S].
7 MS. mou*n*bray.

But for credit,
he and his would
have been over-
whelmed with
debt.

And ȝet, ne had creaunce icome / at þe last ende,

Wiþ þe comunes curse / þat cleued on hem euere,

Þey had be drawe to þe deuyll / for dette þat þey owed.

And whanne þo reot and þe reeuell / þe rent þus passid,   20

And no þing y-lafte / but þe bare baggis,

When all else
failed, they
exacted money
wrongfully,

Þan felle it afforse / to fille hem aȝeyne,

And feyned sum folie / þat failid hem neuer,

And cast it be colis / wiþ her conceill at euene,   24

To haue preuy parlement / for proffitt † of hem-self,

And lete write writtis / all in wex closid,

For peeris and prelatis / þat þei apere shuld,

and made the
sheriffs return
members of par-
liament who
could be won
over.

And sente side sondis / to schreuys abouȝte,   28

To chese swiche cheualleris / as þe charge wold,

To schewe for þe schire / in company wiþ þe grete.

And whanne it drowe to þe day / of þe dede-doynge,

Þat souereynes were semblid / and þe schire-knyȝtis,   32

Þan, as her forme is frist / þey begynne to declare

Þe cause of her comynge / and þan þe kyngis will.

Then the Chan-
cellor arose and
asked for money
to be granted,

Comliche a clerk þan / comsid þe wordis,

And prononcid þe poyntis / aperte to hem alle,   36

And meved for mony / more þan for out ellis,

In glosinge of grette / lest greyues arise.

And whanne þe tale was tolde / anon to þe ende,

and said they
must meet next
day to give their
answer.

Amorwe þei must, affore mete / mete to-gedir,   40

Þe knyȝtis of þe comunete / and carpe of þe maters,

Wiþ citiseyns of shiris / ysent for þe same,

To reherse þe articlis / and graunte all her askynge.

But ȝit for þe manere / to make men blynde,   44

Some members
said that being
paid by their
constituents,
they would never
grant money
wrongfully,
except in case of
war,

Some argued aȝein rith / þen a good while,

And said, "we beth seruantis / and sallere fongen,

And ysent fro þe shiris / to shewe what hem greueth,

And to parle for her prophete / and passe no ferthere,   [*fo.* 119 a.]

And to graunte of her gold / to þe grett wattis   49

By no manere wronge way / but if werre were ;

---

25 MS. propffitt [S].   34 comynge : *nasal abbreviation over y
expunctuated.*   36 prononcid : *nasal abbreviation over second o expunctuated.*   45 Some : *nasal abbreviation over o expunctuated.*
46 sallere : *final e altered to y* ; wages *written above.*   fongen : taken
written above.   48 parle : speake *written above.*

And if we ben fals / to þo us here fyndyth,

Euyll be we worthy / to welden oure hire."   52

Þan satte summe / as siphre doth in awgrym,

Þat noteth a place / and no þing availith ;

And some had ysoupid / with Symond ouere euen,

And schewed for þe shire / and here schew lost ;   56

And somme were tituleris / and to þe kyng wente,

And formed him of foos / þat good frendis weren,

Þat bablid for þe best / and no blame serued

Of kynge ne conceyll / ne of þe comunes noþer,   60

Ho-so toke good kepe / to þe culorum.

And somme slombrid and slepte / and said but a lite ;

And somme mafflid with þe mouþ / and nyst what þey ment ;

And somme had hire / and helde þer-with euere,   64

And wolde no forther affoot / for fer of her maistris ;

And some were so soleyne / and sad of her wittis,

Þat er þey come to þe clos acombrid þey were,

Þat þei þe conclucion þan / constrewe ne couþe,   68

No burne of þe benche / of borowe noþer ellis,

So blynde and so ballid / and bare was þe reson.

And some were so fers / at þe frist come,

Þat þey bente on a bonet / and bare a topte saile   72

Affor þe wynde fresshely / to make a good fare.

Þan lay þe lordis alee / with laste and with charge,

And bare abouȝte þe barge / and blamed þe maister,

Þat knewe not þe kynde cours / þat to þe crafte longid,   76

And warned him wisely / of þe wedir-side.

Thanne þe maste in þe myddis / at þe monþe-ende,

Bowid for brestynge / and brouȝte hem to lond ;

For ne had þei striked a strake / and sterid hem þe better,   80

And abated a bonet / or þe blast come,

Þey had be þrowe ouere þe borde / backeward ichonne.

And some were acombrid / with þe conceill be-fore,   [*fo.* 119 *b*.]

And wiste well y-now / how it sholde ende,   84

Or some of þe semble / shulde repente.

Some helde with þe mo / how it euere wente,

And somme dede rith so / and wolld go no forþer.

---

71 some : *nasal abbreviation over* o *expunctuated.*

Marginal glosses:

for they knew their duty.

Some members were ciphers.

Some were tale-bearers.

Some slumbered

Some talked nonsense.

Some were so stupid that they lost themselves in the argument.

Some were for dashing on at full sail.

But the lords blamed the skipper for ignorance.

The mast bent.

Had they not struck sail,

they would have been blown over-board.

Some knew how it would end.

Some talked
only of the
money which
the king owed
them.

Some parled as perte / as prouyd well after, 88
And clappid more for þe coyne / þat þe kyng owe[d] hem
Thanne for comfforte of þe comyne / þat her cost paied,
And were be-hote hansell / if þey helpe wolde
To be seruyd sekirly / of þe same siluere. 92

Some feared
the lords, and
forsook Do-well.

And some dradde dukis / and Do-well for-soke ;

*   *   *   *   *   *   *   *   *

89 MS. owen [S].   93 Rest of page blank and six ff. missing.

On the last folio is written Summa   xix^cm^a li   vjm^a li   iij^c li   lxxxviij li
xvij s ix d .3. 4.

[FRAGMENT M]

Hovgh þe coroune moste be kepte fro couetous peuple [fo. 1a.] [I have told you] how the Crown should be protected from those who would appropriate its revenues.
Al hoole in his hande and at his heeste eke,
That euery knotte of þe coroune close with oþer,
And not departid for prayer ne profit of [grete],
Leste vncunnyng [comyn] caste vp þe halter   5 If this is not done, the commons will complain of their taxation.
And crie on your cunseil for coigne þat ye lacke,
For þay shal smaicche of þe smoke and smerte þereafter
Whenne collectours comen to caicche what þay habben.
And þough your tresorier be trewe and tymbre not to high, Even if the Treasurer be honest, he can do well for himself, for in two years (men say) he will make enough to live as a lord for twenty years.
Hit wil be nere þe worse atte wyke-is ende,   10
For two yere a tresorier twenty wyntre aftre
May lyue a lord-is life, as leued men tellen.
Now your chanchellier þat chief is to chaste þe peuple See that the Chancellor and all the officers of law show no favour to the rich, but help the poor.
With conscience of your cunseil þat þe coroune kepith,
And alle þe scribes and clercz þat to þe court longen,   15
Bothe iustice and iuges y-ioyned and oþer,
Sergeantz þat seruen for soulde atte barre,
And þe prentys of court, prisist of alle,
Loke ye reeche [not] of þe riche and rewe on þe poure
That for faute of your fees fallen in faire pleyntes ;   20
Haue pitie on þe penylees and þaire pleynte harkeneth,
And hire þaym as hertly as þough ye hure had,
For þe loue of hym þat your life weldeth ;
And graunteth [þaym] for God-is sake and with a good chiere Grant them all legal facilities, with no Chancery fees, and they will be grateful, as they would not be if oppressed by maintenance, or affronted because of their poverty.
The writing of writtz and þe waxe eke ;   25
And þay wil loue you for þe lawe as liege men aughte,
More þenne for mayntenance þat any man vseth,
Or for any frounting for faute of þe coigne.

---

1 Hovgh : how M.   4 departid : parte A.   grete : so A ; MS.
oþer.   5 comyn : so N. ; MS. come yn and : and *marked as* N, *correction missing*.   6 ye lacke : you lacketh N.   8 caicche : caste A.
12 leued : leude A.   14 conscience : consent A.   19 not :
MS. *omits*.   22 hire : hireth B ; th L.   23 your : oure C.
24 MS. hym.   chiere : wille E.

Now ye haue y-herde of þe haselle names
Of officiers withynne and withoute eke,   30
But yit of alle þe burnes þe beste is behinde

Forto serue a souurayn in somer and in wintre,
And most nedeful at eue and at morowe eke,
And a profitable page for princes or for ducz
Or for any lay lord, lettrid or elles,   35
That litel is y-take fourth or his tale lyeued;
And yf ye willeth to wite what þe wight hatte,
Hit is a sothe-sigger þat seilde is y-seye

To be cherisshid of chief in chambre or in halle,
But for his rathe reasons is rebukid ofte,   40
And yf he fable to ferre, þe foote he goeth vndre.
[T]here is no clerc with þe king þat cloþid hym ones,
[B]ut cloþid hym at cristmasse and al þe yere after.
[S]aunder þe seruiselees shuld be his name,
[For] he abidith in no houshold half a yere to þende   45
[But þe] lord and þe lady been loeth of his wordes,

And þe meyny and he mowe not accorde,   [*fo.* 1 *b.*]
But al to-teereth his toppe for his trewe tales.

He can not speke in termes ne in tyme nother,
But bablith fourth bustusely as barn vn-y-lerid;   50
But euer he hitteth on þe heed of þe nayle-is ende,
That the pure poynt pricketh on þe sothe
Til þe foule flessh vomy for attre.
Thenne is þis freeke a-frountid for his feithful tale,

And y-[fulled] vndre foote while falsenes goeth aboute   55
With cautelle and with coigne forto caste deceiptz
Hough trouthe might be trauerssid and tournid of þe weye.
Thenne fareth fals fourth and flatereth atte beste
And lightly is y-lyved withoute long tale,
And euery gome of hym glad, so glorieusely he loketh   60
Thorough þe peynt[ur]e of þe preynte þat in þe palme hongeth.

37 wight: wy D.   42–46 MS. *torn.*   42 cloþid; clothith A;
also L.   43 cloþid *dotted for correction.*   47 *Margin torn away.*
Side-note marked by corrector to stand after l. 48.   meyny: meyne C.
50 barn: burne D.   51 euer *marked for correction.*   55 MS.
y filled; [fe]rked D; *correction torn away.*   61 peynt[ur]e: MS.
preynte, *with a space following it*; peyntours D. palme: paume C.

Right as þe cockil cometh fourth ere þe corne ripe,
With a cleer colour, as cristal hit semeth,
Among þe grayne þat is grene and not ful growe,
Right so fareth falsnesse þat so freysh loketh   65
Thorough þe colour of þe crosse þat many men incumbreth.
But whenne trouthe aftre tornement hath tyme forto kerne
And to growe fro þe grovnde anone to þende,
Thenne fadeth þe flour of þe fals cockil.
That likne I to lyers, for atte þe long goyng,   70
Of euery segge-is sawe þe sothe wol be knowe.

But in the end, falseness will fade before truth as the tares from among the wheat.

Yit is hit not my cunseil to clatre what me knoweth
In sclaundre ne scathe ne scorne of þy brother,
For though þy tale be trewe þyn tente might be noyous,
For whiche þou mighte be harmed and haue þat þou serues. 75

But the truth must not be spoken in malice.

Fort go to þe gospel þat grovnd is of lore,
And þere shal þou see þyself, yf þou can rede,
Whethir I wisse þe wel wisely or elles.

The gospel tells us to rebuke the offender first in private,

He seith þat þou shuldes þe synne of þy brother
Telle hym by tyme and til hymsilf oon,   80
Yn ful wil to amende hym of his mysse-deedes.

Si peccauerit in te frater tuus corrige etc.

And yf he chargeth not þy charite but chideth þe agaynes,
Yit leue hym not so lightly þough he lovre oones,
But funde hym to freyne efte of þe newe,
And haue wittenes þe with þat þou wel knowes,   85

and, if this avails not, then before a witness.

And spare not to speke, spede yf þou mowe,
And he þat moost is of might þy mede shal quite
For suche [soeth] sawes þat sounen into good,
And of a reasonable man rewarde to haue.
For whenne þy tente and þy tale been temprid in oone,   90
And menys no malice to man þat þou spekys,

If we rebuke without malice, he may repent and thank us.

But forto mende hym mukely of his misse-deedes,
Sory for his synne and his shrewed taicches,
And þe burne be y-blessid and balys cunne eschewe   [*fo. 2 a.*]

---

63 semeth: shyneth D.   66 no*ta* de moneta *in margin.*   67 kerne :
keorne D.   69 þe¹: þis D.   70 likne : lyke D.   71 seme*n*
verita*tis* in fi*n*e crescit licet diu i*m*pediat*ur added in margin by* S¹, *last
3 words underlined.*   76 MS. Fort, *with uncrossed* t ; now D.   78 wel
. . . elles : to wit wisdame or elles N.   79 seith : saith A.   80 *Side-note
marked by corrector to stand after l.* 81.   82 yf he : þough A.
84 funde : fonde A.   88 soeth : *so* P (dot and caret).

And thrifty and towarde, þou shal thanke gete.   95

If I were a lord, I would reward a servant who spoke the truth in love.

Were I a lord of a lande þat lawe aughte gouuerne,
Suche a siker seruant shuld haue robes,
Though he seide euer sothe and seruyd of noon other.

B ut now wolde I wite of a wise burne,

I would like to know where to find such a servant, that he might serve the king.

What kynnes creature þat me couthe telle   100
Where to finde þis freek, yf þe king wolde
Haue hym in housholde as holsum were.

A clerk answered me: "No one would be so foolish as to take so perilous a post as to speak the truth to the king, where he might use flattery."

"By Crist," cothe a clerc þat conceipte he had,
"There is no wiseman, I wene, wolde be y-weddid
To suche a simple seruice, a-say where þe liketh,   105
For no maniere [mede] þat þereto belongeth,
Ne ferthryng ne frendship while flatryng helpeth.
For alle þe greet clercz þat with þe king lendith
Knoweth þis as kindely as clerc doeth his bokes :
Hit is no siker seruice but for a somer saison,   110
But yf hit were for a fool þat wold not be ferthred.

But I wonder that there is no man to speak the truth to the king.

He might sey sothe sum while among þaym
And shuld be holde fooly þough hit feul after."
But muche now I meruaille, and so mowen other,

Et nu*n*c reges intelligite erudimini qui iudicatis terram, etc. Dauid.

That oure corouned king is kepte fro þo ludes,   115
Forto [saye] hym þe sothe sum while among
Hough he shuld grece þe griefz er þe woundz gunne festre
And so to leede his life in loue of þe royaulme.

The poor have many neighbours who do so,

For þe poure peuple hath prece of þaym many
Forto telle þaym þaire toyes twyes a woke ;   120

---

103 þat : þo A.   *Cesura mark after* þat.   104 wene : P *adds* þat.
106 mede : *so* A ; MS. soulde.   107 Ne : while A.   ne : and
written above line N.   while : and A.   108 lendith : dwellyn B.
109 Knoweth : knowen B.   115 *Side-note marked to be placed after
this line ; in* MS. *at l.* 120.   S² *adds* And souuerayns sothely / þay serue
but a whiles / yit shuld hit lengthe þayre lyves / and þe lawe mende.
116 saye : *so* B ; MS. telle.   sum . . . among : . . doon growe N ; *a cross
above* sum.   *After the line* S *inserts* :

     thorough mayntenance and mysrewle of maist*er*s above
     And al is *con*sail to þe king he knoweth not þe fawtes
     For lacke of a loresman / þat lesinges hateth
      That wold telle hym þe trouthe and trippe not aside / . . .
S¹ *adds in margin* þe þer . . . out . . . yn . . . hyn . . . wis . . .

117 Hough *marked for correction.*   119 hath prece : haueth pr*e*s C.

And any neighebourgh be nigh on eue or a morowe,
Hit wold not long be lefte, my life durste I wedde ;
And þat is grace and þaire good happe to gouuerne þaym better
And in welthe to be ware / ere þat woo falle.

*and this is a
benefit to them.*

But þe king ne his cunseil cunne not mete with þaym,   125
But cleerly þe cause I knowe not for sothe
But dreede of þe deeth dryveth þaym þens,
Or elles looste of þaire likerous life vppon erthe.

*No one speaks
the truth to the
king, for fear of
the conse-
quences.*

Thus is þe court accumbrid and knoweth not þaire happes
Ne God neither goodman ne þaym-self nothir,   130
Til fortune for foolie falle atte laste,
And al þe world wondre on þaire wilde deedes.

*Hence the court
suffers.*

But yf þe king might knowe þat þe comune talketh
[H]ough grotz been y-gadrid and no grief amendid
[A]nd hough þe lawe is y-lad whenne poure men pleyne,   135
[I] bilieue loyally oure liege lord wolde
[Ha]ue pitie on his peuple for his owen profit
[An]d amende þat were amysse into more ease.

*If the king
knew what the
common people
say, he would
redress their
grievances.*

[B]ut þe cause why þe king knoweth not þe mischief
Is for faute of a fabuler that I bifore tolde of,   [*fo. 2 b.*]
Forto telle hym þe texte, and touche not þe glose,   141
How þe worde walketh with oon and with other.

*He does not
know, because he
has no truth-
teller.*

But whenne oure comely king came furst to londe,
Tho was eche burne bolde to bable what hym aylid
And to fable ferther of fautz and of wrongz,   145
And romansid of þe misse-reule þat in þe royaulme groved,

*When he landed
in this country,
every one was
free to complain,
and was promised
relief.*

And were behote high helpe, I herde hit myself
Y-cried at þe crosse, and was þe king-is wille
Of custume of coylaige þe comunes shuld be easid.

*I myself heard it
proclaimed that
the commons
should be eased
of coylage*

But how þe couenant is y-kepte I can not discryue,   150
For with þe king-is cunseil I come but silde.

*I do not know if
this has been
done.*

---

121 And : yf D.   132 deedes : workes D.   133 might
marked for correction ; margin torn away.   134–139 MS. *torn.*
134 Hough *marked for correction.*   138 þat were *repeated in* MS. *and*
crossed out by O.   into more ease : and mayntenance chaste N.   *At
the bottom of page* D *adds* :

    [And] souuerayns soethly / þay serve but a whiles
    [Yit] shuld hit lengthe þayre lyves / and þe lawe mende

149 custume : and *added by* L *above the line.*

The magpies who once disputed with the parrot were punished, and dare not now complain openly.
But piez with a papegeay parlid of oones,
And were y-plumed and y-pullid and put into a caige.
Sith þe briddes were y-bete þe beke is vndre whinge

Likewise the commons dare not complain to the king and his council.
But yf þay parle priuyly to þaire owen peeris.   155
But þe king ne his cunseil may hit not knowe
What is þe comune clamour ne þe crye nother,
For þere is no man of þe meeyne, more noþer lasse,
That wol wisse þaym any worde but yf his witte faille,
Ne telle þaym þe trouthe ne þe texte nothir,   160
But shony forto shewe what þe shire meneth,
And beguile þaym with glose, so me God helpe,
And speke of þaire owen spede and spie no ferther,
But euer kepe þaym cloos for caicching of wordes.

If any man dares to do so he may suffer death or imprisonment.
And yf a burne bolde hym to bable þe sothe   165
And [mynne] hym of mischief þat misse-reule asketh,
He may lose his life and laugh here no more,
Or y-putte into prisone or y-pyned to deeth
Or y-[brent] or y-shent or sum sorowe haue,
That fro scorne oþer scathe scape shal he neure.   170

Thus is truth so oppressed by princes that he hides himself,
Thus is trouthe doune y-troode and tenyd ful ofte,
Y-bete and y-bounde in bourghes and in shires,
And principaly of princes y-pyned þenne of other,
Y-[halowid] and y-huntid and y-hoote trusse,
That he shoneth to be seye forto shewe his harmes,   175
But euer hideth his heede fro þe hayl-stones,

and is as good seed choked by tares.
And is ouer-woxe with wrong and wickid wedes,
And tenyd with tares and al amisse temprid.

But in time he will grow up and bear fruit;
Yit wol he growe fro [greue] and his grayne bere,
And after sowe his seede whenne he seeth tyme.   180

for truth cannot finally perish.
For alle þe gomes vndre God / goyng vppon erthe
Were neuer so slygh yit forto sle trouthe ;
Though þay batre hym with battz and bete on hym euer,
Trouthe is so tough and loeth forto teere

152 But : yit A.   154 beke : bile A.   159 his : hire B.
165 þe : P *adds* oute.   166 mynde C ; MS. warne.   169 brent :
so A ; MS. blent.   174 MS. haulid ; halowyd B.   179 fro greue :
MS. fro grayen ; oute of greue N.   180 S¹ *adds* That droweth al to
goodnesse and gouuernance after.   183 batre : bale A.   battz :
banes A.

And so pryuy with þe prince þat paradis made   185
That he hath graunt of his lyfe while God is in heuene [*fo.* 3*a.*]
For þough men brenne the borough þere þe burne loiggeth,
Or elles hewe of þe heede þere he a hows had,
Or do hym al þe disease þat men deuise cunne,
Yit wol he quyke agayne and quite alle his foes   190
And treede ouer þe tares / þat ouer his toppe groued,
And al wickid wede into waste tourne.

And þerefore my cunseil (þough þe king knowe hit   *Therefore I advise you to hold by truth,*
And alle þe lordz of þis londe, right lite is my charge)
Ys to be at oone with trouthe and tarre hym nomore,   195   *and admit the truth-teller to your company.*
Leste he tucke at *your* tabart ere two yere been endid,
But ye suffre his seruant to be seye oones
Among you in þe moneth (but yf ye more wil)
Forto saye you þe sothe, þough ye shame thenke.

For hit wol sauere *your* mouthe swetely with-ynne short after   *Then, when fortune turns*
Whenne fortune you fleeth and falleth elles-where ;   201   *against you, it will be the better for you, and the wheel will turn in your favour again.*
And yf ye sauere on his sawe and serue þereafter
And eke wirche by his worde, þe whele wol toürne
And eke chaunge his cours of care and of sorowe,
And tourne into tidewel, terme of *your* lifes.   205

Now is Henry-is hovs holsumly y-made   *The household of Henry IV is now properly planned.*
And a meritable meyny of þe moste greet,
And next I haue y-named as nygh as I couthe,
And þe condicions declarid of alle,
Rehershing no rascaille ne riders aboute.   210

But he hymsilf is souurayn, and so mote he longe,   *He is a most noble king,*
And þe graciousist guyer goyng vppon erthe,   *brave, religious, and full of grace.*
Witti and wise, worthy of deedes,
Y-kidde and y-knowe and cunnyng of werre,
Feers forto fighte, þe felde euer kepith,   215
And trusteth on þe Trinite þat trouthe shal hym helpe ;
A doughtful doer in deedes of armes
And a comely knight y-come of þe grettist,
Ful of al vertue þat to a king longeth,
Of age and of al þing as hym best semeth.   220

---

191 ouer [1]: on B.   195 oone : a ton B.   197 But : P *adds* yf.
200 wol : shal B.   205 Here bigynneth þe disputacion bitwyne mvm
and þe soth sigger *in margin by* S[2].

But hit be wel in his dayes we mowe dreede aftre
Lest feerelees falle withynne fewe yeres.

May God grant
him to rule well !

But God of his goodnes þat gouuernith alle þingz
Hym graunte of his grace to guye wel þe peuple
And to reule þis royaume in pees and in reste,   225
And stable hit to stonde stille for oure dayes.

But I fear lest
evil councillors
may —

But I dreed me sore, so me God helpe,
[L]este couetise of cunseil þat knoweth not hymself
([O]f sum and of certayn, I seye not of alle)
[Th]at of profitable pourpos putteth þe king ofte,   230
[Th]ere his witte and his wil wolde wirche to þe beste—

" Be silent," said
Mum. " Know-
ing that truth-
tellers get no
thanks, you
should have the
sense to keep
quiet."

" Nomore of þis matiere," cothe Mum þenne,   [*fo.* 3 *b.*]
" For I meruaille of þy momeling more þenne þou wenys.
Saides [not] þou þyself, and sothe as me þoughte,
That þees sothe-siggers seruen noon þankes?   235
And þou knowes þis by clergie, how cans þou þe excuse
That þou ne art nycier þan a nunne nyne-folde tyme,
Forto wite þat þy wil / þy witte shal passe ? "

I was put to
confusion, but
yet I wished to
hold debate with
him.

I blussid for his bablyng and a-bode stille
And knytte þere a knotte and construed no ferther ;   240
But yit I thoughte ere he wente, and he wold abide,
To haue a disputeson with hym and spie what he hatte.

" I am Mum,"
said he, " who
dwell with the
great and flatter
them.

" I am Mum þy maister " cothe he " in alle maniere places,
That [sittith] with souuerayns and seruyd with greete.
Thaire wille ne þaire wordes I withseye neuer,   245
But folowe thaym in thaire folie and fare muche þe bettre,
Easily for oyle, sire, and elles were I nyce.

" Thus I prosper,
while you are
hunted down by
officers of
justice.

Thus leede I my life in luste of my herte,
And for my wisedame and witte wone I with þe beste ;
While sergeantz þe sechith to saise by þe lappe   250
For þy wilde wordes / þat maken wretthe ofte.

" You would do
better to follow
me.

Thow were better folowe me foure score wynter
Thenne be a soeth-sigger, so me God helpe,
Oon myle and nomore waye, I Mvm wol avowe.
And þerefore I rede, yf þou reste wilnest,   255
Cumpaignye with no contra yn no kynnes wise,

228–231 MS. *torn.*   232 cothe : saide C.   234 not: *so* P
(*first minim torn away*).   237 nart C.   244 MS. fittith.   247
oyle : oyll A.   250 saise : sese C.   256 Cumpaignye : P *adds* not.

But parle for þy profit and plaise more here-aftre.
For þere nys lord of þis londe ne lady, I wene,
Prince nether prelat ne peer of þe royaulme,
Bachillier ne bourgoys ne no barne elles   260
That yf þay wite what þou arte, þat wil þe desire
Or coueite to his cumpaignie while contra þe foloweth ".

"Now to þis altercacion ", cothe I, "an answere behoueth ;
   For I fele by þy fabelyng þou art felle of werkes
And right worldly wise of wordes and deedes,   265
And euer kepis þe cloos for [casting] bihinde.
Thou wol not putte þe in prees but profit be þe more
To þy propre persone / þou passes not þe bondes
Forto gete any grucche for glaunsyng of boltes.
Thus me semeth þat þou serues þy-self and no man elles,   270
And has housholde and hire to holde vp þy oyles,
And eke bouche of court for colte and for [cnaue];
And [yit] þou suffris þy souurayn to shame hym-self
There þou mightes amende hym many tyme and ofte.
Now suche a-nothir seruant, þe same and noon oþer,   275
Mote dwelle with þe deueil / til Do Bette hym helpe."

Thus after talkyng we twynned a-sundre,
   Bothe Mvm and I, and oure mote endid ;   [*fo. 4 a.*]
But muche mervailled I, whenne Mvm was passid,
Of his opinion þat he heulde euer,   280
And prouyd hit by profitable poyntz [and fele]
That better was a burne to abide stille
Thanne þe soeth to seye þat sitteth in his herte,
Forto warne þe wy þat he with dwellith,
Or mynne hym of mischief þat misse-rewle askith.   285
And euer he concludid with colorable wordes
That who-so mellid muche more þan hit nedeth
Shuld rather wynne weping watre þenne robes.
And cleerly Caton construeth þe same,
And seyth soethly, I saw hit in youthe,   290

Marginal notes:

" No one, high or low, will seek your company as long as you speak contrariously."

I replied : " I see that you are selfish.

" You draw great profit from the court, yet you let scandal fall on the king where you could prevent it. You may go to the devil."

Facientis culpam habet, qui quod potest corrigere negligit emendare in secretis etc.

Thus our debate ended.

Yet afterwards I wondered how he maintained that it was better to be silent than to warn others of evil.

Cato says the same:

---

260 barne : burne D.   264 fabelyng : P *adds* þat.   266 MS.
caſting.   271 oyl (+ *letter or letters torn off* C ; *perhaps* oyle, *cp.*
l. 247).   272 cnaue : MS. caue ; knaue A.   273 yit : *so* A ; MS. yf.
281 MS. y-nowe ; and feble N ; *cp. l.* 1298.   283 sitteth .... herte :
sete on his herte N.

Nam nulli
tacuisse
nocet, nocet
esse locutum.
This troubled me.

That of " bable " cometh blame and of " be stille " neuer,
And a wise worldly worde, as me þenketh,
Of þe whiche I was hevy and highly abawyd,
And for þe double doute as dul as an asse,
And troublid for þe travers, and amisse temprid,   295
That I wente in a wyre a grete while after
For woo I ne wiste who had þe better

Though I
thought over
both our argu-
merts, I could
not tell who was
right.

Of Mvm and of me, and musid faste,
Rehershyng þe reasons of bothe two sides,
The pro and þe contra as clergie askith.   300
But for witte þat I wanne I wolde þat he knewe
I was neuer þe nyre, but as newe to begynne
As clerc is to construe þat can not reede.

Then I consulted
the works of
Sidrac, Solomon,
and Seneca,
wisest of men.

Thenne þoughte I on Sidrac and Salomon-is termes,
And Seneca þe sage I soughte for þe nones,   305
That whilom were þe wisest wies vppon erthe
Forto wise any wighte, what-so hym grieued.
I bablid on þoo bokes þat þoo barnes made,
And waitid on þaire wordes aswel as I couthe,

But they did not
write of these
modern subjects,
but of the old-
fashioned
themes.

But of þe matiere of Mvm might I nought finde,   310
Ne no maniere nycete of þe newe [iette],
But al homely vsage of þe olde date,
How þat [good] gouuernance gracieusely endith.

But in the gloss
I read that if a
man were in per-
plexity, he must
make known his
trouble in the
place where the
remedy might be
found.
Then I under-
stood that I must
apply to men of
learning.

But glymsyng on þe glose, a general revle
Of al maniere mischief I merkid and radde :   315
That who-so were in wire and wold be y-easid
Moste shewe þe sore þere þe salue were.
Thenne was I wel ware what he wolde mene,
That I shulde cunne of clergie to knowe þe sothe,
Forto deme þe doute þat me so dul made.   320
I was wilful of wil and wandrid aboute,

I went to Cam-
bridge, Oxford,
Orleans, and
other places,

Til I came to Cambrigge couthe I not stynte,
To Oxenford and Orleance and many oþer places
There þe congregacion of clercz in scole   [*fo.* 4 *b.*]
Were stablid to stonde in strengthe of bilieue.   325

and related my
argument with
Mum to the
Seven Sciences.

I moeued my matiere of Mvm, as ye knowe,
And of þe soeth-sigger in fewe shorte wordes ;

302 nyre : neer C.   308 barnes : burnes D.   311 MS. yette.
313 good : *so* P.   316 wire : woundid A.   319 cunne : kenne D.

To alle þe vij sci̇́ences I shewed as I couthe,
And how we dwellid in [dwere] / and doute of þe bett*er*.
Sire Grumbald þe grammier þo glowed for anger   330
That he couthe not congruly knytte þaym to-gedre.
Music and Mvm mighte not accorde,
For þay been contrary of kynde, who-so canne spie.
Phisic diffied al [þe] bothe sides,
Bothe Mvm and me and þe soeth-siggre ;   335
He was accumbrid of oure cumpaignye, by Crist þat me bought,
And as fayn of oure voiding as foul [of his make].
Astronomy-ys argumentz were alle of þe skyes,
He-is touche no twynte of terrene þinges.
Rethoric-is reasons me luste not reherce,   340
For he conceyued not þe caas, I knewe by his wordes ;
But a subtile shophister with many sharpe wordes
Sette [þe] soeth-sigger as shorte as he couthe.
But he wolde melle with Mvm ner more ner lasse,
So chiding and chatering [as choghe] was he euert.   345
Ieometrie þe ioynour iablid faste,
And caste many cumpas, as þe crafte askith,
And laide leuel and lyne a-long by þe squyre.
But I was not þe wiser by a Walsh note
Of þe matiere of Mvm þat marrid me ofte,   350
And stoode al a-stonyed and starid for angre
That clergie couthe not my cares amende,
And was in pourpoos to passe fourth right in pure wreth.
But a semely sage þat satte al a-bouue,
Y-chose to þe chaire forto chaste fooles,   355
Whom alle þe vij. sciences seruyd at wille,
Bothe in werke and in worde weren at his heste,
And more bunne at his bede þan boy til his maister,
He satte as a souurayn on a high siege.
A doctour of doutz by dere God he semyd,   360
For he had loked al þat lay to þe .vij. artz ;

Grammar was angry that he could not resolve it.
Music by his nature could have nothing to do with Mum.
Physic scorned both parties.

Astronomy was only concerned with heavenly things.
Rhetoric could not understand the matter; Logic would not oppose Mum.

Geometry made great ado, but I was none the wiser for him.

I was about to depart when I saw a wise man who sat enthroned above the Seven Sciences.

329 MS. dome. and²: for A.   334 MS. y.   337 MS. on þe
skyes : *with* his make N.   343 þe : *so* A ; MS. a.   344 wolde :
P *adds* not.   345 as ... euer : MS. and couche was he neuer ; as
choghe was eu*er* N.   354 semely sage : segge D   356 wille :
nede A.   361 þat lay : þe *lettre* D.

He was as ful of philosophie and vertues bothe
As man vppon molde mighte perceyue.

He called me to
him, and said :
This comely clerc me called agaynes,
And cunseillid me so cleerly þat I caughte ease,   365

"Do you see all
these men who
give themselves
to learning?"
And seide, "soon, seest þou þis semble of clercz,
How þay bisien þaym on þaire bokes and beten þaire wittz,
And how þay loken on þe levis þe [letter] to knowe?
For whenne þay knowen þe scripture þay construen no ferther

Non soli...
sunt atten...
mens imper...
Forto soutille ne to siche no side-wayes.   [fo. 5a.]
But as long as I haue lerned and lokid in bokes,   371
And alle þe vij. sciences y-soughte to þende,

"Neither I nor
they have ever
heard of such a
question as you
have brought
forward. It is
some foolish new-
fangled idea, for
orthodox doc-
trine only tells
us how good
governorship has
good results."
"If you want an
answer, I advise
you to go to
those who, when
they have studied
the text of the
Seven Sciences,
go out into the
world, to live
among the great
and devote them-
selves to the
gloss."
Yit knewe I neuer suche a caas, ne no clerc here,
As þou has y-moeued among vs alle.
Hit is sum noyous nycete of þe newe iette,   375
For þe texte truly telleth vs nomore
But how þat goode gouuernance graciousely endith.
But and þou woldes be wise and wirche as I telle,
I wolde wisse þe to wite where þat þou shuldest
Haue knowlaiche of þy caas cleere to þyn intent,   380
And þy cumberouse question quycly be assoilled.
Now harke and holde and hye to þende.
Sum of þis semble þat þou sees here,
Whenne þay haue loked þe lettre and þe lyfe[z] ouer
Of alle þe .vij. sciences / or sum as þaym liketh,   385
Thay walken fourth in þe worlde and wonen with lordes,
And with a couetous croke Saynt Nicholas þay throwen,
And trauaillen nomore on þe texte, but tournen to þe glose,
And putten þaym to practike and plaisance of wordes.
But þay cunne deme þy doute, by dere God in heuene,   390
I can not knowe of þy caas who couthe elles."

Then I went to
the friars with
my problem.
Thenne ferkid I to freres, alle þe foure ordres,
There þe fundament of feith and felnesse of workes
Hath y-dwellid many day, no doute, as þay telle.
I frayned þaym faire to fele of þaire wittes,   395
And moeuyd my matiere of Mvm, as ye knowe,

365 cleerly: clerkly A.   368 [l]etter: MS. better; lettrure C.
369 *Catch-word* Forto soutille ne to siche etc.   376 telleth: techet
C.   377. S¹ *adds in margin* And þe trouthe to...turment and el...
382 holde: P *adds* hit.   384 lyfez: z L.   386 þe *after with*
crossed out by original scribe.

And of þe soeth-sigger in fewe sho[r]te wordes.
To euery couple I construed my caas for þe nones,
Til the cloistre and þe quyre were so accorded
To yeue Mvm þe maistrie withoute mo wordes,   400
And shewid me exemples, þe sothest vppon erthe,
Nad Mvm be a more frende to making of þaire houses
Thenne þe sothe-sigger, so God shuld þaym helpe,
Hit had be vnhelid half a yere after.

Now ne were thre skiles and scantly þe ferthe,   405
I wolde loue as litel þaire life and þaire deedes
As man vppon molde, til Amendes me prayed.
The furst is a faire poynt forto wynne heuene,
Whenne þay stirid a statute in strengthe of bilieue
That no preste shuld preche saue seely poure freres.   410
But þis [deede] dide þay not, I do you to wite,
For no maniere mede þat mighte þaym befalle,
Ne forto gete þe more good / God wote þe sothe,
But for good herte þat þay haue to hele [men-is] soules.
The secund is a pryvy poynt / I pray hit be helid :   415
Thay cunne not reede redelles a-right, as me þenketh ; [fo. 5 b.]
For furst folowid freres Lollardz [names],
And sith hath be shewed þe same on þaym-self,
That þaire lesingz haue lad þaym to lolle by þe necke ;
At Tibourne for traison y-twyght vp þay were.   420
For as hit is y-seide by eldryn dawes,
†" Þe churle yafe a dome whiche came by hym aftre ".
The thrid is no lesing ne no long tale :
Thees good grey freres þat mouche loue geten
For keping of þaire conscience clenner þan other,   425
Thay goon al bare abouue þe foote and by-nethe double
With smale semyd sockes and of softe wolle,
For þe loue of oure lord harde life induren ;
Thay mellen with no monaye more noþer lasse,
But stiren hit with a sticke and staren on hit ofte   430
And doon þaire bisynes þere-with by obedience of þordre ;

Side-notes:

They all agreed to give Mum their verdict, for he had befriended them more than had the truth-teller.

I would not praise them, but for three (or four) reasons:

Firstly, that they brought forward a project that no priests but friars should be allowed to preach. This they did, not for the sake of gain, but for the good of men's souls.

Secondly, that they have been hanged at Tyburn as traitors.

[Patere llegem quam ipse tulleris.
Thirdly, that they lead a hard life.

They go bare about the legs (yet they have soft woollen socks on their feet).

They touch no money (except with a stick).

But in þe herte ne in þe hande ne may hit not come,
For þenne þay shuld bee shent of þe subpriour.

Fourthly, that
they divide the
country into
districts, each
assigned to a
limiter.
The fourthe poynt is fructuous and fundid al in loue:
Whenne freres goon to chapitre for charite-is sake,   435
Thay casten þere þe cuntrey and coostz aboute,
And parten þe prouynce in parcelle-mele,
And maken limitacions in lengthe and in breede,
Til eche hovs haue his owen as hym aughte.
Thenne hath þe limitour leue to lerne where he cometh   440
To lye and to licke or elles lose his office;

Some limiters
will give small
presents (but
they will take
something better
for themselves).
But sum been so courtoys and kinde of þaire deedes
That with þaire charite þay chaungen a knyfe for a peyre,
But he wol pille ere he passe a parcelle of whete
And choise of þe chese þe chief and þe beste.   445
He is so cunnyng in þe crafte þat where-so he cometh
He leueth þe lasse for þe more deele.

Thus they accu-
mulate goods,
Thus with þaire charite and with þaire fayre chere
Thees good God-is men gadren al to þaym
And kepen hit to þaire owen croppe clene fro other.   450

but will give you
nothing to relieve
your distress.
For þough a frere be fatt and haue a ful coffre
Of gold and of good, þou getys but a lite
Forto bete þy bale, þough þou begge euer.
But þat is no meruail, by Marie of heuene,

But it is useless
to beg from a
Mendicant.
For to begge of a begger what bote is hit   455
But who wolde balle [with] his [browe] to breke harde stones?
Thus þaire conscience is y-knowe and þaire crafte eeke,
That hath be kepte cunseil and cloos many dayes,
Til al þe world wote what þay wolde meene;
And þat is þis trevly, tende who-so wil,   460

They aim at
controlling the
great by means
of the sacrament
of penance.
Thorough crafte of confession to knowe men intentz,—
Of lordz and ladies that lustes desiren,   [fo. 6 a.]
And with þaire wyly wittz wirchen on euer
And mulden vp þe matiere to make þaym fatte,
And gouuernen þe grete and guilen þe poure.   465
Now take my tale as my intent demeth,

454 S² *adds* ne to noo crea*ture* þat can ony reason.   455 MS. Forto.
456 *with*: MS. *omits.*   browe: MS. heede.   who . . . browe: liste
balle wit*h* his browe N.   466 take: th *added by* P.   demeth:
meneth B.

And ye shal wel wite I wil þaym no mischief
By my worde ne by my wille as wissely [for] sothe
As God þat is oure gouuernour me gye at my nede.
For whenne þay come to your cote to craue þat þaym nedeth, 470
Gyfe þaym for God-is sake and with a good wille
Mete or monaye as ye mowe indure,
And yefe þaym sauce þere-with of þe sothe-sigger
Forto preche þe peuple þe peril of synne,
How symonie shendith al hooly churche, 475
And not forbere bisshop ne baron þat lyveth
That þay teche treuly þe texte as hit standeth,
And abide þereby with a bolde herte,
And spare for no spicerie ne no speche elles,
But telle oute þe trouthe and tourne not a-side 480
How Couetise hath caste þe knyght on þe grene,
And woneth at Westmynstre to wynne newe spores,
And can not crepe þens while þe crosse walketh.
He multiplieth monaye in þe mote-halle
More for his mayntenance and manasshing of wordes 485
Thenne with draughte of his swerde or deedes of armes.
And telle þe frere a toquen, þat trouthe wote þe sothe
Why men meruaillen more on þaym þanne on othir,—
That suche a cumpaignye of confessours cunne not yelde
Oon martir among þaym in .vij.† score wynter. 490
Thay prechen alle of penanche as þough [þay] parfite were,
But þay proue hit [in no] poynt þere þaire peril shuld arise.
Thaire cloþing is of conscience / and of Caym þaire werkes,
That fadre was and fundre of alle þe foure ordres,
Of deedes þay doon deceipuyng þe peuple, 495
As Armacanes argumentz, þat þaire actes knewe,
Provyn hit apertly in a poysie-wise ;
For of Caym alle came, as þis clerc tolde.
For who writeth wel þis worde and withoute titil,

When they beg from you, give them what they ask, and with it plain-speaking.

Honora dominum de [tua] substancia proph[eta].

Tell them that they should preach the evil of simony, with no fear of bishop or baron ;

that no bribery should prevent them from attacking covetousness, which has conquered the aristocracy.

Why are there not more martyrs among the friars?

They do not practise what they preach.

They are the children of Cain, as the Archbishop of Armagh has said.

468 for : MS. *omits.*   471 *Side-note marked to stand after l.* 469.
479 ne : P *adds* for *above the line.*   480 tourne : trippe A.   482
S² *adds* At shire and at sessions thaire shoon þay appeire.   484 He :
þay A.   489 That : why A.   490 MS. viij.   491 penanche :
he *crossed out by original scribe and* e *written above* M. þay : *so* P.
492 [in no] : MS. not *with a space after it ; crossed out by original scribe
and* in no *added above line by* M.   494 fundre : fourmour D.

Shal finde of þe figures but euene foure le*tt*res :   500
C. for hit is crokid [for] þees Carmes þou mos take,
A. for þees Augustines þat amoreux been euer,
I. for þees Iacobynes þat been of Iudas kynne,
M. for þees Menours þat monsyd been þaire werkes.

I do not say that they are all like this, but some have innumerable faults.

I seye of þaym þat suche been and cesse agaynes oþer,   505
But wel I wote þat wilful and worldly þay been sum,
And eeke spracke and spitous, and spices wel þay louen,
For Symon-is sermons þay setten al to taske,   [*fo.* 6 *b*]
And feele oþer fautz fourtene hunthrid
Thay lepen ouer lightly, and lyen woundre þicke.   510

I cannot tell their estate : they are not wedded men, though they have wives.

I can not deme deuely of what degre þay bee ;
Thay been not weddid, wel I wote, þough þay wifes haue ;
But knightz yit of conscience I couthe of þaym make,

They may be knights, for they joust against Jesus.

For þay haue ioygned [*in* iustes] agayns Ihesus werkes ;
And forto proue þaym prestes þees poyntz been agayne þaym. 515

I have read that they should be severed from the company of the righteous.

I can not reede redily of what revle þay been,
For hooly churche ne heuene hath not þaym in mynde,
Saue in oon place þaire office and ordre is declarid,

[Aufe]rte gen-tem perfidam [Credentium de f]inib*us*. Deleantur de libro viuen-cium et cum iustis non scribantur.

I sawe hit in a ympne and is a sentence trewe,
And elles-where in hooly writte I herde þaym y-nempnyd.   520
But of þe matiere of Mvm ne of þe sothe-sigger

But this is a divergence. I wished to find an indifferent judge between Mum and the truth-teller.

This is not to pourpoos þe pare of oon pere,
And þerfore my wil is to walke more at large
Forto fynde sum freeke þat of feith were
Not double, but indifferent to deme þe sothe,   525
Wheþer Mvm is more better or Melle-sum-tyme
Forto amende þat were amysse into more ease.

Since the friars were on Mum's side, I left them.

And for þe fikelle freres were fully witholde
And alied to Mvm in many maniere wises,
And eeke ful partie, as prouyd by þaire wordes,   530
I lyeued wel þe lasse þaire lore and þaire deedes,
And forto eschewe chiding I chalanged þaym alle,

---

501 for : MS. *omits.*   505 S² *adds* Hit shal not greue a good frere though gilty be amendid.   507 *Signature* .c. 2. fo. *in right-hand margin.*   508 *Word ending in* ie *torn away.*   510 S¹ *adds* sum and of certayn and [and *crossed out*] I say not of alle.   514 *in* iustes : ioustes A ; MS. iustice.   516 redily : rightfully A.   519 *Side-note* : MS. . . . rte gentem perfidam . . . inib*us* regentem. *Margin torn. First sentence marked to stand after l.* 519 *and second after l.* 520.

And lepte lightly fro þaym, leste I laught were ;
For þaire curtesie is crokid þere þay caste ille,
And þat witen þay wel þat han wrastlid with þaym.   535

Thenne passid I to priories and personages many,   *Then I went to*
   To abbeys of Augustyn and many hooly places,   *the monks*
There prestz and prelatz were parfitely y-closid
To singe and to reede for alle cristen soules.   *They would not*
                                                        admit me because
But for I was a meen man I might not entre ;   540   *of my poverty*
For þough þe place were y-pighte for poure men sake   *though their*
                                                      monasteries were
And eeke funded þere-fore / yit faillen þay ofte   *founded to re-*
                                                      lieve the poor.
That þay doon not eche day do beste of alle.   *Mutaueru**n**t*
                                                      *caritate**m** in*
For þe fundac*i*on † of þe fundours ment   *cupiditate**m**.*
Was groundid for God-is men, þough hit grete serue.   545   *Sapienc**ia**.*
Thay koueiten no comers but yf þay cunne helpe   *If a new-comer*
                                                      brings them no
Forto amende þaire mynstre and to maynteyne þaire rente,   *profit, he is not*
                                                      admitted till they
Or in worke or in worde waite þaire profit,   *have supped.*
Or elles entreth he not til þay haue y-[sopid].
Thus thaire portier for my pourete putt me þens,   550   *Their porter*
                                                      drove me away,
And grauntid me of his goodnesse to go where me luste   *and I went else-*
And to wandry where I wolde withoute þe gates.   *where.*

Thenne raughte I fro religion, redelees of wittes,   *Then I went to*
                                                      the cathedral
   And caried to closes and cathedralle churches   [*fo.* 7 *a*.]   *churches, where*
                                                      men held many
There þat pluralite was prisely y-stablid.   555   *benefices.*
I queyntid me with þe quyre for my questions sake,
And moevid of Mvm more þenne þaym liked.
I was as wise whenne I wente as whenne I came to þaym,
Thay wolde not intremitte of ner noþer side,   *They would pay*
                                                      no attention to
But euer kepte þaym cloos to [cracche] and to mangier,   560   *my problem ;*
                                                      they were given
And fedde so þe foule flesh þat þe velle ne might   *over to gluttony.*
Vnethe kepe þe caroigne but yf hit cleue shuld ;
And nad þe gutte groned þere þay gurde were,

535 wrastlid : wraxlid D. S¹ *adds* :

    Yit [*written over* I *and in margin*] gesse I þat good
        men of grey and of blake
    And of þe white witerly I wote wel been many
    But dan conuent þe co*m*paignie as my credo techeth
    Cunen mo crokes / þan crist eu*er* taught.

543 *Side-note marked to stand after l.* 545.   544 MS. fundac*i*ons.
of : as A.   549 MS. sep*i*d.   560 cracche : *so* D ; MS. racke.

When they ride abroad they are not without money, for they have given nothing to the poor.

Thay had bee sike of swete mete, so me God helpe,

For piking of prouendre passing þassise ;   565

And nadde þay partid with þe poure as prestz doon þaire offryng,

That putten alle þaire masse penyes in þaire purses [bottume],

Nolite possi-dere aurum neque argentum in zonis vestris.

Thay had be blamyd of Belial for þaire bolde riding

Yn gurdellz of good gold or gilte atte leste.

Thenne woxe I wondre wery of wandring aboute   570

Thorough þe wilde weyes þat I wente had,

Ful woo for I ne wiste what was my beste

Then I knew not whether to continue my quest,

Reed—forto reste or rome more at large

Til I wiste wittrely who shulde haue

The maistrie, Mvm or þe sothe-sigger.   575

for every one thought me mad.

And euery man þat I mette mad for my wordes

Wende þat I were / wisten þay non other.

And as I stoode staring, stonyd of þis matiere,

Then Mum himself warned me to desist, for fear of evil consequences.

Mvm with his myter manachid me euer

And cunseilled me to cusky and care for myself,   580

And leste I soughte sorowe, cesse by tyme.

I doutid of his deedes, for his delectacion

Was more in his mynde þenne þe masse-bokes,

But I received a safe-conduct from heaven.

And boode til a baron, blessid be he euer,

(His name is y-nempnyd among þe .ix. ordres)   585

Sent a saufconduyt so þat I wolde

Maynteyne no matiere / to amende myself,

Ne caicche no colour hit came of my wittes,

But [sende fro] a souurayn to shewe hit forth after.

This boldid me to bisynes to bringe hit to ende   590

Thorough grace of þis good lord þat gouuerneth al þing.

I went on for a week, till Saturday evening.

Thenne sought I forth seuenyght and slepte ful silde

And cessid on a Saterday til sunne roose a-morowe

And burnys and belles [bablid] to-gedre,

On Sunday I went to church.

Momeling on þaire matyns and to þe masse after.   595

I satte in a siege my seruice to hire

Til þe prest in a pulpite began forto preche
The peuple to pees and þe peril of synne
And also toffre as ofte as þaym likid.
He taughte þaym by tyme þaire tithing to bringe   [*fo. 7 b.*]
Of al manier grene þat groweth vppon erthe,   601
Of fructe and of floxe in felde and in homes,
Of polaille and of peris, of apples and of [plummes],
Of grapes and of garlik, of gees and of pigges,
Of chibollz and of chiries and of þaire chese eeke;   605
Herbaige and oygnons and alle suche þinges
That growen in þaire gardynes, lete God his parte haue,
Of hony in your hyves and of y*our* hony-combes,
Of malte and of monaye and of all þat multiplieth,
Of wolle and of wexe and [what-]so yow increceth   610
Or newith yow, þe ix partie nymeth to y*our* self,
And trewly þe tithing taketh hooly churche.
And euer I waitid whenne he wolde sum worde moeve
How hooly churche goodes shuld be y-spendid,
And declare þe deedes what þay do shulde   615
To haue suche a harueste and helpe not to erie.
But sorowe on þe sillable he shewed of þat matiere,
For Mvm was a meen and made hym to leue ;
And as wery as I was / yit was I wrothe eeke
With Mvm, for he made þe moppe so lewed   620
To leue men to lerne þe lawe sith he knewe hit.
Thenne ferkid I forth as faste as I mighte
Seuene yere sunnedayes and solempne festes,
Yf prest or prelat or prechour wolde
Sey sothe of hymself and serue þere-after   625
And teche how þe tithinge shuld trewly be departid.
But as wide as I wente was noon of þaym alle

Margin notes:

The priest told the people to make liberal offerings,

and to give tithes of all their produce.

I waited to hear what the church would do with the proceeds.

He said nothing of this, for Mum restrained him.

This angered me, and I wandered on for seven years, listening to sermons.

I found no preacher who

---

599 *Signature* .c. 3. *fo. in right-hand margin.*   603 [plummes]: *so* D ;
MS. notes.   604 S¹ *adds*:

> of lyke and of lynne seede of lambes and egges
> of coltes and of calues / þat þe cow lycketh
> of benes and of boutre / þat bele doo make.

610 [what]: MS. *omits.*   and . . . increceth : or what so ye wynne N.
618, 621 leue : leve C.   623 S¹ *adds* To hire of þair holy nesse for
harvest is sake.

would give any
account of the
spending of the
tithes, for they all
esteem Mum
above the holy
martyrs.

Wolde moeve of þat matiere more noþer lasse.

And why þat þay wolde not wol ye gladly wite,

Thay haue a memoire of Mvm among alle other   630

Ys more in þaire mynde þenne martires of heuene

That token þe deeth for trouthe of tirantz handes.

You may object
that the martyrs
had more power
and more learn-
ing than any one
to-day.

But here a querele or a question quyk mighte þou make :

Martires had more might and more mynde eeke,

And couthe more on clergie þenne cunne now a thousand. 635

But I reply that
they chose death
not because of
their learning,
but through
their love of
God.

But þereto I answere as I am lerid :

Thou, lewed laudate, litel witte has.

Hit was for no cunnyng ne clergie noþer

That þay chosid þe deeth, but for derue loue

And kindenes to oure creatour þat creed vs alle,   640

Propter veri-
tatem dimit-
tam omnem
familiari-
tatem *etc.*

Clergy were not
made known
then by grand
clothing or
luxurious life, as
now, but by their
deeds.

And for pure trouthe þat þay taught [euer].

This made þaym martires more þanne ought elles,

For clercz were not knowe by þaire cloþing þat tyme,

Ne by royal raye ne riding aboute,

Ne by seruice of souuerayns, so me God helpe,   645

Ne by revel ne riot ne by rente nothir,   [*fo.* 8 *a.*]

Ne by þaire double dees / ne þaire deupe hoodes,

Ne by drynkyng of dollid wyne ne by datz at eue,

Ne by worldly workes of writtes ne seelyng,

Ne by no maniere nicete þat þay now vsen,   650

But by þe deedes þat þay dide, I do you to wite.

Though I am
unlearned, I
could show how
the tithes should
be spent.

For I am but lewed and lettrid ful lite,

And yit me semeth þe sentence þat I shewe couthe

And teche how þe tithing shuld trewly be departid,

For in thre lynes hit [lith] and not oon *lett*re more.   655

Now hendely hireth how I begynne :

"God's part"
should go to
the poor after
reservation has
been made
for the support
of the clergy and
the ornaments
of the church.

That ye clepe God-is parte / lete God-is men haue hit,

Reseruyng for yo*ur*self sustenance for yo*ur* foode,

And þe ouerplus ouer þat for ornementz of þe churche.

Though þis be shortly y-seide, yit so me God helpe,   660

Who-so had cu*n*nyng and a clerc were,

Might make a long sermon of þees [lite] wordes ;

634 mynde : witte D.   637 litel : C *adds* þow.   641 eu*er* :
so M; MS. were.   642 *Side-note marked to stand after l.* 641.
647 dees : desys D.   655 MS. light.   656 hireth : herkeneth C.
662 MS. fewe.

And þough he toke to his theme "þe treso*ur* is among þaym
And þe reuylle of þe royaulme and þe richesse bothe,"
He shuld not wende of þe waye two whete cornes.   665

For þay haue tollid so þe tithing þay han þe two dooles,
And been so vsid to ease erly and late
That þay cunne no crafte saue kepe þaym warme.
Thay bisien more for ben*e*fices þenne bibles to reede,
And been as worldly wise and wynners eeke   670
As man vppon molde, and asmuche louen
Mvm and þe monaye, by Marie of heuene,
For mayntenance and mede been þaire two mates.

But the clergy have taken the whole of the tithes for themselves, and are given over to sloth.

They think more of preferment than of study, and love Mum and money as much as do the laity.

"Yit wil þou melle more", cothe Mvm, "þenne hit nedeth.
Be stille lest þou stumble, for þou stondes ful slidre,   675
And þou moeue any more suche maniere wordes.
Thay been not holsum for þy heed ne for þy herte noþer,
For þou mos holde wit*h* þe mo yf þou þy helthe willes;
And so I haue y-tolde þe twyes and oones.

Mum said "It is dangerous for you to speak thus.

Thou art mad of þy mynde, and amysse levis   680
That Mvm hath a maister þere men been of goode;
For Mvm maketh mo men at a moneth-ende
Thanne þe sothe-sigger in seuene score winter;
For he is p*ri*uy with þe pruttist and þere þe price caicchet,
[And] is y-drawe to þe deys with deyntees y-seruyd   685
Whenne þe sothe-sigger dar not be seye.

"You are foolish to think that any one can over-rule Mum.

"Mum has immeasurably more influence than the truth-teller.

For and a matier be moeued at mete or at eue
Or in pryuy places þere peeris assemblen,
Mvm musith þere-on and maketh many cautelles
With a locke on his lippe and loketh aboute.   690
He spendith no speche but spices hit make,
Til he wite whitherward þat wil doo drawe.   [*fo.* 8 *b.*]
But þenne he knittith a knotte and cometh al at ones
And getith hym a greet þanke to go among þe beste.

"He will say nothing unless he is bribed.

Fle fooly þerefor*e*, and frendes þe make,   695
And a-rete, I þe rede, and rome no ferther,
For þou walkis of þe weye forto wynne siluer.
And carpe no more of clergie but yf þou cunne leepe,

"Give up your pilgrimage, which will gain you nothing.

"Say nothing against the

---

664 reuylle : reulle C.   668 warme *written later*.   674 *Space between* melle *and* more *filled in by dash*.   678 willes : willnest D.
685 MS. As.   691 *Signature* .c. 4. fo. *in right-hand margin.*

clergy; if they get you into their power, you will not escape easily."

For and þou come on þaire clouche, þou crepis not þens

Til þou wite right wel *with* whom þat þou mellys."   700

" I will not cease," said I, " for priests are pitiful; they will not harm any one.

"I-wis I wil not," cothe I, " til I wite more;

For prestz been not perillous but pacient of þaire werkes,

And eeke þe plantz of pees and ful of pitie euer,

And chief of al charite y-chose a-fore other;

Forto fighte ne to flite hit falleth not to þaire ordre,   705

Ne to prece to no place þere peril shuld be ynne.

" It is the law that the bishop should leave the court before sentence of death is given.

That proueth wel by parlement, for prelatz shuld be voidid

Whenne any dome of deeth shal be do þere,

Al for cause þaire conscience to kepe vn-y-wemmyd.

" To the clergy one may safely speak the truth without fear."

A man may saye þaym þe sothe sonest of alle,   710

Withoute grucche oþer groyn, but gete many þankes.

Sic luceat lux *vestra* coram homi*nibus* vt videa*nt* ope*r*a v*est*ra bona *etc*.

Thay moste bowe for þe beste, God forbede hit elles,

To shewe vs exemple of suffrance euer."

" Be wary " said Mum, " you do not understand the matter.

"Yee, yit be ware of wiles and waite wel aboute,

For me semeth þat þy sight is sumdele a-dasid   715

And al myndelees ", cothe Mvm / " and al amysse demys;

For þough þou shuldes þy-silf be a sothe-sigger,

Thou has no cleere conceypt to knowe alle þaire werkes.

And þat I pryued by a poynt þou perceipues neuer,

Al a-tw[art] þy intent and þy tale eeke,   720

" Pilate washed his hands to shew his inno-cence, yet he was the most guilty.

For Pilat in þe Passion among al þe peuple

Wilned aftre watre to waisshe with his handes,

To shewe hym by þat signe, of þe bloode-sheding

Of Crist þat vs creed and on þe crosse deyed,

His conscience was clensid as clene as his handes.   725

Yit was he ground of þe grame and moste guilty eeke,

" Every one knows that pre-lates should restrain the wrath of princes.

For euery man þat mynde hath may wel wite

That prelatz aughten haue pite when princz bee moeued,

And reede þaym so þat rancune roote not in hert,

And ere þe grame growe ferre / þe ground so to wede   730

And amende þat were mysse ere any moore caicche

" If a man sees a storm coming and does not seek shelter, he has only himself to blame.

Of man-slaughter or mourdre, as hath many dayes.

For who hath knowlache of a cloude by cours of a-bouue,

And wil stande stille til þe storme falle,

And wende not of þe waye, þe wite is his owen.   735

720 twart: *so* D ; MS. tw *and a space left.*

Though hit heelde on his heede, who is to blame?
For who hath sight of a showre þat sharpely a-riseth,
And wil not caste hym to kepe with couryng abouue   [*fo.* 9 *a.*]
Til hit droppe al a-dovne and dung-wete hym make,
And eeke falle on his frende, in feith as me þenketh,   740
He is auctor of al þe harme and þache
And so pryuy to þe peynes þat [his] peeres induren.
And also in cuntrey hit is a comune speche
And is y-write in Latyne, lerne hit who-so wil :
The reason is "qui tacet consentire videtur".   745
And who-so hath in-sight of silde-couthe thingz,
Of synne or of shame or of shonde outher,
And luste not to lette hit, but leteth hit forth passe
As clerc*z* doon construe þat knowen alle bokes,
He shal be demyd doer of þe same deede.   750
And eeke in lond-is lawe I lernyd by anothir :
Yf a freke for felonye is frayned atte barre
For traison or for trespas / and he a tunge haue
And wil not answere to þe deede he is of indited,
But stont stille as a stoone and no worde stire,   755
But he be deef or dum / to deeth shal he wende,
As atteynt for þe trespas, and is a trewe lawe.
This cursid custume hath cumbrid vs alle ;
The grucching[z] of grete þat shuld vs gouuerne
Han y-shourid sharpely þorough suffrance of clercz,   760
That lightly with labour y-lettid þay mighte,
The conseil of clergie yf þay had caste for hit.
For þere þe heede aketh alle þe lymes after
Pynen / whenne þe principal is put to vnease
(Of sum and certayn, I saye not of alle,   765
But of þe same seurely þat suche maniere vsen.)"
"Now treuly," cothe I, "þy talking me pleasith,
For þou has saide as sothe, so me God helpe,
As euer sage saide sith Crist was in erthe,
For þou has rubbid on þe rote of þe rede galle   770

"And he is re-
sponsible for the
harm that his
companions
suffer.

"Hence he who
sees evil and
does not de-
nounce it, is
guilty as an
accessory.

"The law says
that if a man
accused of felony
will not plead, he
shall be doomed
to death.

"We have all
suffered from the
slowness of the
clergy to rebuke
the great for
their envious
quarrels."

Dum caput
infirmu*m*
cetera mem-
bra dolent.

"Truly," said I,
"you have
probed the root
of the evil.

740 frende : fre *over erasure.*   741 þe ache S.   742 [his] : MS.
omits.   745 qui ... videtur *underlined.*   759 grucching[z] : MS.
grucching.   763 *Side-note marked to stand after l.* 764.   765 and :
of *interlineation by* L.   769 sage : segge C.

And eeke y-serchid þe sore and sought alle þe woundz.

" Say this public-
ly and you will
have great re-
ward."
And yf þou woldes do wel / wende to þaym alle
And telle þe same tale þat þou has tolde here ;
Thou might be man made and mensshid for euer."

" No," said he,
"I will tell no
tales; that is the
counsel of Mum,
my master.
" Nay, þere I leue þe, lucas, go loke [for] an othir ;   775
For I wil wende no waie but wit go bifore,
Ne telle no tales for teryng of hodes,
So taughte me þe [truest] techer on erthe,
My maister and maker, Mvm þat I serue.

" Go where you
like, but keep out
of the way of the
clergy.
Go walke where þy wil is and waite wel aboute,   780
For þou has sought al a-side sith þou begunne
With clercz of Cambrigge and cathedralle churches.
Fare forth þerefore to finde þat þou sechis,
And come not with clergie leste þou a-croke walke,   [*fo. 9 b.*]

" Try the nobility
and the people."
But tourne now to tovnes and temporal lordz,   785
There prece is of peuple, and pray þaym to telle
Yf any sothe-sigger serue þaym long."

Then I went to
the laity, nobles,
and commons.
Thenne ferkid I to fre men and frankeleyns mony,
    To bonde-men and bourgois and many oþer barnes,
To knightz and to comunes and craftz-men eeke,   790
To citezeyns and souurayns and to many grete sires,
To bachilliers, to banerettz, to barons and erles,
To princes and peris and alle maniere estatz ;

But here I found
far more mum-
mers than truth-
tellers.
But in euery court þere I came or cumpaigny outhir
I fonde mo mvmmers atte moneth-ende   795
Than of sothe-sigger[z] by seuene score thousand.

All the courtiers
followed Mum.
For alle þe knyghtz of þe court þat with þe king dwellen,
For þe more partie / [yee], mo þan an hunthrid,
Heulden Mvm for a maister, and more do mighte
With king and his cunseil and al þe court aftre . . .   800

In every town
Mum was the
mayor's dear
friend
And euery tovne þat I trade twelfe moneth to-gedre,
Mvm was a maister and with þe maire euer,
And al of oon lyuraye and looke so to-gedre
That a poure man-is prayer departe þaym ne mighte.
There was no maner man þe maire had levir   805
Bydde of þe burnes in benche þere [þay] satte

---

774 mensshid : menskid C.   775 MS. yf.   778 truest :
so D ; MS. trusty.   783 forth : ferþer D.   789 barnes : burnes D.
796 MS. sigger.   798 MS. ee.   806 þay : *so* D ; MS. he.

As Mvm to þe mete among al þe rewe ;

For he couthe lye and laugh and leepe ouer þe balkes

There any grucche or groyne or grame shuld arise.

He was ful couchant and coy and curtoys of speche,   810

And parlid for þe partie and þe playnte lefte ;

The maire preisid hym apert for his plaisant wordes ;

He was a blessid barne and beste couthe suffre

Whenne souurayns were assemblid to saye what þaym liked ;

He toke no maniere travers tenne yere to-gedre,   815

Among þe comun cunseil lest he caste were,

But euer shewid his seel to sitte among other.

But who-so mvmmeth a mayre to maynteyne his rente,

Maniere were þat þe mayre shuld mvmme hym agaynes

And yelde hym with a yere-is y[i]fte ere þe yere passed.   820

Mvm with þe mayre to þe mete wente,

And euer I after, al vn-a-spied,

For to knowe of my caas couthe I not stynte.

There shuldrid sergeant[z] to serue atte mete

For a male ful of misse-deedz þat Mvm had in keping.   825

I stoode stille as a stoone and starid aboute

And lokid lightly a-long by þe bordes,

Yf any sothe-sigger were sette in þe halle.

But sorowe on þe shyne I sawe of hym þere,

But yf he were a soleyn and seruyd al oon,   830

For alle was huyst in þe halle sauf " holde vp þe oyles ".

[*fo.* 10 a.]

And forto saye sothe and shone long tale,

The sunne and þe sergeant[z] my sight so dasid

That I might not eche messe merke as me luste.

I askid of a eldryn man as I beste couthe   835

Yf any sothe-sigger sate in þe halle,

And he answerid sharply / þat " þe sothe-sigger

Dyneth þis day with Dreede in a chambre,

And hath y-drunke dum-seede, and dar not be seye

Sith Mvm and þe mayer were made suche frendes ".   840

Side notes:

For he was always on his side, and on that of great men.

Naturally, the mayor rewarded him for his support.

Mum went to the banquet with the mayor, and I followed secretly.

Many sergeants served the meat, hoping for reward from Mum.

But I could see no truth-teller.

I asked an old man if there were such.

He told me tha the truth-teller dined alone with Dread, for fear of Mum and the mayor.

---

813 barne : burne D.   817 shewid : showde D.   820 MS. yfte.
823 MS. Forto.   824 MS. a sergeant ; a *crossed out and* z
added to sergeant M.   833 MS. sergeant.   835 eldryn : alder D.
839 dum : doom D.

I went out in anger.

Thenne waxe I woundre wrothe, as I wel might,
And drowe me to þe doreward and dwelled no lenger,
But romed forth reedelees, remembring ofte
That Mvm was suche a maister among men of good.

In the street I saw a truth-teller salving his wounds.

And as I lokid þe loigges along by þe streetz,   845
I sawe a sothe-sigger, in sothe as me þought,
Sitte in a shoppe and salwyn his woundes.

Beati qui per-secucionem paciuntur propter iusti-ciam. euangelium.

Thenne was I ful-come and knewe wel þe sothe
That Mvm vppon molde myrier life had
Thenne þe sothe-sigger, asay who-so wol;   850
But þe better barne to abide stille

Then I under-stood that Mum prospers more in this world, but the truth-teller is the better servant for a lord.

And to lyve with a lord to his life-is ende
Ys þe sothe-sigger, a-say who-so wol.

I grew weak and lay down to rest myself, remembering how I had visited all ranks of men, and found every-where that Mum was master.

Yit was I not þe wiser for waye þat I wente;
This made me al madde as I most nede,   855
And wel fleuble and faynt, and feulle to þe grounde,
And lay dovne on a lynche to lithe my boones,
Rolling in remembrance my rennyng aboute
And alle þe perillous patthes þat I passid had,
As priories and personagz and pluralites,   860
Abbayes of Augustyn and oþer hooly places,
To knightes courtz and crafty men many,
To mayers and maisters, men of high wittes,
And to þe felle freris, alle þe foure ordres,
And oþer hobbes a-heepe, as ye herde haue—   865
And nought þe neer by a note / þis noyed me ofte
That þorough construyng of clercz þat knewe alle bokes
That Mvm shuld be maister moste vppon erthe.

I fell asleep, and slept for seven hours.

And ere I were ware, a wynke me assailled,
That I slepte sadly seuene houres large.   870

I will tell you some of the many marvels which I saw in my dream.

Thenne mette I of mervailles mo þanne me luste
To telle or to talke of, til I se tyme;
But sum of þe silde-couthes I wol shewe here-after,
For dreme is no dwele by Danyel-is wordes,
Though Caton of þe contrarye carpe in his bokes.   875

I was in a lonely country, in a green valley,

Me þought I was in wildernesse walking al oon,
There bestes were and briddes and no barne elles,   [fo. 10 b.]

841 Thenne: Th *in later hand*; Than M.   849 *Side-note marked to stand after l.* 847.   851, 877 barne : burne D.

Yn a cumbe cressing on a creste wise,
Al gras grene þat gladid my herte,
By a cliffe vn-y-knowe of Crist-is owen makyng.   880

I climbed to the top of the hill.

I lepte forth lightly a-long by þe heigges
And movid forth myrily to maistrie þe hilles,
For til I came to þe coppe couthe I not stynte
Of þe highest hille by halfe [of] alle other.
I tournyd me twyes and totid aboute,   885

I looked over a wide landscape— woods, houses, new-mown fields,

Beholding heigges and holtz so grene,
The mansions and medues mowen al newe,
For suche was þe saison of þe same yere.
I lifte vp my eye-ledes and lokid ferther
And sawe many swete sightz, so me God helpe,   890

woods and waters,

The wodes and þe waters and þe welle-springes

green trees and field flowers,

And trees y-traylid fro toppe to þerthe,
Coriously y-courid with curtelle of grene,
The flours on feeldes flavryng swete,
The corne on þe croftes y-croppid ful faire,   895

reaped corn-fields,

The rennyng riuyere russhing faste,

a river full of fish,

Ful of fyssh and of frie of felefold kinde,

trees covered with fruit and flowers.

The breris with þaire beries bent ouer þe wayes
As honysoucles hongyng vppon eche half,
Chesteynes and chiries þat children desiren   900
Were loigged vndre leues ful lusty to seen.
The havthorne so holsum I beheulde eeke,
And hough þe benes blowid and þe brome-floures ;
Peris and plummes and pesecoddes grene,
That ladies lusty loken muche after,   905
Were gadrid for gomes ere þay gunne ripe ;
The grapes grovid a-grete in gardyns aboute,
And oþer fruytz felefold in feldes and closes ;
To nempne alle þe names hit nedith not here.
The conyngz fro couert courid þe bankes   910

rabbits and hares pursued by hounds,

And raughte oute a raundon and retournyd agaynes,
Pleyed forth on þe playne, and to þe pitte after,
But any hovnd hente þaym / or þe hay-nettes.

878 cumbe : . . . mbe (*beginning torn away*) D.   884 [of] : MS.
omits.   910. bankes : b *over an erasure.*

The hare hied hym faste and þe hovndes after ;

For kisshyng of his croupe a-caunt-wise he wente,   915

For nad he tournyd twies his tail had be licked,

So ernestly Ector ycchid hym after.

sheep and lambs, The shepe fro þe sunne shadued þaymself,

While þe lambes laikid a-long by þe heigges.

cows and horses, The cow with hire calfe and coltes ful faire   920

And high hors in haras hurtelid to-gedre,

And preisid þe pasture þat prime-saute þaym made.

deer, by hundreds. The dere on þe dale drowe to þaire dennes,   [*fo.* 11 *a*.]

Ferkid forth to þe ferne and feulle dovne amyddes.

Hertz and hyndes, a hunthrid to-gedre,   925

With rayndeer and roobuc runne to þe wodes,

For þe kenettz on þe cleere were vn-y-couplid ;

And buckes ful burnysshid þat baren good grece,

Foure hunthrid on a herde y-heedid ful faire,

Layen lowe in a launde a-long by þe pale,   930

A swete sight for souurayns, so me God helpe.

I went down to the valley. I moued dovne fro þe mote to þe midwardz

And so a-dovne to þe dale, dwelled I no longer,

The birds sang sweetly. But suche a noise of nestlingz ne so swete notz

I herde not þis halfe yere, ne so heuenely [sounes]   935

As I dide on þat dale adovne among þe heigges,

For in euery bussh was a brid þat in his beste wise

Bablid with his bile, þat blisse was to hire.

So [cheerly] þay chirmed and chaunged þaire notes,

The smell of the fruit and the flowers comforted me for my labour. That what for flauour of þe fruyte and of þe somer floures, 940

The smellyng smote as spices, me þought,

That of my trauail treuly toke I no kepe,

For al was vanesshid me fro þorough þe fresshe sightes.

I saw a franklin's house with a most beautiful garden. Thenne lepte I forth lightly and lokid a-boute,

And I beheulde a faire hovs with halles and chambres,

A frankeleyn-is fre-holde al fresshe newe.   946

I bente me aboute and bode atte dore

Of þe gladdest gardyn þat gome euer had.

I haue no tyme treuly to telle alle þe names

Of ympes and herbes and oþer feele thinges   950

924 to : on D.   935 [sounes]: MS. *omits.*   939. MS. cleerly.

That growed on þat gardyn, þe grounde was so noble.

I passid ynne pryuely and pulled of þe fruytes

And romed þaleys rovnde al a-boute,

But so semely a sage as I sawe þere

I sawe not sothely sith I was bore,   955

An olde auncyen man of a hunthrid wintre,

Y-wedid in white cloþe and wisely y-made,

With hore heres on his heede more þanne half white,

A faire visaige and a vresse and vertuous to [sene].

His eyen were al ernest, eggid to noon ille,   960

With a broode besmet berde / ballid a lite,

As comely a creature as euer kinde wrought.

He was sad of his semblant, softe of his speche,

Proporcioned at alle poyntes and pithy in his tyme,

And by his stature right stronge, and stalworth on his dayes.

He houed ouer a hyue, þe hony forto kepe   966

Fro dranes þat destrued hit and dide not elles ;

He thraste þaym with his thumbe as þicke as þay come,

He lafte noon a-liue for þaire lither taicches.   [fo. 11 b.]

I wondrid on his workes as I wel might,   970

And euer I neyed hym nere as ney as me ought,

And halsid hym hendily as I had lernyd ;

And he me grete agayne right in a goode wise,

And askid what I wolde / and anone I tolde

My wil was to wite what man he were.   975

"I am gardyner of þis [garth]," cothe he, "þe grovnde is myn

　　owen,

Forto digge and to delue and to do suche deedes

As longeth to þis leyȝttone / þe lawe wol I doo,

And wrote vp þe wedes þat wyrwen my plantes ;

And wormes þat worchen not but wasten my herbes,   980

I daisshe þaym to deeth and delue oute þaire dennes.

But þe dranes doon worste, deye mote þay alle ;

Thay haunten þe hyue for hony þat is ynne,

And lurken and licken þe liquor þat is swete,

And trauelyn no twynte / but taken of þe beste   985

Side notes:

I went in and wandered through the alleys.

Here I met an aged man, fairer to look on than any I have ever seen.

He was tending a hive, killing the drones as they approached it.

I asked him who he was.

"I am the keeper of this garden," said he.

"I destroy everything that injures it.

"The worst enemies are the drones, who eat the honey and do no work.

Qui non labo-

954 sage : segge D.   959 sene ; so D ; MS. seme.   961 besmet:
besmyd C.   971 neyed : neghyde C.   976 MS. gate.
978 leyȝttone : leyghtoun C.   985 Side-note marked to stand after l. 986.

rat non man-
ducet. Ber-
nardus.
Of þat þe bees bryngen fro blossomes and floures.

For of alle þe bestes þat breden vppon erthe

"Of all creatures,
the bee is the
most industri-
ous."
For qualite ne quantite, n[o] question, I trowe

The bee in his bisynes beste is allowed,

And prouyd in his propriete passing alle oþer,   990

And pretiest in his wirching to profite of þe peuple."

I asked him to
tell me about the
bees and the
drones.
"Swete sire," sayde I in slepe as me thoughte,

"The propriete of bees I pray þat ye wolde

Declare with þaire deedes, and of þe drane eeke."

"Willingly,"
said he.
"Blethely, burne, þy beede shal bee doo   995

Yf þou wil tende treuly my tale to þende.

' The bees are
ruled by a king
whom they
obey.
The bee of alle bestz / beste is y-gouuerned

Yn lowlynes and labour and in lawe eeke.

Thay haue a king by kinde þat þe coroune bereth,

Whom þay doo sue and serue as souurayn to þaym alle,   1000

And obeyen to his biddyng, or elles þe boke lieth.

"He has the
highest place in
the hive, and
they build their
dwellings below
him.
The highest hoole in þe hyue / he holdeth hit hymself,

For þere þay setten hym in his see by hym-self oone,

And maken mansions by-nethe / þat mervail hit is to knowe

The bilding of þe boures / þat þe bees maken.   1005

"They are the
best builders in
the world.
For þe curiousiste carpintier vndre [cope] of heuene

Couthe not caste þaire coples / ne cuntrefete þare workes.

"They extract
their building
materials from
flowers.
Thaire tymbre and þaire tile stones / and al þat to þaym longeth,

Thay feycchen hit of floures in feldes and in croftes.

"Their hives are
divided, and each
part has a
prince.
Thayr dwellingz been dyuyded, I do hit on þaire combes,   1010

And many a queynt caue been cumpassid [wy]-þynne.

And eche a place hath a *pr*incipal þat peesith al his quarter,

That reuleth þaym to reste / and rise whenne hit nedith,

"The princes are
subject to the
king.
And alle þe principallz to þe prince ful prest þay been at
            nede,

To rere þaire retenue to righte alle þe fautes ;   [*fo.* 12 *a.*]

For þay knowen as kindely / as clerc doeth his bokes   1016

Wastours þat wyrchen not but wombes forto fille.

Thaire workes been right wondreful / wite þou for sothe,

"Some bring
home the flower
juices.
For sum, as þou sees / þay shape þaym to þe feldes

"Some build up
the cells and
To sovke oute þe swettenes of þe somer floures,   1020

And sum abiden at home to bigge vp þe loigges,

988 MS. ne.   995 *An unfinished minim written at the end of* bee.
1006 cope : *so* D ; MS. erthe.   1011 MS. by þynne.

And helpen to make hony of þat þay home bringen,   make the honey.

And doon oþer deedes þorough dome þat is among þaym ;

And sum waiten þe wedre, þe wynde and þe skyes,   " Some watch the weather.

Yf hit be temperate tyme to trauaylle or to leue.   1025

[Thay] eten alle at oones / and neuer oon by hymsilf,   " All eat to- gether, to avoid

Thorough warnyng of þaire wa[r]thour / leste waste were among   waste.
þaym.

The bomelyng of þe bees, as Bartholomew vs telleth,   " Bartholomæus tells us that they

Thair noyse and þaire notz at eue and eeke at morowe,   1029   all know each other's voices.

Lyve hit wel, þair lyden[e] þe leste of þaym hit knoweth.

The moste merciful among þaym and meukest of his deedes   " The king is the most merciful of

Ys king of bees comunely, as clergie vs telleth,   them.

And sperelees, and in wil to spare þat been hym vnder,   " He has no sting, or at least

Or yf he haue oon, he harmeth ne hurteth noon in sothe.   uses none.

For venym doeth not folowe hym / but vertue in alle workes,   " He rules by reason and their

To reule þaym by reason / and by right-ful domes,   1036   consent.

Thorough contente of þe cumpaignie / þat closeth alle in oone.

And yf þe king coueite þe colours to be-holde   " If he wishes to go out, they all

Of þe fressh floures þat on þe feldes growen,   surround him.

Euermore a-myddes as maister of þaym alle   1040

His place is y-properid for peril þat mighte falle ;

And yf he fleuble or feynte / or funder dovneward,   " If he fails in his flight, they bear

The bees wollen bere hym til he be better amended.   him up.

But of þe drane[s] is al þe doute, þe deueil [þaym] quelle,   " But the drones eat more than

For in þaire wide wombes / þay wol hide more   1045   twenty bees, and do no work.

Thenne twenty bees / and trauaillen not no tyme of þe day,

But gaderyn al to þe gutte and growen grete and fatte

And fillen þaire bagges brede-ful / of þat þe bees wyrchen.   Quorum deus venter est et

But hire hough þay ende with al þaire hole cropping :   gloria in con- fusione.

Whenne þay hauè soope þe swete / þe soure cometh aftre,   1050   paulus.

For whenne þe bee-is bisynes is bribed fro þe hyve   " Yet in the end the bees see

Thorough dranes þat deceipuen þaym / and doon no þing elles,   through them, and pay them

Thenne seen þe bees þair subtilite / and seruen þaym þere-after   out.

1026 MS. That.   1027 MS. wauthour.   1030 Lyve: leve C.
MS. lydenys.   1037 content : *altered by* C *in margin and* L *in text
to* consente. closeth : cordeth D.   1042 dovneward : L *adds* z.
1044 MS. drane ; L *adds* z. þe deueil þaym quelle (MS. hym *for* þaym)
þat deye mote þey alle N.   1048 *Side-note marked to stand after l.* 1046.
1049 hough : how D.   1053 seruen : n *written over* t.

"So Bartholo-
mæus tells us."

As Bartholomew þe Bestiary bablith on his bokes,
And of other pryvy poyntz ⁄ but I wol passe ouer."   1055

"At this rate,
there will be
little honey,"
said I.

" By þis skile," cothe I, "þere shuld scant hony
Yf euery hyve hurle þus ⁄ and haue suche a ende."

"Yes," said he,
"unless the
gardener kills
them before they
enter the hive.

" Be certayne," he seide, "þat is a sothe tale
But yf þe gardyner haue grace and gouuerne hym þe bettre
And wisely a-waite whenne dranes furste entren,   1060
And nape thaym on þe nolle ere þay þaire neste caicche;
                                  [fo. 12 b.]

"If they get in,
he can do no-
thing."

For been þay oones ynned ⁄ his eyen shalt be dasid
Fro al kinde knowlache, so couert þaym helpeth."

"I asked him
how he recog-
nized the
drones."

" Yit wolde I wite ⁄" cothe I, "yf your wil be,
Hough to knowe kindely, þorough craft of your scole,   1065
The drane þat deuoureth þat deue is to other,
By colour or by cursidnesse or crie þat he maketh.

"They are long
and thin and
black," said he,
"and come home
empty-handed;
but in six months
they are bigger
and fiercer than
the others."
Nichil aspe-
rius paupero
cum surget in
altum. Gre-
gorius.
I asked why the
bees did not
attack them
earlier.

Kenneth me þe cunnyng, þat I may knowe after."
" Thay been long and lene," cothe he ⁄ "and of a lither hue,
And as bare as a bord, and bringen nought with þaym;   1070
But haue þay hauntid þe hyve half yere to þende,
Thay growen vnder gurdel gretter þan other,
And noon so sharpe to stinge ne so sterne noþer."
" Yit I mervaille," cothe I, "and so mowen other,
Why þe bees wollen not wirwe þaym by tyme,   1075
And falle on þaym fersly furst whanne þay entre,
For so shuld þay saue þaym-silf and þaire goodes."

"They are too
busy," he said,
"in summer
time.

" The bees been so bisi," cothe he, "aboute comune profit,
And tendeth al to trauail while þe tyme dureth
Of þe somer saison and of þe swete floures;   1080
Thayr wittes been in wirching and in no wile elles
Forto waite any waste til winter approche,
That licour þaym lacke ⁄ þair lyfe to susteyne.

"When winter
comes, they see
their labour is
lost, and they
kill the drones."

But as sone as þay see ⁄ þaire swynke is y-stole,
Thenne flocken þay to fighte ⁄ þair fautes to amende,   1085
And quellen þe dranes quicly and quiten alle þaire wrongz."

"Thank you,"
said I, "but the
moral of your
story is too deep
for me.

" Now wol mote ye worthe", cothe I, "for your wise tale,
For hit hath muche menyng ⁄ who-so muse couthe,

1062 MS. shald; shal be dasid S.   1065 How S.   1067 colour:
cry D.   1073 *Side-note against l.* 1074 *in MS., marked to stand after
l.* 1073.   1075 wirwe: wyrwe D.   1085 þair: þe D.   1087 ye:
þou A. your: þy D.

But hit is to mistike for me, by Marie of heuene,
So wol I leue lightly withoute long tale.   1090

" But I would ask you one question, to resolve which I have travelled far.

But and ye dwelle, as I dar, derue I you preye
Oone question to construe þat I come fore ;
For I haue soughte seuene yere and sum dele more,
And mette I neuer man yit þat me wise couthe
Cleere to my knowing, clerc noþer lewed,   1095
Of þe matiere of Mvm þat moste me angrith,
That he shuld haue maisters mor þan oon hunthrid,
Whenne þe sothe-sigger shuld siche his mete.
I haue trauailled tenne yere to temporal estatz,
And spied of spirituel and sparid for no wreth   1100
Forto wite witterly who shuld haue
The maistry, Mvm or þe sothe-sigger.

" Who should have the mastery, Mum or the truth-teller?

For alle þe foure ordres agayne þaire fundacion
Prouyd hit ofte by prechement, for peril þat myght falle,
That Mvm shuld be maister and maynteyne þordre ; 1105
And alle oþer estatz euery after other
Heulden muche more with Mvm þenne with þe sothe-
          sigger.   [*fo.* 13 *a.*]

" The friars uphold Mum,

" and so do all the other estates.

And yf ye deme as þay doon, by dere God in heuene,
By no witte þat I wote I wol go no ferther
Forto seke shadue þere no sunne apperith."   1110
"Swete soon, þy seching," seide þe freke þenne,
" And þy trauail for þy trouthe shal tourne þe to profit,
For I wol go as nygh þe grounde as gospel vs techeth
Forto wise þe wisely to þy waie-is ende.

" If you say the same, I will give up my quest."

He replied : " All the evil and misrule in the kingdom is caused by Mum.

For [of] al þe mischief and mysse-reule þat in þe royaulme
          groweth   1115
Mvm hath be maker alle þees many yeres,
And eek more and moulde, I may wel aduowe ;
And principally by parlement to proue hit I þenke,
When knightz for þe comune been come for þat deede,
And semblid forto shewe þe sores of þe royaulme   1120
And spare no speche þough þay spille shuld,
But berste oute alle þe boicches and blaynes of þe hert
And lete þe rancune renne oute a-russhe al at oones

" This I can prove by what happens in Parliament, where the knights of the shire should speak out boldly their complaints,

1106 *Catch-word* heulden muche more.   1110 seke : sike D.
1115 of : MS. *omits.*

"lest they fester
as an abcess
within their
hearts

Leste þe fals felon festre with-ynne ;
For as I herde haue, þay helen wel þe rather   1125
Whenne þanger and þattre is al oute y-renne,
For better were to breste oute þere bote might falle

"and break out
as rebellion.

Thenne rise agayne regalie and þe royaulme trouble.
The voiding of þis vertue doeth venym forto growe
And sores to be saluelees in many sundry places   1130
Sith souurayns and þe shire-men þe sothe haue eschewed
Yn place þat is proprid to parle for þe royaulme
And fable of þoo fautes and founde þaym to amende.

"They will not
complain of their
abuses, but make
Mum their
spokesman, and
bring back their
grievances un-
cured.

For alle þe perillous poyntz of prelatz and of other,
As peres þat haue pouaire to pulle and to leue,   1135
Thay wollen not parle of þoo poyntz for peril þat might falle,
But hiden alle þe heuynes and halten echone
And maken Mvm þaire messaigier þaire mote to determyne,

Qui potest
contradicere
peccato et non
contradicit
actor est pec-
cati. Sidrac.
"Among the
lawyers Mum is
master.

And bringen home a bagge ful of boicches vn-y-curid,
That nedis most by nature ennoye þaym þere-after.   1140
And in al þe king-is court þere coiphes been and oþer
Mvm is maister þere more þenne men wenen,
For sum of þo segges wolle siche side-wayes,

"They deceive
men so as to
make profit.

Whenne þay witen wel y-now where þe hare walketh,
Thay leden men þe long waye and loue-dayes breken   1145

Fauor et pre-
mium timor
et odium per-
uertunt verum
iudicium.
Canon.

And maken moppes wel myry with þaire madde tales,
Forto sowe siluer seede / and solue ere þay singe,
To haue ynne þaire harueste while þe hete dureth.
Now feithfully, my ful frende, I wol not feyne to þe ;

"All the evil in
this world is
caused by Mum.

There is no wronge on þis world wrought, as I wene,   1150
Treason noþer trespas ne trouble þat falleth,
Felonye ne falshede ne no faute elles,
Rancune ne riotte ne reuyng of peuple,   [*fo*. 18 *b*.]
Courshidnes ne cumbrance ne no caste of guile,
That Mvm nys þe maker and moste cause eeke.   1155
And þat shal I shewe þe by exemples y-nowe ;
For Lucifer þe lyer þat lurketh aboute
Forto gete hym a grounde þat he may graffe on
And to sowe of his seede suche as he vsith,

"Lucifer lies in
wait to ensnare
a man in the trap
of lust or pride
or avarice.

1139 *Side-note marked to stand after l.* 1140.   1143 MS. þo *altered
from* þe.   1146 *Side-note marked to stand after l.* 1148.   1152 *Signature* .d. 1. fo. *in right-hand margin.*

That groweth al to grevance and gurdyng of heedes,   1160
He leyeth his lynes along þat luste may be clepid
Of oure foule flessh þat foundrith ful ofte,
And of gloire of þis grounde his griefz been y-made,
That who be hent in his hoke he shal be holde faste
Til he [be] caste with couetise or sum croke elles.   1165
Thenne fareth he forth felaship to gete,
To holde his opinion ouer alle þingz.
Whenne he is laught on þe lyne he can not lepe þens,
So þe cursid couetise cleueth on his herte,
Or elles dreede forto do wel dulleth his wittz.   1170
But seche what he seche wol and asaye eeke,
There is no sothe-sigger þat wol assent to hym,
But conseilleth hym [þe] contrary and construeth þe doutes
And poynteth hym þe perillz and pleynely telleth
As a sicour seruant, and sheweth hym þe happes.   1175
He shoneth for no salaire ne soulde þat he fangeth,
Ne [for no] likerous lyuelode ne loising of his office,
That he ne telleth þe tirant how hit tourne wol
Hamward by his hows / and harme most hymself.
Thenne fleeth he fro his frend and to his foo tourneth,   1180
For til he mete with Mvm may he neuer reste.
He wol abide with no burne þat botene hym wolde
Ne a-rayne hym arere with reason-is bridel,
So loueth he go large to lepe where hym liketh,
And kiketh faste as a colte þat casteth downe hymsilf,   1185
And fondeth forto finde þis freeke I haue nempnyd,
That fayne is to folowe hym for fees and robes.
Thenne meteth he with Mvm and his matiere sheweth,
That shortly assentith as a shrewed hyne,
And spareth for no spurnyng, but spedith þe matiere,   1190
And wircheth vp with wiles a walle of deceiptes,
Til þe fals fundement falle atte laste,
That þay stumblen after stroutyng and stappen no ferther,

Side-notes:

Semi*n*ator zizanie *et* agricola diaboli.

" But there is no truth-teller who will not freely show him the error of his ways.

" But the man will not listen, and betakes himself to Mum.

" Mum with his deceits brings both to destruction.

1163 griefz: greuys D.   1165 be: *so* P.   1166 *Side-note marked to stand after l.* 1165.   1173 þe: *so* C; MS. be.   1177 for no: *so* M; MS. no for.   1179 S¹ *adds side-note*; Iuris con-sult*us* / Cici*us* debet homo om*n*ia mala pati qu*am* malo co*n*sentire.   1181 reste: stynte D.   1183 a-rayne: *first a crossed out* M.

But lyen dovne on þe diche / as wel nygh y-doluen,
Bothe þe maister and his man y-murid at oones.   1195
Suche maniere medes Mvm can deserue
Forto mende his maister for meete and for hure,

"No Mum shall ever be my servant.
But by þe feith þat I finge atte vantstone
Shal no Mvm be my man and I may a-spie,   [*fo. 14 a.*]
And namely nygh me / but next shal he neuer.   1200

"I adjure you to follow the truth-teller,
And þerefore I fende þe, by feith þat þou aues,
That þou lieue in no lore of suche lewed gomes
That fikelly fablen and fals been withynne,
But sue þe sothe-sigger and seche þou no ferther.

"and in time you will be rewarded.
And þough hit tene for a tyme / hit tideth wel after,   1205
And he þat made þe molde and man with his handes
Shal quite þe with a quitance whenne querellz been vp
Of þis newe nouellerie þat noyeth men ofte.

"He is the best of servants for a king or lord."
Hit is þe holsemyst hyne for halle and for chambre
To bringe boldely a-bedde þe best of þe royaulme   1210
And arise with þe renke, rehershing agaynes
Salomon and Seneca and Sidrac þe noble.
Hit is a sicour seruant forto serue lordes,
And to knightz of þe cuntre his conseil availleth ;
And [thow] he dwelle with a duc and dide not elles   1215
But forto seye hym þe sothe in [seasonable] tymes,
He might serue sum day seuene yeres wages."

"Thank you, gardener," said I, "but I do not know where to find him."
"Grand mercy, gardiner," cothe I, "and God þe foryelde,
For þou has demed deuely þe doute I was ynne ;
But yit wote I not in sothe, ne am not infourmed   1220
How to come to þe court þere þe kempe dwellith."

"He dwells in man's heart," said the sage.
"His dwellyng to discryue," cothe he, "I do hit on alle clercz
That I shal teche [þe] treuly þe tournyng to his place.

In corde fidelis eat habitacio veritatis.
Yn man-is herte his hovsing is, as hooly writte techet,
And mynde is his mansion þat made alle þestres.   1225

"His Father put him in possession of Adam and his descendants.
There feoffed hym his fadre freely forto dwelle,
And put hym in possession in paradise terrestre
Yn Adam oure auncetre and al his issue after.

"God has granted Adam to possess Paradise and afterwards heaven.
He spirith hym with his spirite þat sprange of hymself
To holde þat habitacion and heuene afterwardes,   1230

1201 aues : owes D.   1215 thow : *so* D ; MS. do.   1216 MS. reasonable.   1223 MS. hym

To serue hym in sothenes and no souurayn eschewe
For dreede of deyeng ne no disease elles.
As wold God þat eche gome þat gre hath take in scoles
Wolde holde þat opinion / and ouer-lepe hit neuer,
For hit was neuer so nedeful / as now sith Noe-is dayes.   1235
But Mvm wol be no martir while mytres been in sale,
And but þe sothe-sigger sey þe same wordes
Whenne þou comys to his court, kutte of myn eres.
Now I haue y-wised þe / þe weye to his place,
Hye þe hens to his hows and hippe euene amyddes ;   1240
For þough his loigge be lite / hit is vnloke euer,
That þou mays intre eche day boþe erly and late,
Forto walke where þou wolt wythynne and withoute
And to moeue of his mote in mesurable tyme
And haue concours to Criste and come yn agaynes.   [*fo*. 14 *b*.]
For þay been brethern by baptesme, as þe boke telleth,   1246
And [he] is y-sibbe to þe [sire] abouue þe seuene sterres,
For trouthe and þe trinite been two nygh frendes.
Yf þou wol folowe þis fode, þou mos be faire of speche
And soft of þy sawys, but souuraynete hit helpe ;   1250
For pouerte hath a pressonere / whenne he doeth passe bondes.
And be wel ware of wiles / þe world is ful of mases ;
And loke wel a-leehalf lest þou be beguilid,
For Mvm hath a man þere [þat] is a muche shrewe,
Antecrist-is angel þat eche day vs ennoyeth.   1255
He dwellith faste by þe dore / and droppeth many wiles
Yf he might wynne ouer þe walle with a wron
He debateth eche day with Do-welle withynne,
And þe maistrie among and þe mote wynneth,
And shoueth þe sothe-sigger into a syde-herne,   1260
And taketh couetise þe keye to come ynne when hym liketh.
Thenne dreede with a dore-barre dryueth oute þe beste,
And maketh þe sothe-sigger seche a newe place,
And to walke where he wol withoute on þe grene
Til sorowe for his synnes seese hym agaynes   1265
And þe tenaunt a-tourne to treuthe al his life.

1236 in: at D.   *Side-note marked to stand after l.* 1238.   1244 *No
signature* (d. 2. fo.).   1247 he: MS. *omits.*   sire : *so* D ; MS. fure.
1254 MS. and.

" When you
wake, write
down my words,
that others may
profit.
Though þou slepe now, my soon / yit whenne þou seis tyme,
Loke þou write wisely my wordes echone ;
Hit wol be exemple to sum men seuene yere here-after.

"Speak the truth
in meekness, lest
you anger your
brother.
And loke þou seye euer sothe / but shame not þy brother, 1270
For yf þou telle hym trouthe in tirant-is wise,
He wol rather wexe wrother / þenne forto wirche after.
But in a muke maniere þou mos hym asaye,
And not eche day to egge hym, but in a deue tyme.

" Farewell. I
must depart.
Do þus, my dere soon, for I may dwelle no longer,   1275
But fare to my good frend / þat I fro come.
I haue infourmed þe faire / loke þou folowe after
And make vp þy matiere, þou mays do no better.
Hit may amende many men of þaire misdeedes.

" Be not slack in
writing your
book.
Sith þou felys þe fressh / lete no feynt herte   1280
Abate þy blessid bisynes / of þy boke-making
Til hit be complete to clapsyng, caste aweye doutes
And lete þe sentence be sothe, and sue to þende ;

"Give a copy to
the King ;
knights may
copy it after-
wards."
And furst feoffe þou þerewith þe freyst of þe royaulme,
For yf þy lord liege allone hit begynne,   1285
Care þou not þough knyghtz copie hit echone,
And do write eche word / and wirche þere-after."

Then I awoke.
Thenne soudaynly of sweuene and slepe I abrayed
And woke of my wynke and waitid aboute,

The whole scene
had vanished like
an enchantment,
but the words of
the sage are
worthy of record.
Wondring on my wittz, as I wel aughte,   1290
Where þe gome and þe gardyn and þe gaye sportz   [*fo.* 15 a.]
And alle þe sightz þat I sawe were so sone voidid.
Hit ferde as a fairye / but feithfully þe wordes
Were ful wise of þe wye in þe white cloþes,
And eeke nedeful and notable for þis newe world,   1295
And eeke plaisant to my pay / for þay putten me to reste
Of my long labour and loitryng aboute.

He proved that
the truth-teller
would have the
better of Mum.
For he provid by profitable poyntz and fele
That þe sothe-sigger shuld haue þe better
Of Mvm, and þe maistrie, malgre his chekes.   1300
He made Mvm a man-sleer and a-mys thewed
And likenyd hym to a lorel atte long goyng.
And shortly [hit] sheweth right so by þayr werkes

1291 er *has been erased after* gardyn.   1303 hit : *so* D ; MS. he.

To clercz of conceipte þat construen þaire workes.

He chargid me [cheerly] to change not myn intent   1305   He charged me to write the whole story truly and without fear.
Til þe matire of Mvm were made to þende,
And þat I shuld seye sothe and sette no dreede
Of no creature of clay, for Criste so hym taughte.

And þough sum men of sweuenes sauery but lite,   Though some disbelieve in dreams, yet Daniel interpreted them truly.
Yit þe lore of þe lude shal like me euer,   1310
For Daniel in his dayes declarid ful ofte
Dreemes / and vndide þaym / as deede provid after ;

And Ioseph þe gentil / Genesis þou saye   Joseph dreamed that the sun and moon and the eleven stars bowed down to him.
(The bible bereth witnesse, a boke of bilieue),
He mette þat þe mone and elleuen sterres   1315
With þe shynant sunne soudaynely at oones
A-bowid to his bidding bonairely, hym thought,
And dide hym worship þerewith / þat wroth made after
His brethern þat bisied þaym to bringe hym of dawe.   His brethren tried to murder him, for they interpreted it to mean that they would have to humble themselves before him
Hit semyd by his sweuene / þay sayden þo among þaym,   1320
Shuld falle þat þayr fadre / and þay been fayne eeke
To mete hym with þayre modre in a muke wise,
And pray hym in his pouaire / pite forto haue
Of þaym / and þaym helpe fro hungre and elles.

And so hit feulle sothely / þay sought hym þerafter   1325   And this came to pass, when they went to Egypt to get corn.
Ernestly in Egipte / or elles þe boke lieth,
For hunger þat þay hadde / and helpe couthe þay none
But lowely to loute / his lordship to sike,
Forto graunt of his grayn what hym good likid
That for faute of þayr fode famyne long durid.   1330

And so hit semeth in certayne / þat sum bee right trewe   It seems therefore that some dreams are true.
And sothe of þees sweuenes of sobre men wittes,
And prouen ofte to þe poynt of pourpoos in deede.

And þerefore my doute and dreede is þe lasse   Therefore I will obey the beekeeper, and tell of the evils that beset the government of this land.
To do þat þe burne bade, þat þe bees kepte,   1335
[Forto saye sumwhat / of svth er I passe]
How þe greete of þis ground been y-gouuerned.

Thenne softe I þe soores to serche þaym withynne,   [*fo.* 15 *b.*]   I will apply to its wounds a salve,
And seurely to salue þaym / and with a newe salue

1305 cheerly : MS. cleerly ; cherely C.   1315 the seuene sterres S².
1325 sothely : shortly D.   1336 *So* S² ; *except that* passe *is crossed out and* lafte *substituted.*   1337 Signature .d. 3. fo. *in right-hand margin.*

F

that the truth-
teller could not
obtain because
Mum had carried
it off.

That þe sothe-sigger hath sought many yeres   1340
And mighte not mete þerewith for Mvm and his ferys
That bare a-weye þe bagges / and many a boxe eeke.

For the King's
benefit, I will
open a bag full
of books.

Now for[to] conseille þe king vnknytte I a bagge
Where many a pryue poyse is preyntid withynne
Yn bokes vnbredid in balade-wise made,   1345
Of vice and of vertue fulle to þe margyn,

There is a quire
of receipts for
goods be-
queathed to the
church, and an
account of
moneys received
for condoning for
immorality;

Ve illis qui
vendunt pec-
catum propter
pecuniam.
Lincolniensis.

That was not y-openyd þis oþer half wintre.
There is a quayer of quitances of quethyn goodes,
That bisshoppz han begged to binde al newe,
And a penyworth of papir of penys þat þay fongen   1350
For lemmans and lotebies in þees late dayes,
And lien on þe lettrure, for lawe was hit neuer.
There is a volume of visitacion of viftene leves
How persones and prestis been y-passid ouer
Thorough fauour of fangyng and no faute amendid,   1355
But liggen at London in lorden courtz
And pleyen lille for lalle with many levde [kitte].

There is a
volume telling
how the clergy
leave their
parishes to take
service under
lords,

and how they are
given over to
ignorance and
immorality;

There is a roll
telling how
monks spend
their endow-
ments on them-
selves and not on
the poor;

Thay lusten for to lerne of lettrure no ferþer
Thenne to þe lesson of laudate al þaire life-dayes,
Forto preche þaire parroisshe how Pernelle is arayed   1360
And with þe tolle of þe tithing fetisly a-tired.
Thay been losers of þe lawe / and lewde men maken
The bolder for þaire badnes / and breke þe tenne hestes.
There is a rolle of religion, how þay þaire rentz hadde
Forto parte with þe poure a parcelle oþer-while,   1365
But þay been rotid in a rewe to refresshe greete,
To maynteyne þayre manhode / and matieres þay haue to doo
For pleding and for pourchas, to pasture þaym þe swetter,
So poure þay been and penylees / sith þe pestilence tyme.

There are a set
of pamphlets
concerning the
luxurious lives of
bishops and
pluralists,

Yit is þere a paire of pamphilettz of prelatz of þe royaulme
Yn þe bottume of þe bagge, how boldely þay ride,   1371
Thees persones and þees prebendiers pluralite þat hauen,
[Poperyng] on þaire palefrays fro oone place to an other,
And lernen to lede ladies / and lewed men envien

1343 to : *so* L.   1351 lotebies: P *adds* now.   1352 *Side-note*
against l. 1353 *in* MS. ; *marked to stand after l.* 1352.   1356 at : M *in.*
1357 kitte: *so* D ; MS. light.   1361 tirid C.   1373 MS.
Properyng ; popering D.

To do al þing as þay do / as by þaire deedes proueth.   1375
Thay autorisen with argumentz / and allegen for þaym
That of oon kinde alle came / þere can no [man] seye oþer.

Thus leden þay þaire lyves in lustes and in sportes,
And spenden on þaire speciales / þat þay spare shuld
For pouraile of þaire parroishens / and present to be among þaym   who neglect their flocks.
Forto salue þaire shepe whenne þay sike were.   1381   *Ve pastoribus.*

But how shuld a surgean serue wel his hyre
That cometh not in seuene yere to se þe sore oones,

[*Two folios* (184 *ll.*) *missing.*]

That þay shal not se oon shyne / how soutelly þay wirchen. [*fo.* 16 a.]
I say not but of sum þat suche manieres vsen,   1385
For euery wyman þat is wise, she wircheth to þe beste
And conseilleth al to conscience / leste þere come happes.

Yit is þere a copie for comunes of culmes foure and twenty   There is an account of how
How sum tellen tidingz at home vppon þaire benches,   false rumours spread among
Or elles at eue after souper / or erely atte nale,   1390   the common people.
And lyen on þe lordz,—lorelles and noon other.

Thaire tales been so trouble þat tournen men thoughtz;
The more þat men musen on þaym, þe madder þay been after.
I mervail but þay mette so / how hit might be
That þay finde fables / and been so ferre fro þens   1395
That þough þou ride rennyng, and reste but a lite,   They travel faster than a man
Fro London forth þe long waye to þe land-is ende,   can ride.
And comes right fro þe king-is courte and his cunseil botbe,
Fro prelatz vnto peris in pryuete or elles,
Yit shal tidingz bee y-tolde tenne dayes ere þou come,   1400   Rumores fuge ne incipias
That neuer was of worde spoke ne wroughte, as þou shal hire.   nouus auctor haberi.
Lesingz been so light of fote, þay lepen by þe skyes,
And as swifte as a swalue sheutyng ovte at oones
As falsly forgid / as þough a frere had made þaym.
That harde happes mote þay haue þat Henry so appeiren,   1405   I pray that vengeance may fall

---

1377 MS. may.   1381 *Side-note marked to stand after l.* 1383.
1400 *Side-note marked to stand after l.* 1404.   1403 swalue :
P *adds* þay.   1404 S² *adds after side-note* but caton is al contra, and
his consail bothe.

on those who
spread such
rumours to the
detriment of the
king and the
lords.

They talk as if
they knew better
than the king's
council.

They would not
have liked to
live under
Jenghiz Khan.
I will tell you
how he came to
be king.
The seven
nations, because
of their dis-
union, were en-
slaved by the
neighbouring
princes.
Omne regnum
in se diuisum
desolabitur.

In vision God
told their chief
men to make
Jenghiz their
king.

When he was
crowned, he
made two laws.

The first was
that the leading
men should slay
their eldest sons;

The second, that
they should
deliver up to
him all their
property.
They did both
these things.

Or any lord of þis lande þat loueth pees and reste,

Though þe burne my broþer were, I bid hit with my herte.

Yit wol þay carpe of þe coroune as þay of cunseil were,

And ordeyne more in oon houre þan other half wintre

Al þe king-is cunseil couthe wel bringe aboute.   1410

Thus mellen þay with matieres to moustre þaire wittes,

And grucchen whenne þe gadryng is þat goeth for vs alle.

I seye yf hit be sette so and in suche þinges,

Ful ille couthe þay corde with Changwys-is deedes,

That conquerid many a cuntre as king withynne hymself;   1415

And how he came to his coroune I shal you kenne sone.

The greete God of goodnes þat gouuerneth alle þingz,

He nempned furst his name to þe seuene nacions

That were wel nygh destrued and disware of þaire lives

And in disease and desperat þorough þaire double intentz. 1420

Thaire diuision dide þaym harme / (and so hit doeth elleswhere),

That þay were sette in seruitute by souurayns of þe marches

That had y-wonne and y-wastid wel nygh alle þe landz.

The principal of þis peuple pryuyly by nightz

A voice þaym folowed [in vision] in fourthering of þaymself, 1425

And bade þaym coroune Changwys king of al þaire peuple,

A eildren man of aunsetrie þat aged was a lite.

And so þe deede was y-do / when day and tyme came after,

And when þis Changwys was y-corouned / as cronicle of hym
    telleth,

And sette in his se / with sceptre on his handes,   [*fo.* 16 *b.*]

He stablid two statutz, as storie of hym writeth,

I herde neuer harder / and yit þay holde were.

The furst þat he funded to fele trewe hertz

And his principal peuple to proue and a-saye,

Was þat þe souurayns of þe seuene nacions   1435

Shuld sle þayre soones / þeldest and þaire hoires;

The secund þat þay shuld eeke sese hym in hire [lande]

And yelde hit vp in erniste / and yeue hit hym for euer,

To haue and to holde in his high grace.

And as þe king commandid accordid þay were,   1440

1407 burne : baron D.   1421 *Side-note marked to stand after l.*
1420.   1425 in vision : *so* N ; MS. by nightes.   1427 eildren :
aldre A.   1437 hym in hire N : þaym in his MS. ; MS. handes.

Consentyng to his couetise with crie alle at oones.
Thay sparid not to spille blode þat spronge of þaymself,
Ne to lose þayre lordship and lande at his wille.
Now forto telle trouthe, I trowe hit be no lesing,
Who wolde haue griefed for a grote / he wold haue grucched þere.
Thus proued þis prince his [peuple] and þaire hertz,   1446
And to feil of þaire fiance ful felly he wroughte ;
And [whenne he] wiste þat his wil was not encountrid,
But þat he had þaire hertz al hoole at his wil,
He forgafe þaym þaire graunt and goodely þaym þanked. 1450
Thenne clepid he to cunseil knightz and other,
And wroughte alle *with* oon wil as wise men shuld,
And wanne wisely ayen withynne a while after
The lande and þe lordship þat þay loste had,
And conquerid cuntrees, as Cathay-is lande,   1455
That is the richeste royaulme / þat reyne ouer houeth.
Now by Crist þat me creed, I can not be-þenke
A kindely cause why þe comun shuld
Contre þe king-is wil ne construe his werkes.
I carpe not of knightz / þat cometh for þe shires,   1460
That þe king clepith to cunseil with oþer ;
But hit longeth to no laborier / þe lawe is agayne þaym.
And yit hit is y-vsid with vnwise peuple
And a-vailleth not a ferþing, but vireth þe hertz ;
And tournen with þaire tales þe tente of þe lordes,   1465
That þay leven þe labour þe londe to defende,
To bisye þaym on þe bordures / to bete oute oure foes,
And maynteyne þe marches fro myschief and elles.
Thus clappeth þe comun and knocketh þaymself,
For þe [tayl] of þaire talking teneth þaym ofte.   1470
Thou mays lerne þat lesson in þe nexte lyne,
For and þy heede be hurte / þy [honde] wol apeire ;
And who-so hewe ouer heede / þough his hoode be on,
The spones wol springe oute and spare not þe eye.
Thay finde many fautes / and faillen moste þaymself   1475

When he knew that they would be loyal to him, he gave them back their property.
Then he took counsel with them, and won back the land they had lost, and more besides.

Ecce quam bonum et quam iocundum habitare fratres in vnum.
I see no reason why the commons should criticize the king.
I do not refer to knights of the shire, but to labourers.
This foolish custom takes the lords from their proper business of defending the country.

The people themselves suffer by it in the long run.

They fail in the duty of obedience to the lords.

1443, 1454 lordship : *later contraction mark over* ip.   1446 MS.
pleuple.   1448 whenne he : MS. *omits.*   1457 *Side-note marked
to stand after l.* 1456.   1460 for : fro D.   1470 tayl : *so* D ;
MS. tale.   1472 MS. hoode ; hond D.

Of deedes of deuete that þay do shuld.　　　　[*fo.* 17 *a.*]
Thay shulde loue loyally þe lordz aboute,
That þay mighte lerne a lesson of þaire lowe hertz
To reule þaym by reason and by right lawe.

Potencioribus
pa[res esse]
no*n* possum*us.*
Sap[iencia].

Thay shuld be reedy to ride and renne at þayre heste　　1480
For soulde and for siluer as þay might a-serue,
And obeye to þayre bidding and bable no ferther,

Thus the country
suffers.

For suche lewed [labbing] þe lande doeth a-peire.
But God of his goodnes graunt þaym to amende,

God grant that
they may obey
as did the sub-
jects of Jenghiz.

To knowe what þaire kinde is and commenche bityme　　1485
The cunseille of Changwys and construe no ferther,
But loue so oure liege al oure life-dayes
That he may leede vs with loue as hymself liketh.

There is a scroll
concerning
squires who will
not defend at law
poor men who
are oppressed by
the rich.

There is a scrowe for squyers þat a-square walken
Whenne a tale is y-tolde, yf hit touche greete　　　　1490
That piled han poure men of penys and of goodes;
Thay wol neghen no neer but yf þay noye þenke
And alleigge for þe lord and lawe dovne bere,
Leste soulde and þaire seruice cesse al at ones,
Thus poure men pleyntz been pledid ful ofte,　　　　1495
For reason-is retenue moste reste nedis
There robes rehercyn þe rightz of þe parties.

There is a writ-
ing concerning
men of equal
position who go
to law against
each other.

There is a writte of high wil y-write al newe,
Y-knytte in a cornier of þe bagge-ende,
And is a courssid couraige and coste-ful bothe　　　1500
That serueth al for souurayns of semblable pouaire;
For euer egalite errith and stryueth
More þanne þe [mene] man with his more heigher

Even in a trifling
matter, they will
waste their
estates in legal
proceedings.

For whenne a matiere is y-moeved among men of goode,
Though þere happe no harme / saue her[tz] aggreiggid,　1505
Thay stele into strivyng and strien þaym-self

Their neighbours
will be involved,
because a friend
will believe in
and help his
fiiend's cause.

And stiren so þat stuffure and store doon apeire,
And eeke losen þaire good loos with þaire lewed pride,
And annoyen þaire neighborowes nyne myle aboute.
For euery feithful frend wol funde to helpe　　　　1510
And leue þere he loueth, for lothe or elles;

1481 *Margin torn. Side-note marked to stand after l.* 1482. 　1483
labbing : *so* D ; MS. babling.　　1503 MS. more. 1505 her[tz] : *so* D ;
MS. herg.　　1507 doon : doeth D.　　1511 *Side-note marked to
stand after l.* 1514.　　cato *added by* C.

Suche wilfulnes and wisedame wonen a-sunder.

Thou mays baathe on a brooke to þe breggurdelle ;

But passe not þe polle forþer / for peril þat foloweth.

Thus (seyeth þat oon side) shule [I] obeye   1515

Or make amendes or mukyn myself ?

Nay, are I worke suche a worke / but my witte faille,

Hit shuld stande right straite with stoone of my hovses,

For leuer þenne to lowe me while my life dureth

I wol do a deede þat I dide neuer,   1520

Sille for siluer my sherte and my clothes,

Or borowe til I begge thenne bowe oones.   [*fo.* 17 *b.*]

[And] I were caste in my cuntre and hit knowe were,

I shuld be [eschewid] and ouer-sette ofte.

Ney, I wolmaynteyne my manhoode, maul-greþatgruccheth, 1525

And spare swete spices and spende on my foes.

That other side seyeth right so and þe same wordes,

As wilde [and] as wode and as wrothe eeke,

And braggeth and bosteth and wol brenne watiers

And rather renne in rede blode þenne a-rere oones.   1530

Thus þay blowe as a bore til bothe repente.

Hit is no witte, as I wene, to waste so siluer

For a woode wil and wretthe in þy herte,

And no harme on þy heede in [lande] ne in goodes,

But y-hurte on þe hert with a high pride.   1535

For suche maniere medling al to many tymes,

Though hit gaine in þe bigynnyng, hit groweth so aftre

That lymes been y-loste and lyfes ful ofte.

And eeke hit is no worldly witte, as me þenketh,

To toille þere no trespas is do to a-countz.   1540

But hit semeth to a souurayn þat ynnesight lacketh,

Whenne his mynde is y-moevid to medle in his ire,

That þough his grovnde be not goode / and he gaste were

Or feynte forto folowe / but fersse to þende,

Side notes (right margin):

Ira odiu*m* generat con- cord!a nutrit amorem.

This is foolish ; one should not go out of one's depth.

One party urges submission.

The other party would rather spend his whole estate than give in, lest his neighbours despise him.

Both sides are equally deter- mined not to yield.

[I]ra requie- scit / non [in] sanitas men- tis / [a]c corporis / Salomo*n.* It is foolish to waste money thus where no- thing material is at stake.

Sup*er*bia gene- rat om*n*em malicia*m* vaqu*e* ad mor- te*m.* Salomon.

A foolish man will be afraid that if he does not go to law his reputation will suffer.

1513 brigurdell C.   1515 I: MS. *omits.*   1523 MS. A.
1524 MS. so thewid.   1528 and ¹: *so* P.   a *crossed out in* MS.
after as ¹ M.   1529 *Side-note* *marked to stand after l.* 1530.
Margin torn.   1534 MS. hande.   1535 *Side-note* *marked to*
stand after l. 1538.   on : in P.   1540 acountz: accompte D.
1544 fersse : fers C.

Hit shuld be [aretted] for reprouf whenne hit were rehercyd, 1545
And he y-sette þe shorter at shire and a-boute.
Suche cursid construyng accombreth þe [peuple].

But my counsel
is : when you see
that your cause
is weak, give it
up.

For [cuntre] þat conceipt I can make a reason,
And a trewe, as I trowe, who-so taketh hede :
Whenne rancune þe redeth to reere debatz,   1550
Or angre at attre arteth þy herte
Forto commenche a cause not cleere in þe winde,
Bowe ere þou breste whenne þou arte bette y-fourmyd,
And revle þe by reason and renne not to faste,
But gife hit vp with good wille whenne þy grovnde failleth, 1555
And falle of with fayrenes / leste fors þe assaille.

If you do this of
your own free
will, then when
another time you
continue to
prosecute a
cause, people
will believe that
it is just.

For yf þou leue are þou ligge / þenne wol þy loos springe,
But yf þy tale be trewe, to toylle þou hatis.
So wol þe worde walke with oon and with oþer
And cumforte þy cuntre in cumpas aboute   1560
To be nere at þy nede a-noþer tyme after;
And bilieue loyally, in lawe yf þou were,
Or medlist with a matiere, þy more were trewe,
Elles woldes þou not worche on hit longe.

There is a roll,
drawn up by the
devil himself,
concerning how
by unfair inter-
ference in law-
suits, house-
holders lose
their estates.

There is a raggeman rolle / þat Ragenelle hymself   1565
Hath made of mayntennance and motyng of þe peuple,
Hough þay sheue at sises and sessions aboute,
And halen so þe hockerope / oon halfe agayne oþer   [fo. 18 a.]
Til þe strong[est] steriers and styuest on þe heedes
†Haue haled þe howslord oute atte halle-dore.   1570
Strifen so and streicchen streight adovne þe poure.
Gold and good þaym glewith so / þay wol not go a-sundre
[Til þay haue] drawen hym clene fro his dees / he dysneth þere
nomore.

This evil custom
brings the crown
into disrepute,

This same cursid custume þe coroune doeth a-peyre
And bringeth a bitter byworde a-brode among þe peuple, 1575

1545 MS. sette.   1547 MS. pleuple.   1548 cuntre : *so* D ;
MS. cuntrey.   1560 cuntre : contre C.   1562 bilieue : by
leue B.   1566 made : D *adds* al.   1569 MS. strong. S² *adds*
Han halid oute þe hows lord / oute at his halle dore.   1570 Haue :
MS. Til þay haue. *Line stands in MS. after* 1572.   1572 wol . . .
sundre : cunne goo as . . . N (*margin torn*).   1573 MS. And
Til þay han drave hym fro his dees he disneth þere nom[ore] (*margin
torn*) S².

And is in euery cuntre but a comune tale

That yf þe pouer playne, þough he plede euer

And hurleth *with* his higher / hit happeth ofte-tyme

That he wircheth al in waste and wynneth but a lite.

Thus laboreth þe loos among þe comune peuple   1580

That þe wacker in þe writte wol haue þe wors ende;

Hit wol not gayne a goky a grete man forto plede,

For lawe lieth muche in lordship sith loyaute was exiled,

And poure men pleyntes / penylees a-bateth.

But Dauid demed not so, I do hit on his bokes.   1585

Yit is þere a forelle þat I forgate þat frayed is a lite,

How þe [fleuble] fareth þat folowed bee in shires

Whenne þay griefen greete, þough þe guilte be lite.

And he haue any hors or elles hedid bestes,

He shal be hourled so in high courte and holde so agogge 1590

That hym were bettre lose his lande / þenne long so be toylid;

Suche crokes been y-courid and coloured vnder lawe,

To strue a man *with* [strength] þe status been so made.

For þough men pleede and poursuye and in þaire playntz falle

And newe þaym aftre nonsuyte[s] nynetene hunthred,   1595

Withoute grovnde or guilte / but forto gete a bribe,

Yit shal þay haue no harme / þough þay hurle euer.

But shuld þay picche and paye / at eche pleynte·is ende

And compte alle þe costz of men of court and elles,

And taske al þe trespas / as trouthe wolde and reason,   1600

Thay wolde cesse sum tyme for sheding of þaire siluer.

1 seye aswel of simple men / þat suen ayenst grete,

And of þe poure proute / þat peyren ofte þaire bett*er*,

That causelees accusen þaym to king and to þe lordz,

As I doo of ducz / þat suche deedes vsen;   1605

For lordz and laborers been not like in costes.

Hit wold pese þe peuple and many pleyntes bate

And chaunge al þe chauncellerie / and cheuallerie amende

And ease be to euery man þat been of euene states,

for every one says that it is no use for a poor man to go to law against a rich man.

Munera sup*er* innocente*m* non accipies.

There is an account of the hard fate of poor men who are prosecuted by great men for small causes.

For the great, if defeated once, will go on again without feeling any loss.

But the man who pays ready money will have to stop lest he exhaust it.

It is as wrong for the poor to act thus as for the rich.

It would be a great advantage to all classes if every one bring-ing an action without good

1581 ende : side D.   1587 fleuble : *so* D ; MS. peuple.   1591
toylid : toillid D.   1593 MS. lawe, *followed by blank space* ; strenght
D.   status : statutz D.   1595 MS. nonsuyte.   1599 of ¹ :
for D.   1600 taske : taxe D.   1606 S² *adds* yf þis were y vsid and
y holde lawe.

cause had to pay
a fine, and if the
costs were paid
at the end of
every action.

And solas be to souurayns and to þaire seruantz alle,   1610
And a miracle to meen men þat mote lite cunne,
Were þis oon yere y-vsid as I haue declarid,—
That of euery writte withoute wronge / þere were amendes made,
And paye for alle þe costes at eucry pleynte-is ende,   [*fo.* 18 *b.*]
And tolle for þe trespas as trouthe wolde and reason—   1615
The lawe wold like vs wel, and euer þe lenger þe bettre.

But prerogative
allows any one to
bring proceed-
ings.

But pouaire of prerogatife / þat poynt hath reseruyd
That euery fode haue fredome to folowe vn-y-punysshid.

Canon and Civil
law say other-
wise,

But ciuile seith vs not so / þat serueth for al peuple
That habiteth vndre heuene / hethen men and oþer.   1620
And Crist-is lawe-is y-canonized canon, yf þou loke,

and so does the
Gospel.

And eeke þe glorious gospelle / grovnde of alle lawes,
Techeth vs a trewe texte / þat toucheth þis ilke matiere ;

I feel that in this
matter our law is
partial.

For in my conscience ne in my credo yit couthe I neuer vele
But þat oure lawe leneth þere a lite, as me þenketh.   1625

There is a collec-
tion of books con-
cerning lords
who infringe on
the king's
revenue.

There is a librarie of lordes / þat losen ofte þaym-self
      Thorough lickyng of þe lordship / þat to þe coroune longeth,
And weneth hit be wel y-do / but wors dide þay neuer
Thenne sith þay gunne þat game, I grovnde me on reason.

But every one
knows that it is
good to have a
supreme ruler to
keep the peace.

For euery wighte wote wel / but yf his witte faille,   1630
That hit is holsum forto haue a heede of vs alle,
That is a king y-corouned to kepe vs vnder lawe,
To put vs into prisone whenne we passe boundes.
For but we had a souurayn to sette vs into reste,
Thees rechelees renkes wolde renne on eche oþer.   1635

And it follows
that he must
have sufficient
funds.

Thenne of fyne fors hit foloweth, as me þenketh,
That a certayne substance shuld be ordeynid
To susteyne þis souurayn þat shuld vs gouerne.

It was so once,
but he has been
deprived of
much.

And so I wote wel hit was atte furst tyme,
But now hit is bynome hym þolde and þe newe,   1640

The laws that
should have pre-
vented this have
not been carried
out.

Not-wi[th]standing statutz ful strattely y-made
To stable many statutz and strong lawes make.
But execucion falle what may hit availle
Ne more þenne þe mose may or þe maij floures
To breke dovne bastiles þat beste is y-made.   1645

      1621 lawe-is : is *dotted for correction and crossed out in later hand.*
1623 S *adds* nullum malum impunitum euaungelium.   1641 MS.
wistanding.   1643 falle : followe D. *Space left in MS. after* falle.

Hit is as dede as a dore nayle, þough þe dome come after,
Withoute execucion / þees wise men hit knoweth.
Thees knightz of þe conseil þat nygh þe king dwellen,
And eeke lordz y-lettred of oone lawe and oþer,
Forto kepe his coroune fro couetous peuple,   1650
Han pulled þaym-self þe peres right to þe [pure] stalke,
And lickid so þe leves / he hath þe leste dele,
For þay holden of his honour halfendele and more.
This was grovnde and bigynnyng of gurdyng of heedes,
And eeke more [of] mourdre / and many-folde wronges   1655
That han y-falle for foly withynne þees fourty wintre.
For þegre enuye / þat eche had to oþer
Dide þaym preece to be pryvy and put aweye þe beste,
But muche more for þe mede to make þaym-self riche
Thenne to cunseille þe king of þe comune [wele],   [*fo. 19 a.*]
Or for any deue dome or defence of þe royaulm[e]   1661
This same cursid custume oure coroune hath a-p[ayred],
And cause is most þat comunes collectours haten,
For nedis moste oure liege lord like his estat
Haue for his houshold and for his [haynous werres]   1665
To maynteyne his manhoode / þere may no man seye o[þer],
But of his owen were þe beste, who-so couthe hit bringg[e] ;
To lyve vppon his laboriers, hit may not long indure.
Whenne hit is haled al awey / þenne is wo þe nexte
To you þat shullen siluer to solue þenne were tyme.   1670
For trusteth right treuly, talke what men likeþ,
And wendith and trendith twys in oon wike,
And clepith to your cunseil copes and other,
And pleyne atte parlement, but yf þe deede prouue
That þe coroune in his kinde come ynne agaynes,   1675
Clene in his cumpas with croppes and braunches,
Lite and a lite, right as þe lawe asketh,
Wel mowe we wilne and wisshe what vs liketh

Those lords who ought to protect his revenue have plundered it.

This has been the cause of civil strife for the past forty years.

Jealousy of each other and desire for riches has been more potent with the lords than desire to advise the king or help the commons.

Hence the commons hate the king's tax-collectors.

The king must have money to support his household.

It should come from his own estate, not from taxes, or the people will suffer.

However people may argue in parliament, unless the king gets possession of his revenues again, all classes will be impoverished.

And eeke waite after welthe / but as my witte demeth,
Oure wynnyng and worship wol be þe lasse   1680
With knight and with comune til þc king haue
Alle hoole in his hande þat he haue oughte.

There is an
account of those
who make large
fortunes dis-
honestly, and
leave money for
hospitals in their
wills.

There is a copie of couetise, how conscience is revled
    Whenne he [hath] gadrid a greete bagge and good ·at his
        wil,
And wrongfully y-wonne hit þorough wiles of his hert,   1685
And is y-runne in riches þorough ryfling of þe peuple,
He maketh maisons deu þerewith whenne he may live [no
    len]ger;
But while he had power of þe penyes / þe poure had but lite.

It is indeed a
great help to the
soul to live self-
ishly all one's
life, and give
nothing to the
poor till one
dies.

Hit is a high holynes and grete helth to þe soule,
A man to lyue in lustes alle his life-dayes   1690
And haue no pitie on þe poure, ne parte with þaym nother,
But holde hit euer in his hande til þe herte breke.
But þenne he shapeth for þe soule whenne þe sunne is dovne,
But while þe day durid he delte but a lite;
Now muche moste his merite be þat mendeth so þe poure, 1695
That gifeth his goode for God-is sake whenne his goste is
    pass[ed].

There is a sec-
tion telling how
wills are hidden
away as soon as
they are proved.

There is a [title] of testament[z] þat I tolde neuer,
    How pryuyly þay been provid and y-put a-side,
For so þe siluer be y-soluid for þe seel of þoffice
And þe feis alle y-funge / þay folden þaym to-gedre   17co
And casten þaym in a coffre leste þay copied were,

The executors
say "Let sleeping
dogs lie," and
they do not give
in charity the
dole the testator
left for the good
of his soul.

And sith þay seure þaym by þaymself and seyen þees [wordes]:
"Hit is no wisedame forto wake Warrok while he sl[epeth]"
For þough a quynzieme were y-quethe / oon quita[nce shal be
    geven]
Though executours after-warde execute hit neu[er],   1705

They justify
themselves by
saying; "The
testator gave
nothing while he

[Ne do noght for] þe dede as I do whenne I slepe.   [*fo.* 19 *b.*]
[And yit] þay seyen for þaymsilf right a subtile reason:
"[Why sh]uld we dele for þe dede? / He dide not while he mighte.

1682 D *adds* That . . . (*rest torn away*).   1684 hath: *so* B; MS. *omits*.
1686 ryfling : . . . ng A (*rest torn away*).   1687 no leng*er*: MS. g*er*,
rest torn away.   1689 helth: helpe D.   1696 *margin torn away*.
1697 MS. lite of a testament, *z crossed through*.   1702-5 *margin torn
away*.   1706-12 *margin torn away*.   1706 for: *tail of* f *is visible*.

[He] made vs in his mynde among alle his frendes

[T]o be his trewe attourneys and treete for his debtes, 1710

[F]or so þat þay haue halfendele / þay mowe þaym holde content.

[Y]it wol not þe good go so ferre / so mote we grovnde oure tale,

For I wol seye for myself / seye þou whenne þe liketh,

Yf we do as he dude, may no man deme vs yuel,

Ne rightfully by reason reproue vs here-after. 1715

He was boþe ware and wise while he was on live,

And me lust not be lewed leste I fare þe wors.

His custume was to kepe his good / so lete vs kepe hit eeke,

And þenne after oure deeth day lete dele for vs alle,

For oure executours aftre vs shal haue þe same charge." 1720

Thus þay chiden with charite and chacheth eche other,

That til þe day of dome þe dele is not parfourmid.

Yit is þere a poynt of prophecie how þe peuple construeth

And museth on þe meruailles / þat Merlyn dide deuyse,

And redith as right as þe Ram is hornyd, 1725

As helpe me þe high God, I holde þaym halfe a-masid.

For þere nys wight in þis world þat wote bifore eue

How þe winde and þe wedre wol wirche on þe morowe,

Ne noon so cunnyng a clerc þat construe wel couthe

Ere sunneday a seuenyght what shal falle. 1730

Thus þay muse on þe mase on mone and on sterres

Til heedes been hewe of and hoppe on þe grene,

And al þe wide world wondre on þaire workes.

Yit sawe I þere a cedule soutely indited

With tuly silke intachid right atte rolle-is ende, 1735

Y-write ful of wordes of woundres þat han falle,

And fele-folde ferlees wythynne þees fewe yeris,

By cause þat þe clergie and knighthoode to-gedre

Been not knytte in conscience as Crist dide þaym stable.

For who so loketh on þe lawe may lerne, yf hym like, 1740

Thayre ordre and office / and how þay [ought] wyrche.

For þay folowe no foote of þaire forne-fadres,

I do hit on þaire deeth-day, and deme no ferther,

For seurly sumtyme I sawe hit not late

1721 chacheth eche other *underlined*; *margin torn away.* 1741
[ought]: *so* N; MS. shuld. 1743 I do *underlined*; *margin torn away.*

Once bishops
hated pride and
were examples to
the laity.

Yn cronicle of clercz and kingz lygnees   1745

[H]ow prelatz of prouinces pride moste hatid

[For] þe theme þat þay taughte was tachid on þaire hertz.

[Thay] preched þe peuple and prouyd hit þaymself

[And w]ere lanternes to lewed men to lyve þaym after.

[Thay p]ourchachid no prelacies with prince noþer elles   1750

[Thorough pr]eyer ne povndes / but þorough proufe of þayre
    workes.

    1745 lygnees: lyves D.   1746-51 *margin torn away.*   1748
þaymself: in workes D.

APPENDIX I

Bartholomaeus Anglicus on Bees

(from the 1601 edition)

With a Note by a Practical Bee-keeper

Lib. xii, cap. iiii, p. 520.

Item apes regem sibi creant, ipse sibi populos ordinant, & tamen, licet positæ sint sub rege, ipsæ tamen sunt liberæ, & regem sibi substituunt, & naturali affectu diligunt, & summa defensione defendunt, & pro eo perire pulcrum putant. Regi suo tantam reuerentiam exhibent, vt nullæ de suis domibus exire audeant nec ad aliquos prodire 5 pastus, nisi rex fuerit egressus & volatus sibi vendicauerit principatum. Eligunt autem apes sibi in regem in magnitudine & specie magis insignem, & quod in rege præcipuum est mansuetudine clariorem, nam & si habeat aculeum, eo tamen non vtitur ad vindicandum. Naturaliter autem apes tanto sunt leuiores, quanto cæteris sunt 10 maiores, sed & apes quæ non obtemperant regi propria condemnatione se mulctant, vt aculei sui vulnere moriantur, in apum vero examine nulla est ociosa. Quędam enim certant quasi in bello campestri contra alias apes, aliæ vigilant circa victum, aliæ futuras explorant imbres & speculantur concursus, aliæ ceras de floribus fingunt : 15 aliæ cellulas nunc rotundas, nunc quadratas, mira connexione & æqualitate componunt.

Lib. xviii, cap. xi, p. 1014.

Ordinant excubias suas more castrorum, de nocte quiescunt vsque ad mane, donec vna omnes excitet, gemino aut triplici bombo, vt buccino aliquo, tunc vniuersæ peruolant, si dies fuerit mitis futurus, 20 prædiuinant enim imbres & ventos, & tunc se continent infra tecta. Quando præsciunt cœli temperiem futuram, cum agmine procedunt ad opera, & tunc aliæ flores aggregant pedibus, aliæ aquam ore guttasque lanugine totius corporis simul portant, adolescentiores vero ad opera exeunt & conueniunt & afferunt supra dicta, seniores vero intus 25 operantur. Quæ flores comportant primo onerant pedes anteriores, & post alios donec rostro pleno remeent totaliter oneratæ.

Excipiunt autem sic onustas trinæ vel quaternæ eas, quæ exonerant, secundum quod intus sunt ordinatæ, eorum enim officia sunt diuisa, aliæ enim domus construunt, aliæ poliunt, aliæ cibum parant ex eo 30 quod allatum est, non enim separatim vescuntur, ne inæqualitas [1] cibi

temporis & operis [1] fiat inter eas.　Fauos linealiter & ordinatæ componunt, & in superiori parte suspendunt.　Ceras cadentes fulciunt, primas lineas parum replent de melle, nouissimas autem maxime solent adimplere.　Apes autem gerulæ, quæ necessaria conuehunt
5 timent venti flatus, & ideo volant iuxta terram, & quando sunt onustæ redeunt, ne aliquo flatu impediantur, & quandoque lapillis se onerant, vt lapillorum grauitate sint contra venti impetum magis fixæ.　Mira inter eas est obseruantia disciplinæ, nam inertiam cessantium ab opere notant, & eos mox castigant, immo morte puniunt operari non
10 curantes.　Mira inter eas est munditia, nullęque inter opera sua spurcitiæ permittuntur.　Egestiones apum, quæ operantur intus ne longe recedant, aliæ congerunt in locum vnum & eiiciunt de alueari. Quando aduesperascit, intrant in domos suas & strepunt, donec illa eadem, quæ eas excitauit, circumuolet & eodem, quo excitauit bombo
15 eas inuitet ad quietem, & tunc omnes repente conticescunt.　*Idem in eod.* c. 13.　Item per apes summa æquitas exercetur, feriunt enim omnes earum pacem dissoluentes & earum melle diripere cupientes. Regem siquidem habent apes, qui non aculeo armatus est, sed potius maiestate, *vt dicit idem* cap. 18. vel si habet aculeum, vsum feriendi
20 natura sibi negat, noluit enim natura ipsum sęuum esse ne cito peteret [2] vltionem, & ideo ei telum detraxit & inermem dereliquit, vnde constat apum imperatorem aculeo non vti, miranda autem est circa regem plebis obedientia, nam cum procedit totum examen circa ipsum conglobatur & ab ipso agmine velut acie militum cingitur &
25 vallatur, & prę multitudine obsequentium tunc temporis vix videtur. Cum populus apum in labore est, ipse intus est & circuit similis excitanti, solus à labore est immunis.　Circa quem & apes assunt, quædam habentes aculeum tanquam lictores, qui autoritate assidua regis sunt custodes, & ipse raro procedit foras, nisi quando examen totum debet
30 exire, cuius exitus intelligitur ante diebus aliquot exercitu murmurante, & quasi ad exitum se præparante, vnde siquis tunc regi apum pręscinderet alam, totum examen tunc temporis non exiret, & quando procedunt, singulæ regis obsequio se offerunt, & ei proximæ esse volunt, regem fessum humeris subleuant, & fatigatum totum portant,
35 si qua lassa defecerit, vel ab acie errauerit, odore prosequitur, vbicunque rex præcedit, & vbicunque rex præsederit, ibi cæteræ figunt castra, rege viso totus animatur exercitus, ipsoque amisso, totum agmen dilabitur ad alium, quia sine rege esse non possunt, ad aluearia subintrant quædam falsæ apes, quæ fuci nuncupantur, habentes
40 magnum ventrem, furtimque deuorant mella, & has apes interficiunt, quando eas depræhendunt.

[1-1] MS. Add. 24074 cibi uel operis intemperanter.
[2] MS. Add. 24074 *and* Caxton petere.

p. 1018.

Et apes mellificantes interficiu*n*t masculos nocentes eis, & reges malos, quando eas non bene regunt, sed tantummodo de melle nimis comedunt, & præcipue hoc faciunt quando mel erit paucum, & apes paruæ pugnant cum longioribus, quando non operantur nec laborant, & nituntur eas eiicere de aluearibus.

Mr. W. Hancock, of Uppingham, a well-known beekeeper, kindly sends us the following note :

Beekeepers do not stand at the entrance and kill drones as they enter the hives. Drone-traps are used by some people. The slots in them are of such width that they allow workers to pass through, but the drones being larger are imprisoned and plunged in boiling water and the traps replaced. This is crude and totally unnecessary. Drone-breeding is completely under control if the correct methods are followed. Worker combs only are used, and these are so spaced that drones cannot be reared except in very small numbers. If it were necessary, owing to old-fashioned methods, to catch the drones as indicated in your text, I am afraid all one's time would be occupied with negligible results. For if the bees are allowed to follow their instincts vast numbers of drones are reared. Drones are brought into existence during the *rise* of the population. Normally they are fed on predigested food, but they can feed themselves—when allowed or in need. I agree drones do no work, and if allowed to be reared in-- discriminately they account for a vast quantity of surplus honey which should go to the beekeeper. The inhabitants of the hive all contribute to the common good, and the drones are therefore tolerated during the breeding season only. When the honey-flow is on the wane, the bees by instinct begin to prepare for the winter. Drones are no longer necessary, so food is withheld from them, and when they are in a weak state they are evicted by the workers. The bees feed the drones most liberally during the breeding season, and they may make their homes in almost any hive at such times. They may be reared especially early for mating purposes, and they may be taken and placed in a hive which contains a virgin queen, when at such times sufficient will remain for the purpose of effecting fecundation.

I always feel that the name 'queen' is the name which should be used, and those who watch the queens and notice the graceful shape of their 'persons' will agree with me. Actually, the workers feed the queen in proportion to the honey-flow, and this feeding regulates the queen's egg-laying. If a colony ceases to be prosperous the workers will clear out the drone-brood in all stages, but when prosperity reigns there is an instinctive urge towards breeding for swarming. The

wonderful instinct of the bee reveals, on close inspection, much unnecessary labour and even chaos at times. If this were not so then
the instinctive side would be less developed, and to their detriment.
They are not, moreover, quite so industrious as tradition would have
us believe.

You may take it as correct that there is no question of the bees
finding out about the drones eating all the honey and then killing
them. Many factors are involved. When the bees are gathering
honey in plenty they are good-tempered, and there is little need to
defend their homes at such times; bees will not rob when the natural
supplies are available in plenty.

APPENDIX II

The Story of Jenghiz Khan

(from *The Buke of John Maundeuill*,

ed. Sir G. F. Warner, Roxburghe Club, 1889, pp. 110, 111)

Mes ly emperers de Cathay ne sappelle mie Cham, mes Chan; si
vous dirray la verite coment.

Il nad plus de viii^{xx} anz qe toute Tartarie estoit en subieccioun et
en seruitute des autres nacions enuiroun, qar ils estoient toutz besteaux
5 et ne fesoient qe garder bestes et mener en pasture. Mes entre eux
ils auoient sept nacions principaux, qi estoient souereignez de toutz
eux. Ly primer nacioun ou lignage est appelle Tartar; ces sount ly
plus nobles et ly plus prises. Ly seconde lignage est appelle Tanghot,
ly tierce Eurach, ly quarte Valeir, ly quint Semoch, ly vi. Mengly, le
10 viime Cobooch. Ore auient ensy qe de primer lignage il y auoit vn
prodhomme viel, et nestoit mie riche, quy auoit a noun Changuys.
Cist gist vne noet en soun lit et vist vne auisioun, qe il venoit deuaunt
ly vn chiualer, tout blanc et arme des armes blanches, et seoit sour
vn blanc chiual, et ly dit, 'Chan, dor tu? A toy menuoye le Dieu
15 immortele; et est sa volente qe tu dies a vii. lignages qe tu soiez lour
emperour, qar tu conqueras les pays qi sount entour. Et serront ly
marchisantz en vostre subieccion, ensy qe vous auetz este en lour; qar
ceo est la volunte de Dieu immortele.' Et, quant il vient a matyn,
Changuys se leua et le ala dire as vii. lignages, les quex se mokoient
20 de ly et disoyent qil estoit asotiz; si semparti tout hountous. Et la
noet ensuant cis chiualer blanc vient as vii. lignages et lour com-
maunda de part le Dieu immortel, qils feisent lour emperour de Chan
et ils serroient hors de tout subieccion et tenroient les autres regnes
entour eux en lour seruitute; si qe lendemayn ils eliserount Changuys
25 pur emperour et le ferount seoir sour vn feutre noir et puis ouesque

le feutre ils le leuerount a grant solempnite et lassistrent en vne
chayere et ly firent toutz reuerence et lappellerent Chan, si come ly
blanc chiualer lauoit appelle. Et, quant il fust ensy elist, il voloit
assaier sil poet fier en eux et sils voleient estre obeisantz; si fist
adoncqes plusours estatutz et ordinancez, qils appellent Ysa Chan. 5
Ly primer estatut fuist qils obeissent et croissent en Dieu immortel et
tout puissant, qils les voleit ietter de seruitute et qe toutdis ils apel-
lassent en lour eide en toutes busoignes. Lautre estatut fuist qe toutz
les hommes de pays qi poaient armis porter feussent noumbrez, et a
chescun x. lom baillast un maistre, et a c. un maistre, et a mil vn 10
meistre, et a x. mille vn maistre. Apres il commanda a toutz lez
principaux de ces vii. lignages, qils lessassent et renunciassent a quant
qils auoient de heritage, et de illoqes en auaunt ils se tenissent a
paiez de ceo qil lour dorroit de sa grace; et ils le firent tantost. Apres
il commanda as principaux desusditz, qe chescun feit venir son eisnez 15
fils et de lour propres mainz chescun copast la teste de soun filtz sanz
delay; et tantost ly comandement fust acomply. Et, quant ly Chan
vist qils ne mettoient point de obstacle en chose qil comandast, il
pensoit qil poat bien fier en eaux et commanda tantost qils fuissent
toutz apparilles pur seuir sa baner. Et puis ly Chan mettoit en sub- 20
ieccioun toutes les terres enuiroun.

NOTES

[All line-numbers not preceded by P or a roman numeral refer to Fragment M. Notes to which [S] is affixed are taken from Skeat's editions of *Richard the Redeles*.]

PROLOGUS

P. 1. And: this opening suggests that a preceding portion has been lost. The Prologue, in which Richard is never directly addressed, gives the impression of having been written, or perhaps revised, at least after Passus I and II. We may note, in particular, l. 14, which suggests a reference to the liberality with which Henry rewarded the Percies. The poet begins by addressing Richard directly, as if he were alive (see I. 79), though he is sure that he will not regain his crown (see I. 8). This direct address is continued in Passus I and II. But in Passus III and IV (except III. 338) he speaks of him in the third person, as in the beginning of the Prologue. At P. 43–4, by an ingenious transition, he re-dedicates his poem to Henry IV, for he could hardly expect that other Christian kings would be likely to read alliterative English verse. Henceforward it is Henry to whom the poem is directed, and who is alluded to in ll. 74–81.

P. 2. Bristow: the poet's place of residence saw many notable events of the period: the executions of Scrope, Bushy, and Green in 1399, of Despenser in 1400, and of certain friars who had plotted against the king in 1402 (see Introduction, p. xix). The warfare against Glendower pressed hard on Bristol. Lord Thomas of Berkeley, a Warden of the Marches, was required by the king in 1402 to muster and train men in the counties of Gloucester and Somerset, and in Bristol, to defend the Welsh borders, and was thus employed till 1405 (Seyer, *Memoirs of Bristol*, ii. 174). In 1401 there were riots against the cloth tax in which, according to Adam of Usk, the wives of Bristol took the places of their husbands, and both gave and received wounds (ed. E. M. Thompson, p. 62).

P. 3–4. An allusion to the Church of the Holy Trinity, or Christ Church, described in Barrett's *Bristol*, p. 464. It was in the very centre of the old town, at one of the corners where the four principal streets, High Street, Broad Street, Corn Street, and Wine Street, met. See a plan of Bristol in 1479 in Ricart's Kalendar, edited by Miss Smith for the Camden Society, p. 10. [S.]

In the same picture can be seen the cross, mentioned in l. 148, which stood at the junction of these streets.

P. 7. **dowtes for to deme** : 'and difficulties (arose) to be resolved, because of the fear which was to follow'; cp. ll. 320, 390. The phrase is not quoted in *O.E.D.*

P. 10. **þᵉ wilde Yrisshe** : the first use noted of this phrase, see E. D. Snyder, ' *The Wild Irish* ', *Modern Philology*, xvii. 713.

P. 19. **repeute**: repute, consider. The earliest example of this rare use in *O.E.D.* is from Chaloner, 1549, 'I would my Maisters... shoulde repute with theym selues, how on all sydes theyr myndes are vexed continually'. The sense appears to be that some of those who joined themselves to Henry at Doncaster when he announced that he came to claim his inheritance thought that he should go on to claim the crown. Skeat (reading 'repente') takes the line to mean that 'those who had applauded Henry's acts at Bristol began to turn again to Richard'. This does not seem to have happened. Ziepel (*The Reign of Richard II and Comments upon an Alliterative Poem*, Berlin, 1874) explains it as referring to the Parliament which deposed Richard, many of whose members had sat in the Great Parliament. The reading adopted here makes it easier to interpret 'that' in l. 21. But 'þey' may be indefinite, meaning 'people'.

P. 23. **þat prince was of Walis** : Richard was created Prince of Wales, &c., 20 November, 1376, ceasing to be so on his accession, 21 June 1377.

P. 28. **[g]eue** : MS. ȝeue. This word generally alliterates with hard *g*, see II. 3, 471, 1450, 1555, and probably 1696; also '[g]ifte', II. 96. The only exceptions are 'ȝeue', III. 261, 'yeue', 1438, alliterating with *y*.

P. 29. **a[g]eyn**: MS. aȝeyn; cp. 'agayne', 973, alliterating with hard *g*.

P. 33. Cp. l. 185, 'And so pryuy with þe prince þat paradis made '.

P. 38. Cp. l. 1279.

P. 43. **my lyff durst I wedde** : cp. l. 122.

P. 45. This line stands in the MS. after l. 41. The alteration removes the awkwardness of syntax. It should be noted how often the poet begins a complex sentence with 'and' introducing the subordinate clause, e.g. P. 1, 27, 37, 47, 57, 70, 76; M. 9, 37, 41, 82.

P. 53. Here the author addresses himself to the general reader.

P. 55–6. 'If you enjoy some part, look over the rest of it, for argument is not a thing to be blamed for.'

be þe rode of Chester : the same asseveration is used by Sloth in *Piers Plowman*, A. v. 240 = B. v. 467 ; not in C.

This was probably the cross on the Rood-Eye or Rood-Dee, a piece

of land outside the walls and reclaimed from the sea. The High
Cross which stood in the centre of the city, outside St. Peter's Church,
was destroyed by the Parliamentarians in 1646, the base of the former
was restored about 1858 to its original position. The High Cross was
the scene of city ceremonies, and proclamations were made there, It
was the second station of the Whitsuntide Pageants, which were
performed first at the Abbey Gate and then at the High Cross before
the Mayor. At the cross on the Rood-Eye on Shrove Tuesday, we
read in Archdeacon Rogers's MS. that the Shoemakers and Sadlers
played football for a leather ball which had been first presented in
homage to the Drapers by the Shoemakers. A legend, mentioned
by Ormerod in 1882, tells how a wooden image of the Virgin floated
from Hawarden to Chester, was buried there, and the place of its
interment marked by the Rood Dee Cross. See Ormerod, *History of
Cheshire*, i. 368, 371, 380.

P. 57. **fables**: falsehoods. It may be noted that in ll. 41, 145,
the verb has the more general sense of speaking freely; see also
'fabuler', narrator, 140.

P. 69. 'Since youth always supposes it [i.e. fault-finding, criticism]
to be (a proof of) wisdom.' [S.]

PASSUS PRIMUS

l. 6–7. In the MS. l. 6 ends at 'daiez', and the caesura is placed
after 'riot'. The change obviates the awkwardness of a pause in the
middle of a half-line (after 'wikkid'). For the defective alliteration
of l. 5 (*aaa xx*) cp. ll. 417, 488. The side-note is *1 Tim.* vi. 10.

l. 11–18. This refers specially to the period 1398–9, after Parliament had delegated its powers to a small committee, packed in
Richard's interest. During this time he raised large sums by forced
loans, purveyances, and tallages, though the last-named had been
legally abolished in 1340.

l. 12. **castes of gile**: cp. l. 1154.

l. 17. 'By the appraising of property by men with poleaxes'; cp.
III. 328 and note on it.

l. 26. **har[m]esse**: MS. harnesse. Cp. Chaucer, *Boethius*, ii, Metr.
6 'We han wel knowen how many grete harmes and destrucciouns
weren I-doon by the emperour Nero'.

l. 35. **vertus stones**: 'stones of great power', pearls, rubies,
diamonds, and sapphires, followed by a detailed description of their
virtues. Skeat compares the parallel passages in the description of
Lady Meed, *Piers Plowman*, A. ii. 10–14, B. ii. 10–17, C. iii. 11–16.

Of these it may be noted that B, which is much the most striking of the three, with its mention of

> 'red rubyes as red as any glede,
> And diamantz of derrest pris and double manere safferes',

is the nearest to our poem.

I. 54. 'Rex . . . fecit igitur præparationem maximam per totum tempus Quadragesimæ, et sic deinceps usque ad suum transitum [to Ireland] extorquens pecunias, exigens equos et quadrigas, victualia pro profectione sua rapiens, nihilque solvens; unde factus est suis subditis odibilis et invisus' (Walsingham, *Historia Anglicana*, for year 1399).

I. 57. ȝoure dukys: after Richard's vengeance on the Lords Appellant in 1397 'for the first time in English history the title of duke was made almost vulgar, for it was conferred on no less than five persons on one day. Nottingham was created Duke of Norfolk; Kent, Duke of Surrey; Rutland, Duke of Aumerle; Huntingdon, Duke of Exeter; Derby, Duke of Hereford. In addition, Despenser was made Earl of Gloucester; Scrope, Earl of Wiltshire; Beaufort, Marquis of Dorset.' (Oman, *Political History of England*, iv, 137.)

here double harmes: the very great harm they might inflict. This unusual use of 'double' is found again in ll. 294, 647.

I. 58. Men myȝtten as well haue hun[t]yd an hare with a tabre. We find in Hazlitt's *English Proverbs* the four following: 'Drumming is not the way to catch a hare'; 'It is a mad hare that will be caught with a tabor'; 'Men catch not a hare with the sound of a drum'; and 'You may catch a hare with a tabor as soon'. It must have been a common phrase. [S.] Cp. Whittinton's *Vulgaria* (ed. Miss Beatrice White, E.E.T.S. 187), p. 89, 'I haue as greate appetyte to my booke to daye as an hare to a tabre'.

I. 61. felawis: this can scarcely be right, an abstract noun is required here. Probably the original reading was 'fraunchise', liberality; cp. *Sir Gawain*, 652, 'fraunchyse and felaȝschyp'. Another possible word is 'fredom'.

I. 66–7. The reference is probably to Richard's low-born favourites, such as Bushy, Bagot, and Green. His Chester archers, also, were so encouraged by him that 'Regem reputabant in socium', *Annales Ricardi Secundi*, under the year 1397. See note to III. 317.

I. 76–7. Richard's misgovernment had led to the civil war of 1387, when the Lords Appellant, after their victory at Radcot Bridge, put to death many of Richard's adherents. In July of 1397, while the Commons were still complaining of the abuse of livery and maintenance and the extravagance of the Royal household, Richard revenged himself on the Lords Appellant by the arrest and subsequent murder of the Duke of Gloucester, the execution of the Earl of Arundel, and the banishment of Archbishop Arundel and the Earl of Warwick. In the following year, Richard took advantage of the quarrel between Henry of Lancaster and Thomas Mowbray, Duke of Norfolk, both of whom had sided with Gloucester in 1387 and supported the King in his *coup d'état* of 1397, to banish both from the country, Lancaster for six years and Mowbray for life.

I. 83. cler[l]ie : MS. clergie. Skeat prefixes '[þoru]', but cp. III. 26 and III. 190, where he suggests emendation to 'cler[l]ie'.

I. 88-9. This applies specially to the Appealers of 1397, John Holland, Earl of Huntingdon, the King's brother, Thomas Holland, Earl of Kent, his nephew, Rutland, Nottingham, John Beaufort, Sir William Scrope, Thomas, Lord Despenser, and John Montagu, Earl of Salisbury. 'All, except Scrope, Huntingdon, and Montagu, were very young men' (Oman, *Political History of England*, iv. 135). But when in 1389 Richard had successfully claimed his right to choose his own ministers, he appointed Wykeham Chancellor and Brantingham Treasurer, both of whom had held office under Edward III.

The same accusation is brought against Richard by the Monk of Evesham, *Vita Regis Ricardi II*, ed. Hearne, p. 129. 'Hoc anno [1397] . . . Rex, juvenum & insipientum, & specialiter Johannis Bushe ductus consilio, arrestari fecit Ric. Comitem Arundell, & Thomam Comitem Warwyke, & posuit eos in salva custodia.'

From this passage and P. 64-9, we may conclude that the poet himself is not in his first youth.

I. 90. Hurlewaynis kynne : i.e. the mesnie Hellequin (herlequin, hennequin, &c.), a troop of spirits who hunt or do battle by night. Cp. *Beryn* 8, ' suche nyce Iapis As Hurlewaynes meyne in every hegg that capes'. In *De Nugis Curialium*, IV. xiij, Walter Mapes refers to them under the title of Herlethingi. Their last appearance, he says, was on the borders of Wales and Hereford in the first year of King Henry II. See Godefroy's *Dictionnaire* under Hellequin, Grimm's *Teutonic Mythology*, trans. Stallybrass, on the 'furious host', pp. 918–50, especially p. 941. In the seventeenth century, in the form Hellwain, it becomes the name of a minor devil, see *O.E.D.* The people alluded to are such men as Bagot, Bushy, and Green.

I. 95. oried : the subject pronoun is understood.

I. 99. Richard's revenge on the Lords Appellant. There may be a pun on the name of Bushy, cp. II. 39.

I. 107-9. The false deed is the murder of the Duke of Gloucester, see Ziepel, *The Reign of Richard II*, Berlin, 1874, p. 15. John Holland, the king's half-brother, was leader of the armed band which seized Gloucester. According to Froissart, Gloucester had plotted with the Earl of Arundel to seize the king's person, but John Holland frustrated the plan by informing Richard. This, however, was a fabrication to prevent Richard's action from appearing to be his revenge for the events of 1387. Holland was one of the Appealers, and was rewarded with the Dukedom of Exeter.

I. 109. Cp. l. 1407.

PASSUS SECUNDUS

II. 2. The key to the whole passage at the beginning of this Passus is to observe that the author is inveighing against the king's servants, and in particular against their wearing of badges. *Livery* (*leuerey* in l. 2, *leuere* in l. 26) is used here in the particular sense of *uniform*, though it also meant a grant or allowance to servants of a more general kind ; as when, for instance, Spenser defines it as an ' allowaunce of horse-meate, as they commonly use the woord in stabling, as to keepe horses at liverye' ; *View of the State of Ireland*, Globe edition, p. 623. The author complains that the king had *marked* his servants (l. 20) with badges or ' signes ' (l. 21). which were made of silver (l. 45) and which bore the image of a *hart* (l. 4). The whole passage is aptly illustrated by the following remarks. ' The *White Hart* was the favourite badge of Richard II. At a tournament held in Smithfield in 1390, in honour of the Count of St. Pol, Count of Luxemburg, and the Count of Ostrevant, eldest son of Albert, Count of Holland and Zealand, who had been elected members of the garter, " all the kynges house were of one sute ; theyr cotys, theyr armys, theyr sheldes, and theyr trappours were browdrid all with *whyte hertys*, with crownes of gold about their neck, and cheynes of gold hanging thereon, which *hertys* was the *kynges leverye* that he gaf to *lordes*, *ladyes*, *knyghtes*, and *squyers*, to knowe his household people from others "; Caxton's Chronicle at the end of *Polychronicon*, lib. ult. chap. vi.'—*The History of Signboards*, by Larwood and Hotten, p. 112. This tournament is described by Froissart, *Chron.*, Bk. IV, c. 23. Richard probably took this badge from the cognisance of his mother, the ' fair maid of Kent ', which was a white hind. See Mrs. Palliser's *Historic Devices*, p. 363.

Lingard's remarks are also very applicable here. Speaking of the Statutes passed at the beginning of the reign of Henry IV, he says : ' A fourth forbade, under the heaviest penalties, any person besides the king to give liveries to his retainers. These badges had long been the principal expedients by which the great lords were enabled to increase their power, and to maintain their quarrels. Whoever wore the livery was bound in honour to espouse the cause of the donor ;

and it was worn not only by those who had received fees, or were engaged in actual services, but by as many as were willing to accept it as an honour, or in token of friendship, or with a view to future emolument.' Lingard's reference is to *Rot. Parl.* iii. 428, 442; Stat. 1 Hen. IV, c. 10, 14. [S.] But lords could give liveries to men of law.

The Wilton Diptych, a late fourteenth-century work, stated by the National Gallery authorities to be probably of the French school, shows the young king presented by St. John the Baptist, St. Edward the Confessor, and St. Edmund to the Blessed Virgin and her Child. The court of angels accompanying them bear the badge of the White Hart on their tunics.

II. 3. [g]af: MS. ȝaf: see note to P. 28.

II. 9. the egle. That the *Eagle* means Bolingbroke is placed beyond all doubt by Passus III. 69. An eagle was one of the numerous badges of his grandfather, Edward III. [S.]

II. 25. hassellis: cp. l. 29, 'þe haselle names Of officiers withynne and withoute eke'. Skeat glosses it as 'obviously a French spelling of OHG. *heistalde* or *hagestalt*, mod.G. *hagestolz*, a bachelor, cognate with AS. *hago-steald*, *hæg-steald*, *heh-steald*, an unmarried person, young warrior, young man . . . Cp. Low Lat. *haistaldi*, *hestaldi*, retainers'.

II. 42. 'For every *hart* which you marked on a badge, you lost ten score of loyal *hearts*.' I believe there is also a play upon the word *mark*, which sometimes signifies to *hit*, *succeed in hitting* (as in Passus III. 268), and is here opposed to *miss*. This smart saying is attributed to the *townmen*, as being sharper than *countrymen*. [S.]

II. 49. A finite verb, such as 'did', must be supplied. The side-note is from *Luke* xi. 17.

II. 53–4. 'Yet I am ignorant, and manifest little of any good quality which could entitle me to covet', &c.

II. 64. [wankel]: MS. feble, caught from line above. 'Wankel' has a suitable meaning, and preserves the alliteration.

II. 83. 'True in his faith, living on his own', i.e. independent, as the next line explains. For the use of the pp. in active sense, cp. 'vnstombled' in the previous line, and see Einenkel, *Historische Syntax*, 1916, p. 5.

II. 92. 'And a righteous intention in granting and giving.'

II. 96. [g]ifte: MS. ȝifte; see note on P. 28.

II. 108. priuy: manifest. Apparently a ME. adjective 'preue', proved, manifest, was confused by scribes, with 'preue', privy. For other examples of this word and the adverb formed from it see Glossary, also *Siege of Jerusalem*, E.E.T.S. 188, l. 163 (of the Holy Vernicle), 'Peynted priuely and pleyn, þat no poynt wanteþ', and

the note on the passage, *Cleanness* 1107, and perhaps *Pearl* 12, 24.
It is not likely to be connected with OF. preu, valiant, which is only
used of persons ; more probably it derives from OF. prové, with the
vowel of the strong stem pruev-. This suggestion receives support
from the passages in *Pearl*, where in the refrain ' Of þat (*or* My)
pryuy perle wyth-outen spot ', ll. 12, 24, the adjective in the next three
stanzas is ' precios '. The two adjectives are found together in *Isa.*,
xxviii. 16, ' lapidem probatum, angularem, pretiosum ', Wyclif ' a corner ston precious, proued '.

II. 110. 'To give my opinion concerning the rightness of your
action.' Cp. *Troy Book*, 11260–1 :

> ' Sothly, Syr kyng, hit sittis not now
> 3our discresion to dem with no du reason.'

II. 111. **hertis**: here again, as in II. 42, there is a pun.

II. 113. **þe good greehonde**: Mr. Wright suggests the Earl of
Dorset (John Beaufort), as the badge of the Beauforts was a greyhound. But he was of no great mark ... In this difficulty, Mr. G. E.
Adams, Somerset Herald, has kindly suggested the solution—' Why
should not the greyhound stand for Ralph Neville, created Earl of
Westmoreland by Richard II, and of his Privy Council, Constable of
the Tower of London, &c.? He was one of those who greatly con-
tributed to raise Henry to the throne. In Surtees' *Durham*, vol. i,
plate 8, are two seals of the Earls of Westmoreland supported by
greyhounds. The supporters granted to Elizabeth Widville were a
lion (of March), and a *greyhound*, which latter Sandford says was in
allusion to the supporters of the Nevilles, from whom Edward's
mother was descended.' Besides, he may easily have taken the badge
of the greyhound from his alliance with the Beauforts. In the *Annals
of England*, p. 216, note k, we read—' Ralph, lord Neville, had been
created Earl of Westmoreland by Richard II, ... but he was the
brother-in-law of Henry of Lancaster, and rendered him most essen-
tial service *against* his benefactor. He married, for his second wife,
Joan Beaufort, daughter of John of Gaunt.' [S.]

The ballad of *The Rising in the North* (1569) describes the Earl of
Westmoreland's ensign :

> ' The Erle of Westmoreland, he had in his ancyent
> The dunn bull in sight most hye,
> And three doggs with golden collers
> Were sett out royallie.'
> (Child, *English and Scottish Popular Ballads*, p. 426.)

On the other hand, Sir E. M. Thompson identifies the greyhound with
Bolingbroke himself, from the passage in Adam of Usk, p. 25, ' Iste

dux Henricus, secundum propheciam Merlini juxta propheciam, pullus aquile, quia filius Johannis. Set secundum Bredlintoun merito canis, propter liberatam collariorum leporariis conveniencium; et quia diebus canicularibus venit, et quia infidos cervos, liberatam scilicet regis Ricardi in cervis excistentem, penitus regno affugavit.' He also quotes a reference to Henry's greyhound badge in a Latin chronicle, B.M. Harl. 1989, f. 381, describing Richard's removal from Flint to London in 1399, and points out that the expression 'cheff of ȝoure lese' is far more likely to apply to Henry Bolingbroke than to Dorset or even Westmoreland (*Chronicon Adæ de Usk*, 1904, p. 173.)

II. 114. **lese**: originally the thong in which hounds were held, then a set of three hounds. In 1526 the *Household Ordinances* mention the 'officers of the lesh', or the department of the household which had the care of the hounds, see *O.E.D.* under 'leash'.

II. 126. **anon to þe skynnes**: probably this should read 'to þe pure skynnes', cp. II. 32.

II. 134. **harde**: perhaps a scribal alteration for 'vnsofte', which would restore the alliteration. 'Soft' in ME. and in Northern parlance used of the weather = mild, genial. Cp. *Sir Gawain*, 509–10, 'Bryddeȝ busken to bylde, and bremlych syngen For solace of þe softe somer', Henryson, *Robene and Makyne*, 97–8, 'the nicht is softe and dry, the weddir is warme and fair'. In *Prompt. Parv.* it glosses *calmus*.

II. 137. **Deus, &c.**: cp. *Ps.* ix. 37-8, 'Desiderium pauperum exaudivit Dominus . . . judicare pupillo et humili'.

II. 139. **mesure is a meri mene**: the first example of this proverb; cp. *Piers Plowman*, A. i. 33, 'mesure is medicine, thauh thou muche ȝeorne', so B, C (MS. I), other MSS. 'wylne'. *John Russells Boke of Nurture*, 107 (E.E.T.S. 32, p. 8) has 'Mesure is a mery meene'.

II. 140. **[rend] be þe rotus ȝoure raskall endurid**: Skeat translates this without emending: 'lived upon roots'. But the alliterative phrase is common, e.g. *Leg. of Good Women*, 2613, 'The flour, the lefe, is rent up by the rote' and 'to endure by' for 'to live on' is unusual. The 'rascall' had been deprived of their lands, ll. 136-7.

II. 147. **feedrin**: plumage, from OE. feðer-hama. *O.E.D.* gives no examples of this word between 1175 and 1470. Douglas (*Aeneid*, IV. v. 93) has 'feddrame'. Skeat took the word as a weak plural, quoting *Ayenbite*, p. 270, 'hou moche uayr is ine þe ueþeren of þe pokoce'. But apart from the fact that weak plurals, common in *Ayenbite*, are rare in R., it seems clear that 'feedrin' is a different word from 'fedris' in the following line. It is possible that 'hem' was originally 'his'.

II. 151. **her sothes**: the truth about themselves; cf. *Knight of La Tour Landry*, p. 124, 'to tell*e* hym his sothes and trouthe withoute flat*er*ie', and Gower, *Confessio Amantis*, vii. 2347–50:

> 'Whan Rome was the worldes chief,
> The Sothseiere tho was lief,
> Which wolde noght the trouthe spare,
> Bot with hise wordes pleine and bare
> To Themperour hise sothes tolde.'

II. 152–4. A clear allusion to *Bushy, Green*, and *Scrope*. [S.] Sir John Bushy was speaker in the Parliaments of 1393–4, 1397, and 1398, and all three were on the standing committee to which this Parliament delegated its duties. Sir Thomas Green was one of Richard's household knights. Sir William Scrope, Chamberlain of the king's household, was one of the eight Appealers of 1397, who accused Gloucester, Arundel, and Warwick of high treason. For this service he was created Earl of Wiltshire. On this occasion Bushy and Green, together with Sir William Bagot, acted as prolocutors to demand, on the king's behalf, the repeal of the pardons granted in 1388. On Richard's departure for Ireland, he left the kingdom in charge of these four as councillors to the Regent, the Duke of York, and the subsidies were given them to farm. When Henry invaded England, Bagot went to Ireland to warn Richard, while Bushy, Green, and Scrope fled to Bristol. On Henry's arrival outside Bristol, the governor gave them up, and they were beheaded after a very short and irregular trial.

II. 155. **hand-m[el]le**: MS. hand molde. Skeat translates without emending 'He so mixed the metal with the hand-mould (i.e. so moulded events), that they lost', etc. But a 'hand-mould', a word not found elsewhere till 1875, would not be used for mixing metal, and 'hand-mell' is found for a hand-mallet in the Surtees *Vestry Books* in 1600. The verb 'mell', to hammer, occurs in *Allit. Morte Arthure* 2950 and *Allit. Troy Book* 10994.

II. 157. **þis faukyn**: i.e. the eagle, Henry IV, mentioned in ll. 145, 152, 176 of this Passus. Apparently the change is due to the need for new alliterative formulas.

II. 158. **kuyttis**: such men as Bushy and Green. The poet suggests that Henry, after dealing with them, attacked an adversary of higher rank.

II. 164–75. There is here an allusion to Sir William Bagot, Sheriff of Leicestershire, 6 and 7 Richard II. [S.] Before escaping to Ireland (see note on II. 152–4) he secured for himself grants from the crown. When Henry the younger came from Trim Castle to join his father, he 'brought with him in chains Sir William Bagot, a knight of low degree, who had been raised by the king to high places'. (*Chronicon Adæ de Usk*, ed. Sir E. M. Thompson, 1904, p. 180). He was brought up for trial, and committed to the Tower, but in 1401 he was pardoned and his lands restored (see note to *Cronica Tripertita*, iii. 388, *Gower's Works*, ed. Macaulay, iv. 414). The possibility of his being eventually pardoned is alluded to in the penultimate verse of '*On King Richard's Ministers*', Wright, *Pol. Poems and Songs*, i. 363–6.

II. 165. **pulter**: probably answers to the Swed. *paltor*, rags, and the Scottish *peltrie*; we still use the adjective *paltry*, from the same root. [S.]

The word is parallel to 'loby', five lines later. Bagot, as Treasurer, took the very rags of the poor.

II. 172. This appears to refer to Bagot's capture in Ireland.

II. 178. **kareyne**: this is derived from NF. caroigne, late L. *carōnia. It is possible that the ME. forms with 'ei' arose analogically from such doublets as 'peise-poise', where OF. ei had become oi in C.F. Similarly we have ME. pikeis, picois, a pick-axe, from OF. picois, late L. picōsium.

II. 182. **a reclayme**: Francis de Sales uses the same figure in his *Amour de Dieu*, I. xvi, ed. 1610, 'Le perdreau qui aura esté esclos et nourry sous les ailes d'une perdrix estrangere, au premier reclam qu'il oyt de sa vraie mere, qui avoit pondu l'œuf duquel il est procedé, il quitte la perdrix larronnesse, se rend a sa premiere mere et se met a sa suite'. The passage is evidently from the same ultimate source as III. 37–61; note the similarity of 'il quitte la perdrix larronesse' and 'And leueth þᵉ lurker'.

PASSUS TERCIUS

III. 1. **restore**: there is no example in *O.E.D.* of this intransitive sense; the nearest is *Allit. Troy Book*, 10399, 'His strenkith restoris stithly agayn'. Skeat takes 'restore' with 'That whi', and renders it 'establish the reason why'. But 'whi' introduces the object of 'schewe', and we may translate: 'Let us leave this bird (till I return to it) in favour of a subject I am interested in, namely, that I will show why', &c.

III. 13–25. The origin of this is found in Pliny, *Historia Naturalis*, viii. 32, 'et his cum serpente pugna: vestigant cavernas, nariumque spiritu extrahunt renitentes', and in xxviii. 9, 'Exitio his [serpentibus] esse cervos nemo ignorat ut, si quæ sunt, extractas cavernis mandentis. nec vero ipsi spirantesque tantum adversantur'; Isidore

Etym. XII. i. 18, 'Hi serpentium inimici, cum se gravatos infirmitate persenserint, spiritu narium eos extrahunt de cavernis, et superacta pernicie veneni eorum, pabulo reparantur'. The origin of the legend as to the stag's age when this happens is probably due to Pliny's having added a note as to its age of more than a century. Hugh of St. Victor (*De Bestiis*, ii. 14), following Isidore, says that they live for 900 years before they become weak.

III. 13–16. 'I mean, with regard to the harts of strength that has come with years, pricked on by good living and their lusty age, that when they have lived 100 years, they grow weak', &c. Cp. l. 922 'And preisid þe pasture þat prime-saute þaym made', also the saying 'Provender pricks'. For the rather unwieldy arrangement of the sentence, compare II. 1–7, where in the same way 'of' governs an object with dependent clauses, separating the principal verb from its object by several lines.

III. 21. This refers to the Appellants who caused the Earl of Arundel's execution in 1397; see note on III. 26.

III. 26. The sense is that the harts should have attacked venomous adders, and not colts, horses, swans, or bears. The *horse* is Richard Fitzalan, Earl of Arundel, beheaded on Tower Hill, A.D. 1397; the *colt*, his son Thomas, who fled to join Henry, and was one of the small company who landed with him at Ravenspurgh; the *swan*, Thomas, Duke of Gloucester, Richard's uncle, so treacherously murdered by his orders at Calais, about the same time that Arundel was beheaded; and the *bear*, Thomas Beauchamp, Earl of Warwick, seized with Arundel by Richard's orders, and banished by him for life to the Isle of Man, though afterwards released by Henry. They were named from their badges, the *white horse* being that of Arundel, the *swan* that of the Duke of Gloucester, which he had adopted from his father, Edward III, who sometimes used it; and the *black bear* that of the Earl of Warwick. See *Political Songs*, ed. Wright, vol. i, p. 419. [S.]

Wright quotes from the argument of the first book of Gower's *Chronica Tripertita*, 'Tres namque tunc regni nobiles super hoc specialius moti, scilicet Thomas Dux Glouernie, qui vulgariter dictus est *cignus*, Ricardus Comes Arundellie, qui dicitur *Equs*, Thomas Comes de Warrewyk, cuius nomen *Vrsus*'.

III. 28. **sholle**: very probably a scribal error for 'sholde'; cp. P. 24.

III. 29. Side-note. The leading passage in the Civil Law is the Institutes of Justinian, I. t. 16. 1, where among those who lose their liberty are 'Liberti ut ingrati condemnati'. The whole subject is treated of by W. W. Buckland, *The Roman Law of Slavery* p. 422 sqq.

The texts of the decrees from Claudius to Constantine are given by Hunter, *Roman Law*, 4th ed., p. 170.

There is nothing resembling this in the English *Stimulus Conscientiæ*.

III. 30–1. 'Public opinion was much shocked by the fact that the guard of Cheshire archers which led [Arundel] to the block was commanded by two of his nearest relatives, by Nottingham, who had married his daughter, and Kent his nephew.' Sir C. Oman, *Political History of England*, iv. 136.

III. 37. þat þe bough spareth: i.e. that build their nests on the ground.

III. 43–61. Cp. Bartholomaeus Anglicus, lib. xii, c. 31, 'And is soo gyleful that the one stelyth the egges of the others | and syttyth a brood on theym | But this frawde hath noo fruyte | for whan yᵉ byrdes ben haughte . and here yᵉ voyce of their owne mod*er* . they forsake her yᵗ brooded theym whan thei were egges . & kepte theym as her owne byrdes . and torne & folowe theyr owne moder naturall as Ysydre sayth & Ambrose also | '

Isidore, *Etym.* XII. vii. 63, 'Adeo autem fraudulenta, ut alteri ova diripiens foveat, sed fraus fructum non habet ; denique dum pulli propriæ vocem genetricis audierint, naturali quodam instinctu hanc quæ fovit relinquunt, et ad eamdem quæ genuit revertuntur.'

The present account differs from this in that the partridge does not steal the eggs, but takes their owner's place ; this is obviously more suitable to the political meaning of the allegory.

III. 45. congion: a term of abuse. The word generally implies deformity or lack of intellect, as in (i) *Prompt. Parv.* sub Coonyone, congeon or dwerfe ; *King Alis.*, 1718, 'Alisaundre! thou conioun wode' ; (ii) *Piers Plowman*, A. xi. 86–7, 'And nou cometh a conioun and wolde cacchen of my wittes, What is Dowel from Dobet! nou daffe mot he worthe' ; *Chester Plays*, ii. 601, 'Say, thou cayteife, tho conioyne, Wenes thou to passe me of renowne ?' The earliest English form is 'cangun', a deformed person or idiot, in *Holy Maidenhood*, c. 1230. Godefroy has 'changon', 1427, as a term of abuse. Hence *O.E.D.* derives from late L. cambiōnem, a changeling, popularly supposed to grow up deficient in form or intellect.

III. 50. þe hue : cp. *Chester Plays*, iii. 123–4, 'Of cleane fowles seaven alsoe, The hee and shee together'.

III. 59. Skeat glossed 'leued' as '(they) lived', which seems an unnatural construction. Sir William Craigie suggests OE. gelēfed, made weak. Or we might substitute 'leue' and 'lened', and read 'that their loins were weak and made lean by hunger'. The adj. 'leue' might be derived from OE. lēf, debilis.

III. 68–72. The poet speaks here as if Henry were king by right of inheritance. The words of his claim are recorded in the Rolls of Parliament : ' als I y^t am disendit be right lyne of the Blode comyng fro the gude lorde Kyng Henry therde, and thorghe yat ryght yat God of his grace hath sent me, with helpe of my Kyn and of my Frendes to recover it' (*Rot. Parl.* iii. 423). Apparently the reference is to a story circulated by his adherents that Edmund, Earl of Lancaster, his maternal ancestor, was the elder son of Henry III, but because of his deformity had been set aside in favour of Edward I. See Oman, *Political History*, iv. 152–3. Cp. also III. 92–3, and Gower's *Address to Henry IV* (*Works*, ed. Macaulay, III. 481) :

> ' Thi title is knowe uppon thin ancestrie,
>   The lordes folk hath ek thy riht affermed ;
>   So stant thi regne of God and man confermed.'

III. 75. Another allusion to Bushy.

III. 81. **twynte** : this rare word, occurring in both fragments, is only found elsewhere in the *Tale of Beryn*, 433, 'nat a twynt'.

III. 94. The Earl of Warwick, imprisoned in the Isle of Man in 1397, removed to the Tower in 1398, was liberated by Henry in 1399.

III. 98. **Bosse** : evidently a nickname for the bear. The noun ' boss ', from OF. boce, signifies a protuberance, and from the sixteenth century was applied to a water conduit, running from a tap, and specially to the Boss or water-tap of Billingsgate, which was built by Richard Whittington in the form of a bear. See Miss B. White's introduction to Whittinton and Stanbridge's *Vulgaria*, E.E.T.S. 187, p. xxviii. Whittington's mayoralties were in 1397, 1406, and 1419. The first of these fell in a very troublous time, and his great benefactions to the City belong to a later date. Hence the Boss of Billingsgate could not have given rise to the nickname. Possibly the bear-shape was traditional before his time.

III. 100. **þe heeris** : i.e. of those who had fallen, the young Earl of Arundel and the Duke of Gloucester's son.

III. 101. **gaglide** : this word is only used of geese ; cp. the company term, 'a gaggle of geese'. Either it refers back to the ' swimmers ', followers of the Swan of Gloucester, l. 86, or some lines have been omitted after l. 98 or l. 190. In the poem *On King Richard's Ministers*, Wright, *Pol. Poems and Songs*, i. 363–6, Rolls. Series, the peacocks and geese are spoken of as joining with the eagle immediately on his arrival in the North, and being fed with corn from the bag (Bagot). This can scarcely refer to any but the Percies and the Earl of Westmoreland, Henry's first important adherents, who were lavishly rewarded by him (see Oman, *Pol. Hist.* iv. 160). Robert

Neville, eldest son of the third baron, who was killed in a border raid in 1318, was called 'The Peacock of the North'. The present line may therefore refer to the followers of the Percies.

In *Archaeologia*, xxi. 90, W. Hamper identifies the peacocks and geese with the Lords and Commons.

III. 102. **felons oastis**: devices of wicked men; or else this is an example of the ME. adj. 'felons', from OF. nom. s. 'felons' of ' felon'. Cp. *Erkenwald*, 231, 'þe folke was felonse & fals '.

III. 105–6. The Earl-marshal was Thomas de Mowbray, Duke of Norfolk, son-in-law to the Earl of Arundel. The latter was executed by Richard's orders; and, as Froissart tells us, the Earl-marshal actually bandaged his father-in-law's eyes at the execution, see Froissart, bk. iv, c. 92. Such was, at any rate, the common story, as given also by Walsingham. [S.]

olo[y]ed: MS. cloþed; emended by H. Bradley, *Modern Language Review*, xii. 202. 'Cloy', perhaps an aphetic form of 'accloy', OF. encloyer, is given by Palsgrave as to prick a horse with a nail in shoeing. In the general sense of laming a horse, it is found as a variant of 'accloy', 'encloy', in *Piers Plowman*, C. xxi. 296.

III. 111. **[passith]**: MS. *persith* ; cp. P. 17 ; 238.

III. 113. **Cursidnesse and oombraunoe**: cp. l. 1154.

III. 116. **That were**: that would be, indeed! Ironical. [S.] For a similar tone, cp. ll. 1689–96.

III. 118. **in turmentours wede**: cf. 'Hii ben degised as *turmentours* that comen from clerkes plei ', *Pol. Songs*, ed. Wright, p. 336. [S.] The allusion is to the new squires of the reign of Edward II, who are compared to the Roman soldiers of the Miracle Plays; cp. Towneley '*Scourging and Crucifixion* ', where they are called Primus Tortor, &c.

III. 122–5. The dislocation of order here was probably due to the scribe being misled by two lines beginning with 'For'. Similarly l. 127 was temporarily omitted owing to the three consecutive lines beginning with 'And'.

III. 128. **endauntid**: made much of; cp. dawnte, *blanditractare*, *Cath. Angl.* 92. In *Prick of Conscience*, 1078, dauntes = love; in *Lay Folk's Mass Book*, p. 140, l. 445, endaunt = to charm (the adder). The sense passes from 'to tame' to 'to soothe through taming', and hence 'to cherish '; as in *Life of St. Christina*, ed. Horstmann, *Anglia*, viii. 132, 'Wiþ siche woordes and cosses dauntynge hir body', where the sense is 'cherishing '.

III. 129. For the side-note, see *Luke* vii. 25 'hominem mollibus vestimentis indutum ? . . . in domibus regum sunt'.

III. 136–7. In early times criminals to be hanged were brought to the gallows on a cart, which was driven away, leaving them suspended. The fixed platform with a drop was first used at Tyburn in the middle of the eighteenth century, see *The Hangmen of England*, by H. Bleackley, 1929.

III. 139. **chepe** : the market, the site of which in London is recorded in 'Cheapside'. In *Winner and Waster*, ll. 472 ff., the king ordains the chepe as the most suitable dwelling for Waster.

III. 140. The line perhaps means—'And use all their silver for ornamenting girdles or drinking-horns'. [S.] Cp. l. 569, also *Visions of Tundale*, 201–2 (addressed to the soul of Tundale) :

> ' Wer is thi streynthe and thi myght
> And thi hornys soo gayly dyght ?'

and *Sir Gawain*, 162–3 :

> ' Boþe þe barres of his belt and oþer blyþe stones
> þat were richely rayled in his aray clene.'

In the illustrations to MS. Harl. 4425, a fifteenth-century *Roman de la Rose*, reproduced by the B.M. as postcards, the Lover wears a golden belt with long gold pendants.

III. 141. Cp. *Piers Plowman*, B. v. 242–3 :

> ' I lerned amonge Lumbardes and Iewes a lessoun,
> To wey pens with a peys and pare þe heuyest.'

III. 145. The first (and only medieval) reference to the proverb quoted by Fuller, *Worthies*, i. 399 (ed. 1840) : ' First hang and draw, Then hear the cause by Lydford Law ', which had no power to pass such a sentence. See Chambers's *Book of Days*, ii. 327 (quoted by Skeat), 'Lydford itself is the chief town of the Stannaries, and the proverb probably was levelled at the summary decisions of the Stannary courts which, under a Charter of Edward I, had sole jurisdiction over all cases in which the natives were concerned, that did not affect land, life, or limb.' For other references see Apperson, *English Proverbs and Proverbial Phrases*, *sub* Lydford Law.

III. 152. Skeat compares *Parson's Tale*, 415, &c. See also the Monk of Evesham, *Vita R. Ric. II*, ed. Hearne, pp. 172–3 : ' In primordio hujus Regis [Henry IV] excrescebat nimis insolentia indumentorum in Regno, & maxime togarum cum profundis & latis manicis, vocatis vulgaritur *Pokys*, ad modum *Bagpipe* formatis, adeo ut eis tam a servis, quam a Dominis indifferenter utebatur. Quæ quidem receptacula Dæmoniorum recte dici poterant. Quia quicquid furtive apprehendi posset, mox in eis recondebatur. Aliæ autem earum adeo latæ & largæ fuerunt, ut usque ad pedes, vel saltem ad genua, plenæ scissuris et dæmoniis, dependerent. Cum autem ad mensam servi

Dominis eorum de potagio, de salsiamento, vel hujusmodi liquore, servire deberent, statim in eis demergebantur, de hujusmodi liquore prius gustantes quam Domini. Et ita quod eis deliberatum, donatum seu acquisitum erat ad utendum, seu utiliter tegendum eorum miserabile corpus, in istis *Pokys* vel manicis, truncato alio habitu, superflue expendebatur.'₁

Long sleeves are mentioned as early as 1352, in *Winner and Waster*, 410–11.

> 'Nysottes of þe new gett, so nysely attyred,
> With [si]de slabbande sleues, sleght to þe grou*n*de.'

III. 156. **Pernell**: Purnel (short for Petronilla), a common female name, particularly used of a woman of loose character. Another such name was *Felice*, which is used in l. 160. [S.]

Cp. ll. 1360-1 (and note on the passage):

> 'Forto preche þaire parroisshe how Pernelle is arayed .
> And with þe tolle of þe tithing fetisly a-tired.'

The two names occur in the same passage in *Piers Plowman*, A. v. 26–9.

III. 159. Hard and soft *g* appear to alliterate here: cp. l. 314, 'But glymsyng on the glose, a general revle'. Schumacher, *Studien über den Stabreim in der ME. Alliterationsdichtung*, pp. 162–3, takes the former line to be defective in alliteration, though he allows it as 'eye-rhyme' in the *Alexander Fragments*.

III. 162-6. See note on III. 193.

III. 170. **side tales**: long tales. There appears to be a play upon words here, in allusion to the sleeves which trail along the ground in III. 152. This is the only example in *O.E.D.* of 'side' in the sense of 'long-lasting'. A foot-note to *Catholicon Angl.*, p. 339 quotes from Fitzherbert's *Boke of Husbandry* 'to be *syde* tayled' as a property of the fox. We may note also l. 1470 'þe [tayl] of þaire talking', the conclusion, result of their speech, where the MS. has 'tale' corrected in the gloss to 'tayl'.

III. 172. Cp. *Piers Plowman*, A. Prol. 889, 'Thow mihtest beter meten the myst on Maluerne hulles Then geten a mom of heore mouth til moneye weore schewed.'

III. 186. **beringe vppon oilles**: the use of flattery . . . Perhaps *vppon* should be altered to *vp of*. [S.]

Cp. ll. 247, 271, 831; also Trevisa, *Polychr.* iii. 447, 'A greet deel of hem . . . hilde up þe kynges oyl (*magna convivantium parte assentiente*; (Gower, *Confessio Amantis*, vii. 2194-5, 'Bot holden up his oil and sein That al is wel, what evere he doth'; vii. 2583-4, 'Prophetes false manye mo To bere up oil'. Both passages refer to flattery of kings.

III. 193. **dagges**: see an illustration in Fairholt, *Costume in England*, I. 125, from the French metrical *Histoire du Roi d'Angleterre Richard II*, also in *Archaeologia*, vol. xx, opposite p. 13. Cp. Harding's *Chronicle*, ch. cxciii :

> 'Cut werke was greate both in court and tounes,
> Bothe in me*n*nes hoddis and also in their gounes.'

Duche cotis. In the *Book of the Knight of La Tour Landry*, E.E.T.S. 33, p. 159, the French original of which was written in 1371-2, is the story of a young squire, rebuked by an old knight for appearing before the company 'clothed in a cote hardy upon the guyse of Almayne'. The knight professed to take him for a minstrel; whereupon the squire gave the offending tunic to a pursuivant (in the French 'un menestrel'), and put on another gown. See Sir I. Gollancz, *Cleanness*, i, pp. 83-4.

III. 194. **se[h]or[n]**: MS. scort, glossed by 'scorne'. Cp. *Paston Lett.*, III. 185, 'The fawcon Which is alofte, tellith scorne to loke a down'. No such phrase as 'tell short' is recorded, though *Piers Plowman*, B. xii. 124 has 'sette short be here science'. In III. 236 the verb 'schorned' alliterates with *sl* and *sh*, but in l. 73 the noun alliterates with *sk*.

III. 207-10. Somewhere earlier a passage seems to have been omitted describing how Wisdom came to the court and was slighted by the graceless courtiers.

III. 216-18. Ziepel quotes Harding's *Chronicle*, ch. cxciii :
> 'Truly I herd Robert Ireleffe saye,
> Clerke of the grenecloth, y^t to the houshold
> Came euery daye for moost partie alwaye,
> Ten thousand folke by his messis tould,
> That folowed the hous aye as thei would,
> And in the kechin three hundred seruitours,
> And in eche office many occupiours.'

III. 218. 'And for thair jugement, the kyng leet make a long and large hous of tymber in the paleis at Westmynstre, that was callid an Hale; couered with tile3, and open on bothe side3 and atte endis, that alle men myghte se thorough' (of the trial of the Earl of Arundel, *English Chronicle of Richard II*, Camden Society, 1856, p. 9).

III. 222-3. For a similar turn of humour cp. ll. 551-2.

III. 228. Cp. l. 174, and note on it.

III. 234. þe **sleues** þat **slode vppon þe erthe**: cp. III. 152 and note on it.

III. 249. The 'three degrees' or ranks were, in olden times, the

Oratores (here Counsellors), l. 250; *Bellatores* (Warriors), ll. 251, 252; and *Laboratores* (Labourers), l. 253. [S.]

III. 253. Cp. *Piers Plowman*, A. vii. 259, 'And leorne to labre with lond, leste lyflode faile' (similarly C; B 'for lyflode is swete').

III. 262. Cp. Ray, *Proverbs*, 1768, p. 225, 'As nimble as a cow in a cage'; Heywood, *Proverbs*, pt. ii, ch. i, 'as comely as is a cowe in a cage'.

It may be noted that a variant form of 'chough' was 'cow'; cp· *Wife of Bath's Prologue*, 232, 'Shal bere hym on hond the cow is wood', where the cow is a caged talking bird; see Skeat's note. There may be a play of words behind the simile.

III. 272. 'And not to rule like bats (awake only at night), and rest all day.' [S.]

The Monk of Evesham says that Richard was 'luxuriæ nimis deditus, vigilator maximus, ita ut aliquando mediam noctem nonnunquam usque mane totam noctem in potationibus & aliis non dicendis insompnem duceret' (*Hist. R. Ric. II*, ed. Hearne, pp. 169–70).

III. 284. **letith**: 'they' must be understood before this. The spelling 'him' in III. 286 is probably due to a scribe taking the verbs to be singular.

III. 293. **heuene** [-ȝate]: cp. *Piers Plowman*, B. v. 603, 'Of Almesdedes ar the hokes that the gates hangen on', and *Genesis and Exodus* 1620, 'Her heuenegate amongus us' (non est hic aliud nisi ... porta cæli).

III. 299. **kew-kaw**: the sense of the passage is that the justices have to be bribed; cp. the proverb quoted first by Heywood, 'Ka me, ka the, one good tourne askth an other'. A variant is 'claw me, claw thee', and 'claw' = 'flatter' is common from the 14th century. 'Þouȝ he come late' suggests that this is a new practice; cp. the following line.

III. 301. This refers probably to the judges on circuit.

III. 307. **billis**: the bill in civil cases was the 'narration' (see p. xxix), which the judge would abate as showing no cause of action. In criminal cases it was the presentment or accusation which when received by the jury became the indictment.

III. 316. Cp. *Piers Plowman*, A. iii. 71, 'For theose be men vppon molde that most harm worchen' (similarly in B, but C has 'For thees men doth most harme to the mene puple'). Here it refers to the retail traders, who oppress the poor.

III. 317. **chyders of Chester**: see *Annales Ricardi II*, (Rolls Series, ed. Riley, 1866, p. 208) under the year 1397: 'Ipse vero Rex, ut efficacius perficere posset nequam conceptus, congregari fecit malefactores de Comitatu Cestriæ, ad vallandum latus suum, quorum

tutelæ totaliter se commisit, ad numerum magnum valde : qui, natura
bestiales, parati erant ad omnem nequitiam perpetrandam; ita ut
expost tanta surrexit eis insolentia, ut Regem reputabant in socium,
et alios, quanquam valentes et dominos, haberent in despectum. Et
hii non erant de generosis patriæ, sed tracti vel de rure, vel sutoria,
vel alia quavis, arte ; ut qui domi vix digni reputati fuerant detrahere
calceos magistrorum, hic se reputabant pares et socios dominorum.
In tantum crevit eorum importuna superbia, fastus, et crudelis audacia,
ut expost, cum Rege transeuntes per regnum, tam infra hospitium
Regis quam extra, fideles Regis ligeos impune verberarent, vulne-
rarent, et occiderent, nimis crudeliter, et bona populi prædarentur,
nihil pro suis victualibus solvere statuentes . . . nec expediebat quen-
quam contravenire tantis impietatibus, crudelitatibus, vel oppressioni-
bus ; quia, si quisquam se conquesturum Regi protestaretur, mox
sine misericordia trucidabatur indilate. Siquis resistere paravisset, a
superveniente multitudine opprimebatur, et cultello vel gladio neca-
batur. Fuit nempe talis eorum conditio, quod soli nunquam
præsumerent obviare soli, non quidem vivorum minimo ; sed cum
placeret malefacere, et in aliquem vindicari, glomeratim currerent ad
opprimendum unum solum hominem, et suam malitiam exercendum.'
See also *Chronicon Adæ de Usk*, ed. Sir E. M. Thompson, 1904,
p. 23, where their number is given as 400, who guarded the king day
and night wherever he went, wearing their armour. In the Monk of
Evesham's *Vita Ricardi II*, ed. Hearne, 1729, pp. 133-4, we read that
there were about 2,000 of them, and how at the Earl of Arundel's
trial in 1397 they guarded the Parliament house, and actually began
to shoot their arrows on the people.

III. 319. **pledid pipoudris** : settled all manner of cases summarily,
as in the Court of Piepowders. This was a 'summary court formerly
held at fairs and markets to administer justice among itinerant dealers
and others temporarily present' (*O.E.D.*); cp. *Liber Albus*, i. 67
(1220-1), 'Terminare querelas transeuntium per villam qui moram
non poterunt facere, qui dicuntur *pepoudrous*'. As there is no mention
in the Chronicles of the Cheshire men intruding into the courts at
Westminster, the passage probably means that, when accompanying
the king on his progresses, they interfered with local courts.

III. 322. **till þey a fyne had** : *see* Introduction p. xxix.

III. 323. 'They understood no legal pleading, as the commons
reported.'

III. 328. We may compare an occurrence related in *Paston Letters*,
no. 518 (ed. Gairdner, 1900). The Duke of Suffolk claimed to be the
rightful owner of John Paston's manor of Drayton. In August 1465,
when Paston's servants went to hold the manor-court there, the

Duke's men, 'with a lx. persones or more be estymacion, and the tenauntes of the same town, sum of hem havyng rusty pollexis and byllys, comyn in to the maner yard to kepe the courte'. They seized one of Paston's men, bound his hands behind his back, and delivered him into the custody of the bailiff.

III. 351. *Degon* is clearly a term of contempt; see note to l. 362 below. [S.]

Cp. the use of Hob as a common noun in I. 90. Jamieson quotes ' diggot' as a 'contemptuous designation given to a child, implying the notion of dishonourable conduct '.

III. 352–71. Divine judgement fell upon Richard and his Chester men. Apparently God is the sun, and Bolingbroke and his army the moon and stars.

III. 352. Cp. l. 1247.

III. 362. **Degon and Dóbyn**: evidently Diggon and Dobbin, both common names for country bumpkins, here used in contempt of the upstarts who used to burst in men's doors and rob them. Spenser introduces *Diggon* and *Hobbinol* into his Shepherdes Kalender for September. [S.]

III. 363. **y-dubbid of a duke**: rewarded by Richard for their interference with justice (cp. III. 351). Here, as three lines earlier, ' duke ' has the sense of leader, ruler.

PASSUS QUARTUS

IV. 7. **Marohe and Moubray**: Roger Mortimer succeeded to the Earldom of March in 1381, at the age of seven. His estates were farmed by the Earl of Arundel and others. Thomas de Mowbray, afterwards Duke of Norfolk, succeeded to the barony of Mowbray in 1383, at the age of seventeen. The Chancellor, Richard, Baron Scrope, father of the Scrope who was later King Richard's favourite, objected to the king's extravagant action in thus granting the lands, and was deprived of his office; see Walsingham, *Hist. Angl.* ii. 68–70.

IV. 13. Cp. *God Spede the Plough*, 25–32 (E.E.T.S. 30, p. 70):

> ' The kyngis puruiours also they come,
> To haue whete and otys at the kyngis nede ;
> And over that befe and mutton,
> And butter and pulleyn, so god me spede !
> And to the kyngis courte we moste it lede,
> And our payment shal be a styk of a bough ;
> And yet we moste speke faire for drede —
> " I praye to God, spede wele the plough ".'

IV. 14. **poundage**: in the Parliament of 1397 the Commons

granted Richard 12*d*. on every pound of merchandise and 3*s*. on every tun of wine entering or leaving the kingdom for the next three years.

IV. 24. The Parliament of Shrewsbury, January 1398, was the same packed Parliament which had condemned Arundel and Warwick the previous year. On the proposal of Speaker Bushy it delegated its powers to a small committee, by the help of which Richard governed for the remainder of his reign.

IV. 26. **writtis all in wex closid**: i.e. 'writs close', letters addressed by the sovereign to particular persons and sealed with the privy seal, in contradistinction to 'letters patent' which were addressed to ' omnibus ad quos presentes litteræ pervenerint ' and were under the great seal. This Parliament was, in fact, the same one which had been adjourned after the ennoblement of Richard's followers in September 1398 ; see note to IV. 33–8.

IV. 33–8. ' Lundy apres la Quinzeine de Seint Hiller proschein venant, le Roy & les Seigñrs Espirituels & Temporels, & les Chivalers des Contees, Citezeins & Burgeis, a Salopbirs assemblez en Parlement solonc l'ejournement d'icell, le Chaunceller rehercea, Coment le Parlement feust commencez a Londres, & la cause de Somnons d'icell ' (*Rot. Parl*. iii. 356, Jan. 1397–8). This was the regular form for opening Parliament. After the conventional allusions to the need for preserving the liberties of the Church and of the lords, citizens, and burgesses, the Chancellor ' monstra as Comunes, Coment le Roy vorroit estre enfourmez par eux coment le Charge serroit portez pur la Defense du Roialme . . . & auxi pur la Marche d'Escoce, en cas q'ils ne tiegnent mye les auncienes Treves qi feurent prises pur quatre ans '.

IV. 39. **anon to þe ende**: cp. l. 68. Both lines are of type *aa xx*, which makes it possible that each is a scribal stop-gap.

IV. 40–92. The result of this discussion is given in the Rolls of Parliament: ' Item, le Marsdy proschein ensuant, Monśr Johan Bussy rehercea au Roy en Parlement, coment le Chanceller & Tresorer monstrent a luy & ses Compaignons la Necessite & busoignables Charges du Roy & du Roialme, & dist, Coment q̃ les Communes feurent a graunt povert, nientmeyns ils sont & serront prestz come loialx lieges de faire leur devoir a leur poair. . . . Item, mesme le [Joefdy], les Communes du Roialme, par assent des Seigñrs Espirituels & Temporels, granterent au Roy la Subside des Leyns, Quirs, & Peaux lanutz a terme de sa vie, & une Quinszisme, & Disme, & une dimy-Quinszisme & dimy-Disme.' (*Rot. Parl*. iii. 359, 368).

IV. 55. **Symond**: the reference is to Simon Magus ; they had taken money for their vote, cp. 'Symon-is sermons', l. 508, and the poem ' On Bishop Boothe ', *Pol. Poems* (Rolls), ii. 225 :

> 'Boothe, be ware, bisshoppe thoughe thou be,
> Sithe that Symoun hym selff set the in thy sete, . . .
> Thy goode and thy catelle made the to mete
> With the churche of Chester.'

Ziepel connects the line with Sir Simon Burley, the king's old tutor, executed by the Lords Appellant in 1388, on the charge of having led Richard in his youth to form a corrupt court.

IV. 71–82. This nautical metaphor is especially natural on the lips of a Bristol man.

IV. 78. **at þe monþe-ende**: a favourite expression; cp. ll. 682, 795.

IV. 86. **helde wiþ þe mo**: agreed with the most part. There is no other example of the phrase in *O.E.D.*, but cp. l. 678, 'þou mos holde wiþ þe mo'.

IV. 93. **Do-well**: see note on l. 543.

M

1–6. Cp. the proceedings of the Parliament of September, 1402 ; Introduction, p. xx ; and *Cont. Eulog. Hist.* (Rolls), pp. 395–6.

5. **caste vp þe halter**: cast off restraint. Perhaps 'þe' should be inserted before 'vncunnyng'.

7. **smaicche of þe smoke**: this might mean 'get an inkling of state secrets', cp. *State Papers*, 1526, 'many strange thinges, wherof I smelt a smoke at Calays'. The context, however, suggests that the sense is 'to be irritated', as is the throat by smoke.

9. Cp. *Piers Plowman*, A. iii. 76 (of the retail tradesmen): 'For toke thei on trewely, thei timbrede not so hye.'

17–23. Cp. *Piers Plowman*, A. Prol. 85–9:

> 'Seriauns hit semeth to seruen atte barre,
> Pleden for pons and poundes the lawe,
> Not for loue of vr lord vn-loseth heore lippes ones.
> Thow mihtest beter meten the myst on Maluerne hulles
> Then geten a mom of heore mouth til moneye weore schewed.'

þe **prentys of court**: answering to the modern barristers.

25. Cp. Introduction (pp. xxvi ff.).

38–41. We may compare a passage from the *Ayenbite of Inwyt*, p. 256: 'þise greate men hi ssolden wel ham loki | þet hi hiereþ | and þet hi leueþ. þet hi vindeþ veawe | þet zoþ ham zigge. Ac ulatours | and lyeʒeres | byeþ to grat cheap ine hare cort. þe meste dierþe þet is aboute ham | is of zoþnesse ¡ an of trewþe. and þeruore hi byeþ ofte y-giled. þet hi yhereþ bleþeliche | and y-leueþ liʒtliche þet me ham zayþ and þet ham likeþ. Senekes zayþ. þet þer ne lackeþ to greate lhordes :

bote zoþ ziggeres. Vor hi habbeþ lye3eres | and vlatours: to greate
cheape. and veawe zoþ ziggeres.'

43. 'But he had to provide his own clothes.'

61. þe peynt[*ur*]e of þe preynte : this expression is parallel to
'þe colour of þe crosse' in l. 66.

66. þe colour of þe crosse : i.e. the cross which was engraved on
the backs of coins. Cp. *Piers Plowman*, B. xv. 506–7 :

> ' Bothe riche and religious that rode thei honoure,
> That in grotes is ygraue, and in golde nobles.'

67. tornement : turning, overthrowing ; cp. l. 57.

68. anone : the weakness of the word suggests a stop-gap ; cp.
note on IV. 39. Perhaps the original was ' as grayne ', cp. l. 64 and
the textual note to l. 71.

80. Cp. *Matt.* xviii. 15, 'Si autem peccaverit in te frater tuus,
vade et corripe eum inter te et ipsum solum.'

84. of þe newe : afresh, also in III. 161.

87–9. 'He that is most of might shall . . . have regard of a
reasonable man', i.e. thyself. 'To haue' and 'quite' are parallel, the
second infinitive taking 'to', as often happens; cp. ll. 117–18, also
l. 1272, where 'forto' is used before the second infinitive.

99–102. Henry appears to have had such a servant in Philip
Repyngdon, Abbot of Leicester, who was his chaplain, confessor, and
personal friend. In the *Chronicon* of Adam of Usk (ed. E. M.
Thompson, 1904, pp. 65–9) is a letter which Repyngdon wrote to
Henry in May, 1401, to tell him of the disorders of the realm, and of
the failure of the high hopes with which Henry had been received on
his landing. Quoting *Proverbs* xxvii. 6, 'Faithful are the wounds of
a friend', he reproaches the king with the state of the country, from
which law and justice are banished, and where oppression of the poor
is rife. ' Ideo, in justam penam et vindictam negligencie et ommis-
sionis gubernatorum populi, Deus judex justus permittit plebeos,
tanquam feras bestias, irregulariter et irracionabiliter judicare, et
regimen superiorum innaturaliter presumere, et erga superiores, equales,
et inferiores, sine discressionis libramine, bestialiter desevire ' (p. 67 ;
cp. ll. 1457 ff.).

109. Cp. l. 1016, also *Piers Plowman*, A. vi. 29, 'I knowe him as
kuyndeliche as clerk doth his bokes', similarly B; C has 'as clerkus
don hure bokes '.

112. þaym : this should probably be omitted ; cp. l. 116.

114. Side-note from *Ps.* ii. 10.

130. Ne God neither goodman : see a letter in *The Times
Literary Supplement*, August 13, 1931, by Dr. C. T. Onions, giving

examples of the phrase 'God and good men', with examples from the *Peterborough Chronicle* for the year 1137, Minot's poem on Bannock-burn, ii. 14, and *Piers Plowman*, C. vi. 67 (not in A or B, but it is also found in B. xiv. 8). In *T.L.S.*, September 17, 1931, A. J. Barnouw stated that the phrase was known in Dutch, but only in the negative form, e.g. Vondel, *Joseph in Dothan*, ii. 668–9:

> 'Waer ben ick nu gekomen
> Daer Godt woont noch goedt mensch !'

The negative form is found in *Jack Upland's Rejoinder* (*Pol. Poems*, Rolls, ii. 99), 'Ffor God ne any godeman appreved never this symonye.' The expression seems to be a forcible synonym for 'all good men'; cp. the example from *Piers Plowman*, C. vi. 67, quoted by Dr. Onions, 'lordes kyn . . . Bothe god and good men'.

138. Cp. l. 527.

141. **glose**: gloss, with a play upon its secondary meaning of 'flattery'; cp. ll. 162, 388.

144-6. Though it seems at first sight as if the author had changed his opinion about Richard's misrule, it is probable, judging by the other examples of the first two in both texts, that none of the words 'bable', 'fable', 'romansid', have any depreciatory meaning. On the other hand, the noun 'fable' definitely means a falsehood in P. 57.

148. **at þe crosse**: presumably of Bristol. Here Despenser was executed by the men of the city without trial in 1400; see Monk of Evesham, *Vita R. Ric. II*, ed. Hearne, p. 167, 'ad crucem, ibidem in mercatu stantem'. The market-cross was everywhere the place where proclamations were made.

152-5. 'Once some of the commons discussed their grievances with some one of higher rank, and consequently suffered fines and imprison-ments. Now they dare not speak, except privately among themselves.' It is not clear what this refers to, but ll. 154–5 seem to point to some occurrence in Henry's reign. There is nothing recorded which fits the case, but in Rymer's *Foedera*, viii. 255–6, there is a letter sent by Henry in 1402 to the authorities in the counties of Somerset, Dorset, Devon, and Cornwall, saying that certain of his subjects in different parts of the kingdom had been spreading lies in taverns and other meeting-places to the effect that he had not kept his coronation promises. He therefore calls upon the authorities to contradict these falsehoods, and arrest and imprison all these preachers of sedition. Some unrecorded incident arising out of this measure may be re-ferred to. Similar complaints had been made in the parliament of January, 1404, see Introduction, p. xxi.

The present passage sounds as if it might be an answer to the later or the earlier of these charges, with a reference to some folk-lore story of a chattering magpie and a parrot.

152. **of oones**: once. The phrase is not given in *O.E.D.*, but 'of' is required by the metre.

162. **glose**: flattery; also, as contrasted with 'texte', l. 160, marginal comment.

166. **[mynne]**: the line is repeated at 285.

169. **[brent]**: MS. 'blent', probably a scribal error, as blinding had ceased to be, if it ever was, a legal punishment.

174. Cp. III. 228, also *Piers Plowman*, A. ii. 194, 'Bote ouur-al i-hunted and hote to trusse'; B 'yhowted', C 'houted out', 'i-hunted', 'hountyd'.

183. **Though þay batre hym with battz**: for the alliterating words A has 'bale', 'banes'. But it is not easy to see what these mean, and both 'baterid' and 'battis' are found in the first fragment; see Glossary.

185. Cp. P. 33, 'For to [preie] þe prynce þat paradise made.'

188. The line is probably derived from *Habakkuk*, iii. 13, 'per-cussisti caput de domo impii', which is read at Lauds for Good Friday, a part of the office of Tenebrae.

205. **terme of your lifes**: a legal phrase; cp. 'The whiche shoppe I woll that letice my wif have *terme* of here lyf'. Guildhall, *Pleas & Memoranda*, A. 62, f. 3 *r* (1435).

210. **rascaille**. See Introduction, p. xxi.

211–20. During his earlier life Henry had won great renown in the tournament and on the field. Before he was twenty Froissart had praised his knightly skill, and he had distinguished himself in jousts at London. He had been foremost in the victory at Radcot Bridge in 1387, and with Warwick led the army which was gladly admitted by the citizens of London. After 1389 he gradually regained Richard's favour, and won fame in tournaments and crusades. He attended the great jousts at Saint-Inglevert, 1390, where the French agreed that he was the best of the English knights, overshadowing Richard, who was also there. He afterwards joined the expedition of the Teutonic knights into Lithuania, and also went to Jerusalem.

222. Cp. *Piers Plowman*, A. Prol. 62, 'Mony ferlyes han bi-falle in a fewe ȝeres', and l. 1737.

234–5. Mum must be referring to ll. 165–78 or possibly ll. 38–57. He therefore, as well as the clerk of l. 103, has overheard the author's soliloquy. Judging by ll. 241–3, this is Mum's first appearance in the poem.

238. 'Seeing that thy desire (to talk) will set aside thy under-standing.'

240. **knytte þere a knotte**: broke off what I intended to do. Cp. Lansdowne MS. of *Squire's Tale*, l. 670 and following:

> 'And þere I left I þenke aȝeine be-gynne
> Bot I wil here nowe maake a knotte
> To þe time it come next to my lotte.'

See also l. 693.

252. **Thow were bett*er***: it would be better for thee. The original construction was 'thee were better'; the first example in *O.E.D.* of the substitution of the nom. for the dat. is 1430; see under 'be', B. 19.

254. **Oon myle and nomore waye**: i.e. 'oon myle waye and nomore', for only twenty minutes; cp. *Astrolabe*, I, § 16, '5 of these degres maken a myle wey, and 3 mileweie maken an houre.'

256. **Cumpaignye with no contra**: have nothing to do with contradiction.

259-60. These lines represent a traditional formula; cp. *Winner & Waster* (1352-3), 327-8:

> 'Ne es nothir kaysser ne kynge ne knyghte þat the folowes,
> Barone ne bachelere ne beryn that thou loueste',

Piers Plowman, A. x. 133-4:

> 'Kynges and knihtes and alle cunne clerkes,
> Barouns and burgeis and bonde men of tounes',

Siege of Jerusalem (c. 1390-1400), 489-90:

> 'Her nys king noþ*er* knyȝt comen to þ*is* place,
> Barou*n* ne burges ne burne þa*t* me folweþ.'

273. **shame**: for the sake of the metre, this should read 'shamen'.

274. The side-note is attributed in the *Speculum Christiani* (E.E.T.S. 182) to Gregory (see pp. 63, 125, 137, 239). See note to l. 1139.

281. **[and fele]**: MS. y-nowe; gloss 'and feble'; a corruption of 'and fele', cp. l. 1298.

289. *The Distichs of Cato* was a popular medieval school-book. It was a sort of delectus of moral sentences, written in the third century A.D. by Dionysius Cato, and divided into four books with prefaces about the time of Charlemagne. It consists of 144 couplets. The best text is that of Baehrens, *Poetae Latinae Minores*, 1881. The couplet quoted is I. 12 (p. 218, vol. iii).

291. From *Great Cato*, E.E.T.S. 117, p. 565:

> 'Rumores fuge, ne incipias nouus auctor haberi,
> Nam nulli tacuisse nocet, nocet esse locutum.'

293. **abawyd**: amazed, confounded. In Lydgate and Robert of

Brunne it rimes with 'saved'. *O.E.D.* suggests derivation from
O.F. *abavir, developed from O.F. ababir, to astonish. Bense, *Dict.
of Low-Dutch Element in English Vocabulary*, suggests Flemish origin
or influence.

294. **þe double doute**: the very great doubt; cp. I. 57.

304–5. Sidrac refers to a collection of questions and answers com-
posed towards the end of the thirteenth century treating of things in
general. It was called—among other names—the 'Trésor des
Sciences'. Cf. 1212 and p. xxvi.

308. Following the medieval custom, he read to himself aloud;
cp. Rule of St. Benedict, ch. xlviii, 'qui voluerit sibi legere, sic legat
ut alium non inquietet'.

313. **[good]**: omitted in MS., but supplied by P.; cp. III. 223,
'for his good *gouer*naunce'. 'How good behaviour leads to a happy
issue.'

314. See note on III. 159.

318. **he**: the writer of the gloss.

323. The University of Orleans was famous for its Faculty of Law,
which in the fourteenth century was unrivalled in Western Europe.

329. **[dwere]**: MS. dome; cp. Hilton, *Scala Perf.*, II. xi. 'Therefore fallen some in dowte and dwere.'

330. **Sire Grumbald**: the name suggests Grimbart the badger in
Reynard the Fox.

glowed for anger: cp. 'starid for angre', l. 351.

334. **al [þe] bothe**: 'tous les deux'; *O.E.D.* quotes 'all bothe',
from *Chron. Vilod.* 892, *c.* 1420.

337. **[of his make]**: the MS. reading is caught from the line
below.

342. **a subtile shophister**: i.e. Logic.

343. **Sette [þe] soeth-sigger as shorte as he couthe**: cp.
l. 1546. The phrase is instanced in *O.E.D.* for the year 1639, where
it means 'kept short of food', see *set*, vb. 25 b. The more usual
medieval construction is 'set short by', see *Piers Plowman*, B. xii.
124, 'sette schort be here science'.

345. Cf. '*Reply of Friar Daw Topias*', *Pol. Poems* (Rolls), ii. 40,
'chidyng with blasfemie or chyteryng as chowȝes'.

346. Cp. *Troy Book*, 8394 (of the images in the great hall of Ilion),
'*Wi*th gematry Justly aioynet to gedur.'

366–7. Cp. *Piers Plowman*, A. i. 5–6:

'And seide, "sone! slepest thou? Sixt thou this peple
Al hou bisy thei ben a-boute the mase".'

The B-text is the same, and C (MSS. I, B); the others substitute
'Wille' for 'sone'.

368. [letter]: MS. better, A, lettrure; but cp. l. 384.

374. among vs alle: cp. l. 630, 'among alle other'. The metre of both lines would be rectified by reading 'among[es]'.

387–8. With a trick taught by covetousness they overthrow St. Nicholas, i.e. escape from study (St. Nicholas being the patron of scholars), and betake themselves to flattery of their patrons. There is a play of words on 'glose' = gloss, and 'glose' = flattery; cp. ll. 141, 162.

393. felnesse: wisdom, shrewdness. Wiclif uses it to translate *astutia* in *Job* v. 13, *Prov.* i. 4.

398. The friars, according to their rules, went about in couples, see *Piers Plowman*, A. ix. 8, and *Piers Plowmans Crede* 340. In the *Reply of Friar Daw Topias*, *Pol. Poems* (Rolls), ii. p. 101, the Friar justifies the custom by the example of Barnabas and Paul, Paul and Timothy, the two tables of the law, and the two cherubim in the Temple. Jack Upland in his Rejoinder, *ibid.* p. 42, compares the friars to the foxes which Samson bound two and two together, to spoil the corn and vines.

399. the cloistre and þe quyre: the cloister was the general living place, used for exercise and also for ablutions. For a description of a cloister in a house of Dominican friars, with tin conduits and latoun lavers, see *Piers Plowmans Crede*, ll. 191–8. The sense of the line, therefore, appears to be that in all departments of the friars' houses, from the religious to the more secular, Mum was lord.

409–10. According to medieval theory, only the cleric having charge of souls had permission to preach, except by the licence of the bishop. After the rise of Lollardism, this licence would be obtained more easily by the friar than by the secular, who might be suspect of heresy. Hence the Wyclifite tract, 'Of Prelates', complains that friars have leave to preach where true priests cannot obtain it (*Wyclif's English Works*, E.E.T.S. 74, pp. 59, 105–6). In 1401 the Statute *De Heretico Comburendo* again forbade unlicensed preaching, and in 1409 the *Constitutions* of Archbishop Arundel, which had already been promulgated at the Synod of Oxford in 1408, legislated still more strictly in the same direction. On March 10, 1410, Archbishop Arundel issued an order that the four orders of friars should be free to preach in the province of Canterbury (*Cont. Eulog. Hist.* 417, where the expression 'statutum fuit' is used). The present passage probably points to an unsuccessful attempt on the part of the friars to get a similar exemption after the Statute of 1401.

417–20. See Introduction, p. xix. The sense clearly is that friars first gave Lollards their names, and now they must have the same name given them. The quotation from *Little Cato* (*Minor Poems of Vernon MS.*, ed. Horstmann, E.E.T.S. 117, p. 560) is thus translated:

> 'Soffrez en dreit de tei
> Meymes cele ley
> Ke tu as done. . . .
> Such lawe as þou hast brouȝt
> And haunted hast bi-fore,
> þou most hit mekely suffre
> For winnyng or for lore',

and l. 422 emphasizes the same moral. 'Folowid', which generally means 'baptized', must be taken as 'gave as in baptism'. Its identity of form with the verb from OE. 'folgian' confused the scribe, who altered 'names' to 'manieres'. A has corrected both words; unfortunately his first gloss is torn away.

The name of Lollards was first given during the fourteenth century in the Netherlands to some of the various sects such as the Fraticelli who split off from the Franciscans; this may be the meaning of l. 417. More probably it refers to the opposition of the friars to Wyclif's Eucharistic doctrines, which divided Oxford into two hostile parties, 'Lollard' and 'Catholic'. See *Camb. Med. Hist.* vii. 492.

421-2. Cp. the story of Haman in the book of *Esther*, who was hanged on the gallows he had caused to be erected for Mordecai. The line appears to be a proverbial saying, cp. the parallel passage, l. 65-7. It is notable that there is no alliteration.

424. **grey freres**: Franciscans.

426-7. According to their rule, they should have gone barefoot: cp. *Piers Plowmans Crede*, 298-300:

> 'Fraunces bad his breþeren barfote to wenden;
> Nou han þei bucled schon, for bleynynge of her heles,
> And hosen in harde weder y-hamled by þe ancle.'

Skeat explains 'y-hamled' as 'cut short at the ankle, so that people should not easily see that they had hose on'.

430. According to the rule of their founder, Franciscans were to receive no money, either directly or through another person. This was evaded by counting out the money with a stick, see *English Works of Wyclif*, E.E.T.S. 74, p. 49.

435-9. At the Provincial Chapter the province was divided into districts, in each of which one special convent had the right of begging.

442. Cp. *Sir Gawain*, 1525, 'And ȝe þat ar so cortays and coynt of your hetes'.

443. A pear stands for a trifle, cp. P. 73, also 'þe pare of oon pere', l. 522. A knife was a popular present, cp. *Canterbury Tales, Prologue,*

233–4, and apparently it was then, as now, unlucky to give as a present anything with a cutting edge. The friar took care, however, to get a more substantial equivalent; cp. *Song against the Friars* (*Pol. Poems and Songs*, i, Rolls, p. 265):

> ' Ther is no pedler that pak can bere,
> That half so dere can selle his gere,
> Then a frer can do.
> For if he gife a wyfe a knyfe
> that cost bot penys two,
> Worthe ten knyves, so mot I thryfe,
> he wyl have er he go.'

444–5. Cp. *Poem on the Times of Edward II*, Wright, *Pol. Songs*, p. 331:

> ' And 3it there is another ordre, Menour and Jacobin,
> And freres of the Carme, and of Seint Austin,
> That wolde preche more for a busshel of whete,
> Than for to bringe a soule from helle out of the hete ',

and Skelton, *Colin Clout*, ed. Hughes, pp. 124–5:

> ' As many a frere, God wote,
> Preches for his grote,
> Flatterynge for a newe cote
> And for to have his fees;
> Some to gather chese.'

461–2. To know men's purposes, e.g. those of lords and ladies who, &c. Perhaps 'men' is a scribal slip for 'þe'.

471. The quotation is *Prov.* iii. 9.

479. **spicerie**: bribery, cp. ll. 507, 691. *Piers Plowmans Crede*, 301, refers to Franciscans carrying round spices as presents, 'And spicerie sprad in her purse to parten where hem lust.' Skeat quotes Wright, *Pol. Poems*, i. 265, 'And also many a dyuers spyse In bagges about thai bere.' But here apparently the friars are bribed with spices, as in l. 507.

482. The line added by S here and the correction in l. 484 cannot possibly be original. The subject of the sentence is the knight, see l. 486. Overcome by Covetousness, he seeks to gain victories in the law-courts and by 'maintenance' instead of by military service. For the omission of the subject pronoun, cp. I. 95, III. 284; 1452.

483. **while þe crosse walketh**: while money is going. Cp. note to l. 66, and Usk, *Test. Love*, I. vii. 97, 'the valewe of the leste coyned plate that walketh in money'. There is a play of words on the Good Friday ceremony of the Veneration of the Cross; cp. *Piers Plowman*, B. xviii. 428, 'And crepeth to the crosse on knees and kisseth it for

a Iuwel.' Henry VIII's proclamation (26 Feb. 1538-9) allows the ceremony (Wilkins' *Concilia* iii. 842).

489-90. Note the play on the words ' Confessors ' and ' Martyrs '—two of the classes of saints in the Liturgy. See note to l. 830.

490. vij: MS. viij. But seven is the conventional number for such formulae, cp. ll. 683, 796.

496. Armacanes: Richard FitzRalph, Archbishop of Armagh, who preached before the Pope at Avignon against the friars in 1357. We do not find the reference to Cain in his printed works, nor is it at all likely that he is the author of it. It probably originated in the University of Paris.

498. Allusions to the derivation are common in Middle English: as *Piers Plowmans Crede*, l. 486, and *Song against the Friars* (Wright, *Pol. Poems*, i. 266). Wyclif continually alludes to the Friaries as ' Caymes castels', and gives the derivation in *Trialogus*, iv. 33, ' Et in testimonium istorum, quattuor literae hujus nominis *Caim* inchoant hos quattuor ordines, secundum ordinem temporis, quo finguntur a fratribus incepisse, ita quod C Carmelitas, A Augustinenses, J Jacobitas et M Minores significat.'

499. withoute titil: without an abbreviation-mark over the ' y ' for an ' m '; cp. Wyclif, *Matt.* v. 18, ' oon i or titil shal nat passe fro the lawe '. The late Latin ' titulus ' was used in this sense, and may have affected the spelling of ' tituleris ', IV. 57, triflers, tittlers.

500. figures: letters; cp. *Erkenwald*, 53, ' Fulle verray were þe vigures', of the inscription on a tomb. The earliest example of this use in *O.E.D.* is from *Timon of Athens*.

508. Symon-is sermons: see note to IV. 55.

514. Cp. *Sir Gawain*, 97, ' To joyne wyth hym in iustyng.'

519. a ympne: the hymn for the Vespers of All Saints, ' Placare Christi servulis', or 'Christe redemptor omnium', see Daniel's *Thesaurus*, i. 256. The second quotation is *Ps.* lxix. 28 (A.V.) = *Ps.* lxviii. 29 (Vulgate).

527. Cp. l. 138.

535. The gloss here seems to refer to *Piers Plowmans Crede*.

537. abbeys of Augustyn: houses of Austin Canons.

543. do beste: cp. IV. 93, 'and Do-well for-soke', also l. 1258, ' He debateth eche day with Do-welle withynne.'

551-2. Cp. III. 222-3. The same dry humour is visible in l. 599.

555. pluralite: the holding of more than one benefice having a cure of souls ; it had been forbidden by the Constitutions of Archbishop Peckham at the Council of Reading, 1279 (Wilkins, *Concilia*, ii. 33). Those disobeying, unless they had Papal dispensation, incurred excommunication, see *Jacob's Well*, E.E.T.S. 115, p. 18.

560. [c]rac[ch]e : MS racke. The word is used of a horse's manger in *William of Palerne*, l. 3233.

561-2. ne ... Vnethe : 'unethe' is used in ME. both with and without a negative, e.g. Lydgate, *Chron. Troy*, i. 3392, 'Wel onethe he ne my3t endure', and Chaucer, *Book of the Duchess*, 712, 'Unnethe myghte I lenger dwelle.'

566. The offering at Mass was supposed to be divided into three parts ; see note on ll. 657-9.

568. The side-note is from *Matt.* x. 9. The meaning of the reference to Belial is not clear. Perhaps the sense is : 'Having given nothing to the poor, they travel with money in their purses. Hence (though they may be blamed by Christ), they will never be blamed by the devil.' For another reference to the 'bold riding' of cathedral clergy, see l. 1371, and cp. *Piers Plowman*, B. iv. 124, 'Tyl bisschopes baiardes ben beggeres chambres.' Belial became a representative devil in the late Middle Ages owing to the religious romance of Palladinus written in 1382. The infernal powers, considering themselves wronged by the forcible entry of Jesus into Hades, and his removal of certain souls there detained, bring an action before the Almighty for damages and reinstatement. They appoint Belial as their proctor and spokesman. The Almighty, as he is alleged by Jesus to be his father, delegates the hearing of the case to Solomon, the wisest of men, and the hearing of the case proceeds in conformity with all the technicalities of Civil Law.

584. a baron : i e. God, the good Lord who governs all things (l. 591), and is glorified by all the angels (l. 585). The line added after l. 589, which seems to be based on l. 1206, may have been put in to make this clear.

594. Perhaps 'belles' is a scribal error for 'burdes'.

596. During the fourteenth century, fixed seats were introduced into churches, as can be traced in the consequent rise of the pier-bases (see F. Bond, *Gothic Architecture in England*, p. 447). They appear to have been first appropriated to women (see *Piers Plowman*, C. vii. 143-4) :

> 'Among wyues and wodewes ich am ywoned sitte
> Yparroked in puwes.'

In Myrc's *Instructions for Parish Priests* (E.E.T.S. 31, p. 9) the only postures are standing and kneeling, and the former is not approved, except at the Gospel.

597-8. For the construction, cp. *Piers Plowman*, A. iii. 216, 'Prestes that precheth the peple to goode'.

600. The priest asks for the lesser tithe, that on the increase of

small crops.   The greater tithe, that of the main produce, was evidently alienated to a monastery.

600–12.   This speech turns from reported to direct speech.   On the eagerness of the secular clergy to demand their tithes, see Owst, *Preaching in Medieval England*, p. 46.   He quotes from the *Dispute between a Good Man and the Devil* (*Minor Poems of the Vernon MS.*, p. 348):

> 'But euer a-mong al oþur nede
> His oune erende wol he bede,
> Þat þei brynge heore offrynges
> To chirche, and heore typinges.
> Wel þou wost þat þis is soþ:
> Al for his owne gode he hit doþ;
> Kepeþ he nouȝt of heore comynge,
> But ȝif þei wole him eni good bringe.'

It is only fair to say that this is the devil's point of view.   Myrc in his *Instructions to Parish Priests*, ll. 356–9, says with humorous moderation:

> 'I holde hyt but an ydul þynge
> To speke myche of teythynge,
> For þaȝ a preste be but a fonne,
> Aske hys teyþynge welle he conne.'

Jacob's Well, E.E.T.S. 115, pp. 37–47, devotes two chapters to the regulations of tithe-paying.

604.   Note: cp. *Piers Plowman*, C. xiii. 190, 'As lynne-seed and lik-seed.'

605.   **Of chibollz and of chiries**: cp. *Piers Plowman*, A. vii. 281, 'Chibolles, cheef mete, and ripe chiries monye.'

617.   **But sorowe on þe sillable he shewed of þat matiere**: he did not utter a single syllable; cp. l. 829, and *Poem on the Times of Edward II* (*Pol. Songs*), Camden Society, 178, 'Sorwe on that o frere that kepeth come thare', where the meaning is that not a single friar comes.   Otherwise in ME. the expression is an imprecation; the first example quoted by *O.E.D.* as a negative use is in 1573.

623.   **sunnedayes and solempne festes**: i.e. on days when sermons were preached.

628.   Cp. *Piers Plowman*, C. ii. 123, 'Ac of this matere no more meuen ich nelle', *Troy Book*, 7206, 'But of þat mater was meuit no more at þat tyme; also *Piers Plowman*, A. ix. 113, 'I durste meue no mateere.'

630.   **among**: cp. note to l. 374.

637. **laudate**: the first of the seven Hours was Lauds, which always contained *Pss.* cxlviii–cl (Vulgate), beginning with 'Laudate'. The 'laudate' appears to be the clerk who knows no more than the first of these Hours, cp. l. 1359.

645. **seruice of souuerayns**: cp. *Piers Plowman*, B. Prol. 95-6:

'And some seruen as seruauntz lordes and ladyes,
And in stede of stuwardes sytten and demen.'

647. **þaire double dees**: daises above the ordinary height.

þaire deupe hoodes: Jack Upland rebukes the friars for their great hoods; Friar Daw Topias replies:

' My greet hood behynde shapun as a sheeld,
Suffraunce in adversitee sothely it scheweth,
Herbi to reseyve repreef for oure Goddis sake
Or ellis bisynesse of oure feith it may wel bitokene.'

(*Pol. Poems*, ii, Rolls, pp. 19, 69-70). Here, however, the parish clergy are under discussion.

649. See note on l. 25.

655. Cp. *Piers Plowman*, A. viii. 94, 'In two lynes hit lay, and not a lettre more'; so C; B, 'nouȝt a leef more'.

657-9. The tithes and offerings were supposed to be divided into three parts, for the support of the parish priest, the upkeep of the fabric, and the relief of the poor.

God-is men: i.e. the poor. Cp. ll. 541, 545; also *Piers Plowman*, B. iii. 71:

'[leueth] to greden after goddis men whan ȝe delen doles . . .
nesciat sinistra quid faciat dextra.'

Skeat takes it to refer to the friars, but more probably it means the poor, and the sense of the passage is that lords are not to be ostentatious in almsgiving. Cp. 'goddes gest', *Plowman's Tale*, 747.

663-4. The text meant is not obvious; it might be *Isa.* ii. 7, 'Their land also is full of silver and gold, neither is there any end of their treasures.' Since the scribe is very careful not to double consonants unnecessarily (see Introduction, p. xxxiii), **reuylle** probably = revelry, luxurious living; cp. *Sir Gawain*, 538, ' With much reuel and ryche of þe Rounde Table.'

666. **þe two dooles**: i.e. the two other shares, besides their own.

687. **mete**: dinner, cp. Wyclif, *Luke* xiv. 12, 'a mete ether souper' = 'prandium aut cœnam'.

692. 'Till he knows which way desire will tend,' i.e. which is going to be the popular side. A possible emendation would be to read 'þe doo wil drawe', the metaphor being taken from deer-hunting, cp. l. 1144, 'Whenne þay witen wel y-now where þe hare walketh.' Or the

'doo' might be (in Fifeshire) the wooden ball used in the game of shinty (Jamieson). The line would then mean, 'till he knows which way the cat will jump', a metaphor presumably taken from the game of tip-cat.

693. See note to l. 240.

694. 'And gets for himself a great reward, which may be accounted among the best.'

703. **þe plantz of pees**: cp. *Piers Plowman*, A. i. 136–7, 'loue is . . . þe playnt of pees', where MSS. TUHH₂ have 'pla(u)nte', B, 'plente', C, 'plonte'.

707–8. According to the Constitutions of Clarendon, § xi, the bishops could not, as ecclesiastics, take any part in a sentence of death. See Anson, *Law and Custom of the Constitution*, i. 238.

713. The side-note is from *Matt.* v. 16.

720. **a-tw[art]**: a variant of 'athwart', no form of which is recorded in *O.E.D.* until Blind Harry's *Wallace*, 1470. In *Ricart's Kalendar*, 1479, p. 10, we have 'a-twhert the lande'. The figurative use is not recorded till 1594.

727–42. See Introduction, p. xxiv.

733. **by cours of a-bouue**; by the movement of the sky, clouds. This use seems unnatural; and perhaps 'a-bouue' was caught by the scribe from l. 738, and replaces some noun.

745. **qui tacet consentire videtur**: cp. Epistle of Gregory to Syagrius, Migne, Lib. ix, Indict. ii, Epist. cxiii, 'Nam consentire videtur erranti, qui corrigenda ut resecari debeant, non concurrit' (*Grat. dist.* 83, c. 5). The text in Gratian is: 'qui non occurrit, consentit erranti'.

751–7. In trials for felony the prisoner was first asked if he were guilty or not. If he pleaded 'Not guilty' he was asked how he would be tried, to which he must answer, 'By God and my country'. Till he answered he could not be tried. If he refused to answer he was said to 'stand mute', and a jury had to decide whether this was 'of malice' or 'by the visitation of God' (i.e. if he was deaf or dumb). If the latter, the trial proceeded; if the former, he was imprisoned until he could be compelled to plead or died. In the third year of Edward I, the First Statute of Westminster enacted that 'les felons escries, et queux sont appertment de male fame, et ne se voilent mettre en enqueste des felonies que l'on mette sur eux devant justices à le suit de roy, soyent mises en la prison fort et dure, come ceux queux refusent estre al comen ley de la terre'. In the thirty-first year of Edward III, a certain Cecilia de Rygeway, refusing to plead to the murder of her husband, was imprisoned without food for forty days, and then pardoned. In the eighth year of Henry IV, two thieves who remained mute were condemned to be imprisoned and pressed down with weights and fed on bread and water on alternate days until they died. (See Year Books of Henry IV ; also Barrington, *Observations on the Statutes*, ch. xii ; Sir J. Stephen, *History of the Criminal Law of England*, i. 297–30 ; Pollock and Maitland, *History of English Law*, ii. 651–2.)

761–2. 'Which (quarrels) the Church might easily have prevented by its action, if it had devised wise counsel against the occasion.'

763. 'Cui caput infirmum cetera membra dolent', *Song on the Corruptions of the Time* (reign of Henry III), *Pol. Songs* (Camden Soc.), p. 31, where the metre, however, requires a hexameter. Cp. *Invectio contra Avaritiam* (attributed to Walter Mapes), ibid., p. 15, 'Membra dolent singula capitis dolore'; also Gower, *In Praise of Peace*, 260, 'Of that the heed is syk, the limmes aken', belonging to the first year of Henry IV; *O Deus Immense*, 85, 'Quo caput infirmum, nichil est de corpore firmum' (ed. Macaulay, iv. 364).

779. Apparently the author has forgotten that it is Mum who is speaking.

800. A line has been omitted, to the effect of: 'Thanne þe sothesiggere in seuene score winter', l. 683, or 'Thenne þe sothe-sigger, asay who-so wol', l. 850.

829. **shyne**: glimpse; cp. l. 1384. The only other instance recorded seems to be J. Bell, *Haddon's Answ. Osor.*, 483 *b* (1581), 'You may putt all your winninges in your eyes, and see never a shine the lesse.'

830. Cp. *Piers Plowman*, B. xii. 198–205 (of the penitent thief):
'Riȝt as sum man ȝeue me mete, and sette me amydde the flore,
Ich haue mete more than ynough, ac nouȝt so moche worship
As tho that seten atte syde-table or with the souereignes of the halle,
But sitte as a begger bordelees bi my-self on the grounde,
So it fareth bi that feloun that a Gode Fryday was saued ;
He sit neither with seynt Iohan, Symonde ne Iude,
Ne wyth maydenes ne with martires, confessoures ne wydwes,
But by hym-self as a soleyne and serued on the erthe.'
In such a way did the 'tall clownish younge man' seat himself on the floor at the Faerie Queene's annual feast, 'unfitte through his rusticity for a better place'.

839. **hath y-drunke dum-seede**: cp. Skelton's phrase 'to eat sauce', 'She asked yf ever I dranke of saucys cuppe' (*Bowge of Court*, 73). The phrase suggests an imitation of the Shakespearian 'We have the receipt of fern-seed, we walk invisible', *1 Hen. IV*, II. i. 96, but this is not found before Shakespeare.

849. The side-note is from *Matt*. v. 10.

862. **knightes courtz**: see Cowell's *Interpreter*, 1701. '*Knighten-Court*, Is a Court-Baron or Honor-Court, held twice a year under the

Bishop of *Hereford* at his Palace there; wherein those who are Lords of Mannors, and their Tenants holding by *Knights Service*, of the Honor of that Bishoprick, are Suiters.'

874–5. In *Piers Plowman*, A. viii. 135 ff. and B and C, the opinions of Daniel and Cato are similarly contrasted. The advice of Cato is 'Somnia ne cures', II. 31, ed. Baehrens.

876. Cp. *Piers Plowman*, A. Prol. 12, 'That I was in a wildernesse, wuste I neuer where', similarly B, but there is no wilderness in the C text.

885 ff. The description of a far-spreading prospect is not common in Middle English poetry (see Introduction, p. xvii). We may compare *In Memoriam*, xi (though this is of Lincolnshire):

> ' yon great plain
> That sweeps with all its autumn bowers
> And crowded farms and lessening towers,
> To mingle with the bounding main.'

The prospect is a typical view of the West Country; cp. William of Malmesbury's enthusiastic description of Gloucestershire in *De Gestis Pontificum*, iv (Migne, clxxix, 1595): 'Terra omnis frugum opima, fructuum ferax hic et sola naturæ gratia, illic culturæ solertia, ut quamvis tædiosum per socordiam provocet ad laboris illecebram: ubi centuplicato fenore responsura sit copia, cernas tramites publicos vestitos pomiferis arboribus non insitiva manus industria, sed ipsius solius humi natura. Ipsa se terra sponte subrigit in fructus eosque sapore et specie cæteris plurimum præstantes, quorum plures ante annum marcescere nesciunt, ut omnes usque ad novos successores præstent officium. Regio plus quam aliæ Angliæ provinciæ vinearum frequentia densior, proventu uberior, sapore jucundior. Vina enim ipsa bibentium ora triste non torquent acredine, quippe quæ parum debeant Gallicis dulcedine, villæ innumerabiles, abbatiæ præstantes, vici frequentes, quibus omnibus accedit ad gloriam, fluvius Sabrina, quo nullus in hac terra alveo latior, gurgite rapacior, arte piscosior.'

The tenor of this is very like our poet's picture; as we might expect, however, the later writer has no monasteries in his panorama.

888. þe same yere: 'that very year'. The time was just after hay-harvest, which took place at the end of June; see Fitzherbert's *Book of Husbandry*, English Dialect Society, p. 32.

922. prime-saute: vigorous, spirited; apparently from the French 'de primsaut, de prinsaut', at a bound, suddenly. The *Dictionnaire de l'Académie française* has ' Esprit prime-sautier, pour dire, Un esprit qui saisit et rend ses idées avec promptitude, sans passer par les idées intermédiaires '. Cp. 'pasture prikkyth', III. 14.

926. **With rayndeer and roobuo** : these animals are constant companions in the Middle English alliterative landscape ; cp. *Morte Arthure*, 922, 'The roo and þe rayne-dere reklesse thare ronnene.' In Lydgate's *Reason & Sensuality*, 3728, Adonis has the permission of Venus to hunt 'reyndere and the dredful roo'.

939. **[cheerly]** : MS. 'cleerly'; cp. l. 1305, where the same scribal error is corrected by A, cp. also III. 203. The change makes the alliteration regular.

968. See FitzHerbert's *Book of Husbandry*, ed. Skeat, 1882, p. 76, 'and also there is a bee called a drone, and she is greatter than an other bee, and they wyll eate the honny and gather nothynge : and therfore they wolde be kylde.' In FitzHerbert's idiom this means 'should be killed' (see App. II, p. 81).

985. **Side-note.** In the *Speculum Christiani*, E.E.T.S. 182, p. 65, these words are attributed to 'the Apostle'. See 2 *Thess.* iii. 10, 'siquis non vult operari nec manducet'. This is quoted by St. Bernard in *Sermon* LV, *De sex hydriis spiritualibus*, Migne, vol. 183, § 1188, col. 679.

989. **The bee in his bisynes** : 'a Besynes of flyes' is found in a list of company terms in Lydgate's *Horse, Sheep and Goose*.

1010. **Thayr dwellings been dyuyded** : this translates 'eorum enim officia sunt diuisa', see p. 79, l. 29. Trevisa renders it 'for here office ben diu*er*se'. The first example of the English word 'offices' meaning rooms in *O.E.D.* is from Hall's *Chronicle*, 1548. But this use was common in medieval Latin ; see Du Cange.

1016. See note on l. 109.

1017. **Wastours þat wyrchen not** : cp. *Piers Plowman*, A. vii. 290, 'And tho nolde the wastor worche, but wandren aboute.'

1028. **Bartholomew** : see p. xxv.

1030. Cp. *Alex. Fragment A*, 601, 'Þe ludene of þat language lelli þei knowe', they know the language of birds.

1037. The glosses 'consente' and 'cordeth' are perhaps better, but the reading of the text is possible.

1048. The side-note is from *Phil.* iii. 19.

1051. **þe bee-is bisynes** : see note on l. 989.

1054. Bartholomaeus Anglicus is not called Bartholomew the Bestiary in any other work.

1073. The side-note is from. Claudian, *In Eutropium*, i. 181, 'Asperius nihil est humili, cum surgit in altum.'

1087. **wise tale** : for the satirical expression cp. *Piers Plowman*, A. Prol. 48, 'with mony wyse tales'.

1093. He had spent seven years in listening to sermons ; cp. l. 623.

1117. **more and moulde** : the latter word might mean mould, pattern, or mould, earth from which the 'more' grew; but probably the expression = root and crown, cp. *Troilus*, v. 25–6:

> 'As she that was the sothfast crop and more
> Of al his lust or joyes her-bifore.'

1118 ff. None of Henry's early parliaments seem to have been characterized by any slowness of the Commons to speak of grievances. The most peaceful was, perhaps, that held at Gloucester in October 1407, after which no parliament met till that of January 1410, which was mostly concerned with attempts at disendowment of the Church.

1139. Side-note. 'Qui ergo potest contradicere et non contradicit, peccat & videtur fautor esse, secundum illud Gregorii, "Non caret scrupulo societatis occultæ, qui manifesto facinori desinit obviare"', from Matthew Paris's account of the last words of Bishop Grosseteste, *Historia Anglorum*, under year 1253. Not in the common text of Sidrac.

1146. Side-note: cp. *Opuscula quædam R. Grossetest, Epist.* 51 (*Fasciculus Rerum Expetendarum & Fugiendarum*, E. Brown, 1690, ii. 340), 'quem etiam à veritate judicii non flectant amor aut odium, timor aut spes, preces aut pretium'.

1147. sowe siluer seede, to bribe with silver. The expression is not quoted in *O.E.D.*

solue: to *sol-fa* is to practise singing the scale of notes. See a poem on Learning to Sing, pr. in *Reliq. Antiq.* i. 292, 'I *solfe* and singge after', &c.; and see *solfa* in the Index to Dyce's edition of Skelton (Skeat's note to *Piers Plowman*, C. viii. 31, 'ʒut can ich nother solfye ne synge').

1154. caste of guile: cp. l. 12.

1166. The side-note appears to be a reference to the Parable of the Tares, *Matt.* xiii. 24–30, 36–43, especially 38–9. Can the last three words be a corruption of 'in agro est diabolus'?

1187. for fees and robes: [for] inserted before 'robes' would rectify the metre.

1206. See note to l. 584.

1212. Cp. ll. 304–5, also *Tale of Beryn*, E.E.T.S., E.S. 105, l. 2666, 'Seneca & Sydrak & Salamonys sawis.'

1221. kempe: in both Old and Middle English this regularly means a fighting man, a champion. But in the *Siege of Jerusalem*, 1328, it is used of Pilate's jailer.

1225. Cp. *Prov.* xiv. 33. 'In corde prudentis requiescit sapientia'; and *Piers Plowman*, B. v. 615, 'Thow shalt see in thi-selue Treuthe sitte in thine herte.' The truth-teller is here identified with the eternal Veritas. God gave Him possession of Paradise in the person of Adam and all his issue. Through the Holy Spirit, God inspires

Adam (representing mankind) to possess Paradise and afterwards Heaven, to serve God in truth, and to give reasonable obedience to all rulers.

1236. The side-note, with slight differences, comes from *John* x. 1.

1247. Cp. III. 352.

1250. **but souuraynete hit helpe**: unless our position of authority requires us to be dictatorial. If this is the correct meaning, it is a very early use of 'help' = 'cause to be otherwise'. The first in *O.E.D.* is 1589, 'But this last inconvenience may be holpen.' The natural verb to use in ME. would be 'make', cp. *Piers Plowman*, C. xi. 157, 'And semblable in soule to god, bote yf synne hit make.'

1251. Cp. l. 1633.

1255. **Antecrist-is angel**: this appears to be the only example in ME. of 'angel' being used of any messenger not sent from God. The whole passage is suggestive of the description in *Piers Plowman*, B. xx of Antichrist besieging Holy Church. Here it is the heart of man (cp. l. 1224) which is besieged.

1257. Cp. *John* x. 1, 'He that entereth not by the door into the sheepfold, but climbeth up some other way, the same is a thief and a robber.' See side-note to l. 1236.

1262. **dore-barre**: a convenient weapon of defence in old times, cp. *Sir Beues*, E.E.T.S., E.S. 46, p. 88 :

> ' The dore barre he toke yn honde
> And slewe all þat he þere fonde,'

and *Gammer Gurton*, V. ii. 99, 'Onles thy head and my doore-bar kyste.' Under the name of door-tree, it was used by Havelok :

> ' Hauelok lifte up þe dore-tre
> And at a dint he slow hem þre' (ll. 1806–7).

1265. **hym**: i.e. the tenant, the soul of man.

1272. **forto**: see note on ll. 87–9.

1279. At the beginning of the poem, in P. 38, the author states his object in the same words.

1285. **allone hit begynne**: i.e. read it before any one else can.

1289. **And woke of my wynke**: cp. *Piers Plowman*, A. v. 3. ' Thenne wakede I of my wink' (MSS. T.U.H, wynkyng; so B, not in C).

1296. **plaisant to my pay**: cp. the beginning of *Pearl*:

> ' Perle plesaunte to prynces paye.'

1302. **atte long goyng**: in the long run ; cp. l. 70, and also cp. III. 136, which both Skeat and *O.E.D.* take to mean 'at death', which makes no sense here.   But the more general meaning covers all three instances.

1304.   The last word should probably be 'dedes'.

1311 ff.   *Piers Plowman*, A. viii. 137–51, similarly instances Daniel and Joseph ; cf. note to ll. 874–5.

1315.   **elleuen sterres** : so *Genesis* xxxvii. 9 and *Piers Plowman*. The gloss 'the seuene sterres' can scarcely be right, as the sun and moon should be included among them.   It is just possible that the 'seven stars' may mean the Great Bear, as in *Book of the Duchess*, 823–4, which says that the sun is fairer

> 'Than any othere planete in heven,
> The mone, or the sterres seven '.

1330.   'To those who for a long time endured famine.'

1338.   **Thenne softe I þe soores** : cp. *St. Marherete*, 14/2, 'Lauerd ... softe me mi sar', *Siege of Jerusalem*, 87, 'To softe þe grete sore þat sitteþ on my cheke.'

1345.   **bokes vnbredid in balade-wise made** : cp. *Pol. Songs* (Camden Soc.), p. 156 (of the lawyers in the Consistory Court) :

> 'Heore boc ase un-bredes (r.w. bi-ledes, redes, gredes)
> Heo wendeth bokes un-brad ' (r.w. a-mad, had).

The metre and sense of the first line are improved by reading 'heore bokes heo un-bredes'.   The word may mean 'spread out, opened', from OE. *unbrǣdan ; cp. OE. unlīesan, ME. unleesen, to unloose. The p.p. 'un-brad' makes it unlikely that the word could be from the ME. brēden, to twist, from OE. bregdan, brēdan, and could mean that the leathern thong which tied the book up was unfastened.   Cp. 'bokis y-bounde', III. 296.

1350–1.   Cp. *Canterbury Tales, Prologue* 653–7 :

> 'And if he foond owher a good felawe,
> He wolde techen him to have noon awe,
> In swich caas, of the Ercedekenes curs,
> But-if a mannes soule were in his purs ;
> For in his purs he sholde y-punysshed be.'

1353–63.   This section refers to the Archdeacon's visitation.

1354–6.   The errors of parish priests are ignored (because of their bribery) when they should be punished, and no fault of theirs is amended, but they live in London, &c.

lorden : weak genitive plural.   Final -e (OE. -ena) is required for the metre.

1357.   **[kitte]** : so A ; MS. light ; cp. *Piers Plowman*, C. viii. 304, Ich may nat come for a Kytte, so hue cleueth on me.'

1359.   **laudate** : see note to l. 637.

1360. **Pernelle**: a stock name for a woman of light character and showy dress; cp. *Piers Plowman*, A. v. 26–7, 45–9, and especially 163, 'Sire Pers of Pridye and Pernel of Flaundres', where she is evidently the parish priest's mistress. Cp. III. 156 and note on the passage.

1364–9. A section dealing with religious houses which devote the patrimony of the poor to the expenses of lawsuits, etc.

1367. **To maynteyne þayre manhode**: cp. *Piers Plowman*, A. iii. 177–8:

'For ȝit I may as I mihte menske the with ȝiftes
And meyntene thi monhede more then thou knowest.'

Cp. l. 1666.

1369. Cp. *Piers Plowman*, A. Prol. 81, 'That heore parisch hath ben pore seththe the pestilence tyme.' This is the complaint of the parish clergy, but the monasteries were equally affected; see Coulton, *Five Centuries of Religion*, i. 420.

1370–83. A section dealing with prelates and prebendaries who neglect their duties and lead worldly lives at the expense of the poor of their flocks.

1371. Cp. l. 568.

1372. **Poperyng**: so D; MS. properyng. Cp. *Piers Plowman*, A. xi. 210: 'Poperith on a palfrey to toune and to toune', B, 'A priker on a palfray', C, 'And priked a-boute on palfrais.'

1374–7. 'The higher clergy vie with the common people in immorality, as we see by their deeds. They justify themselves by arguments, declaring, in their own support, that all are the children of Adam, as is certain.'

The undoubtedly orthodox theory that all the sons of Adam are equal could be pressed to give awkward results. Dr. Owst (*Literature and Pulpit in Medieval England*, pp. 290 ff.) shows how in the fourteenth century it inspired communistic agitators. Here, apparently, it furnishes an excuse for the clergy whose morals were no better than those of the laity. Perhaps 'seluen' is lost from the end of l. 1376.

1381. The side-note is from *Jer.* xxiii. 1.

1383–4. Here two folios seem to have been lost. Besides the attack on women, of which we have the last four lines, there was probably one on friars. Judging by the author's feelings towards these latter as expressed in ll. 392–535, this may well have filled up the missing 184 ll.

1386. Cp. *Prov.* xiv. 1, 'Sapiens mulier aedificat domum suam; insipiens exstructam quoque manibus destruet.'

1388–1488. A section dealing with the spreaders of rumours, including the story of Jenghis Khan.

1392. ' þay' must be understood before 'tournen'.

1404. Perhaps a reference to the stories of Richard spread by the friars. See Introduction (p. xix).

1404. Side note. Cato Distichs I. 12.

1407. Cp. I. 109.

1413–56. For the story of Jenghiz Khan, see Appendix II, p. 82, and Introduction, p. xxiii.

1413. 'If such a lot were appointed (to them) and under similar circumstances.'

1419. **disware of þaire lives**: bewildered concerning their hope of life; cp. *Guy of Warwick* (A), 6003, 'A kniȝt icham deswarre (r.w. charite)'. If we read '[in] disware', we might connect the word with ME. 'without diswere, disware', 'without a doubt', which comes from ME. 'were', doubt.

1421. Side-note from *Luke* xi. 17.

1425. **[in vision]**: so N; MS. by nightes; cp. *Mandeville's Travels*, E.E.T.S. 153, p. 147.

1437. **sese [hym] in [hire lande]**: MS. sese þaym in his handes. N glosses 'þaym in his' by 'hym in hire', thus following a MS. which retained 'hire' for 'their', as does R. Cf. Saisin, to put a man in possession of his estate.

1450. **He forgafe þaym þaire graunt**: this is not according to Mandeville's story.

1452. 'þay' must be understood before 'wroughte'.

1456. Cp. *Piers Plowman*, A. iii. 201, 'That is the riccheste reame that reyn ouer houeth', also in B, but omitted in C.

1457. Side-note from *Ps.* cxxxii. 1 (Vulgate).

1465–8. See Introduction, p. xxiv.

1470. **þe [tayl] of þaire talking**: MS. tale. Cp. 'the taille of the tixte', *Piers Plowman*, B. iii. 347 (not in A, omitted in C).

1472. Cp. 'Cui caput infirmum cetera membra dolent', note on l. 763.

1473–4. A common medieval and Tudor proverb; cp. the collection of proverbs in E.E.T.S., E.S. 101, p. 132:

> 'He that heweth to hye, þe chippis wil fall in his ye
> Qui nimis alte secant, hos quisquile cito cecant.'

The nearest parallel to our version is in Robert of Brunne's translation of Langtoft's Chronicle, ed. Hearne, p. 91:

> 'Þat hewis ouer his heued, þe chip falles in his ine.'

1489-97. A section dealing with squires (or jurors) who give false verdicts against poor men.

1498-1563. A section against wasting one's substance by going to law.

1498. of high wil : of great purport.

1511. Side-note from *Great Cato, Minor Poems of Vernon MS.,* E.E.T.S. 98, 117, p. 573. Distichs I. 36, ed. cit.

1529. brenne watiers : this looks like an early version of the late eighteenth-century 'set the Thames on fire'. In 1787 Peter Pindar has 'Whose modest wisdom . . . never aims to . . . burn the Thames' (*Sir J. Banks & Emp. of Mor.*, Proëmium).

1531. blowe as a bore : cp. *Avowynge of King Arther*, xv :
> 'Alle wrothe wex that sqwyne,
> Blu, and brayd vppe his bryne.'

1534. in [l]ande : although the emendation spoils the alliteration, 'there seems no reasonable sense to be attached to the MS. reading 'in hande', unless it could be taken as 'in person'. In both parts of the poem there are several lines of the type *aa xx*, see p. xlii.

1544. 'If he were slow to prosecute, though eager for his object.'

1552. cleere in þe winde : clear in the direction it is going to take ; cp. the proverb 'to know which way the wind blows'. Possibly it might be taken as 'clearly to the windward', as in hunting ; cp. l. 1095, 'Cleere to my knowing'.

1557-8. 'If you stop before you are defeated, then the report will be spread concerning you that, unless your story is a good one, you will refuse to go to law.'

1565-85. A section against maintenance and riotous interference with justice.

1565. raggeman rolle : see *O.E.D.* under 'Ragman' and 'Ragman('s) Roll'. It is so called from the ragged fringe of seals at the foot. 'Rageman' first appears in 1276 as the name of a statute of 4 Edward I ; by 1290 it has given its name to a game, which in 1400 is called 'Ragmane roelle'. The present seems to be the first example of 'Ragman roll' for a rolled-up document.

Ragenelle : an inferior devil. In *Chester Plays*, xxiii. 655, Antichrist calls for help on Satan, Lucifer, Beelzebub, and Ragnell, 'Ragnell, Ragnell, thou art my deere.' In the *Digby Mary Magdalene*, ll. 1200-1,
> 'ragnell *and* roffyn *and* other In þe wavys
> gravntt yow *grace* to dye on þe galows',

he seems to be connected with the sea. Hence, perhaps, his invocation by the sailor in Jonah's ship in *Patience*, 188 :
> 'þer Ragnel *in* his rakentes hy*m* rere of his dremes.'

In his first edition of this poem, Sir I. Gollancz advanced the view that the name stood for Raguel, who was the angel of chastisement in the apocryphal *Enoch*. In the second edition he alluded to this identification as a possible one. Although in most MSS. of the period *n* and *u* are indistinguishable, the metre of the lines quoted, and the spelling in our text, point to 'Ragnel' as the correct form.

1568. **hockerope**: Hock-tide is the Monday and Tuesday following the second Sunday after Easter. 'On Hock-Monday, the women "hocked" the men ; that is to say, they went abroad with ropes, caught and bound any man they came across, and exacted a forfeit. On Hock-Tuesday, the men retaliated in similar fashion upon the women. Bishop Carpenter of Worcester forbade this practice in his diocese in 1450.' (Sir E. K. Chambers, *The Mediaeval Stage*, i. 155, q.v. for further descriptions of Hock-tide customs.) The description here, however, more resembles a tug-of-war.

1577. Cp. *Piers Plowman*, A. iii. 161, 'For the pore may haue no pouwer to playne, thauȝ hem smerte' (of bribery in the law-courts).

1582. **goky**: cp. the only other recorded example of the word, *Piers Plowman*, B. xi. 296–301 :

> 'A chartre is chalengeable byfor a chief iustice,
> If false Latyne be in the lettre, the lawe it inpugneth,
> Or peynted parenterlinarie or parceles ouer-skipped ;
> The gome that gloseth so chartres for a goky is holden.
> So is it a goky, by god, that in his gospel faileth,
> Or in masse or in matynes maketh any defaute.'

Here the meaning is evidently 'fool, ignorant person'; in our poem it appears to mean a poor person who would not have a legal education. It is probably connected with ON. gaukr, cuckoo ; see *O.E.D.* under 'gowk', where the meaning 'fool' is instanced first in 1605 ; see also 'gawky', of similar meaning and unknown origin, first appearing as a noun in 1724, which may have affected the ending.

1585. Side-note from *Ps.* xiv. 5 (Vulgate) with 'accepit' for 'accipies'.

1586–1625. A section on the woes of a poor defendant in a suit brought by a rich man.

1586. **forelle**: sheepskin parchment covering for a book ; cp. Horman, *Vulgaria*, 84 *b*, 'I hadde leuer haue my boke sowed in a forel : than bounde in bourdis'; *Piers Plowman*, C. xvi. 103, 'What he fond in a forel of a freres lyuynge' (B, 'freyel', evidently corrupted from 'forel').

1623. Foot-note. The passage is from Innocent, *De Contemptu Mundi*, Bk. iii, ch. 15. See Skeat's note on *Piers Plowman*, C. v.

140, in E.E.T.S. 67, p. 83. The Gospel text referred to may be *Matt.* xvi. 27, 'and then he shall reward every man according to his works', or the description of the Judgement in *Matt.* xxv. 31-46.

1626-82. A section dealing with encroachments on the king's revenues required for good government.

1627. **lickyng of þe lordship þat to þe coroune longeth**: see Introduction, p. xx.

1633. Cp. l. 1251.

1640. **þolde and þe newe**: the regular revenues of the Crown, and the taxes and subsidies voted by Parliament.

1646. **as dede as a dore nayle**: cp. *Piers Plowman*, A. i. 161. ' And dede as a dore-nayl, but the deede folowe ' (so C ; B, dore-tre),

1649. **lordz y-lettred of oone lawe and oþer**: i.e. bishops ; cp. *Piers Plowman*, A. viii. 13-14 :

> ' Busschops that blessen and bothe the lawes cunnen,
> Loketh on that on lawe and lereth men that other.'

B :   ' Bisshopes yblessed, ȝif thei ben as thei shulden,
>   Legistres of bothe the lawes, the lewed there-with to preche ' ;

C substitutes for the second line :

> ' Leel and ful of loue, and no lord dreden.'

The two laws are the Canon and Civil Law ; cp. ' doctor utriusque juris '.

1650. Cp. l. 1.

1656. **þees fourty wintre**: it was after the Treaty of Bretigny, in 1360, that Edward III began to fall under the influence of favourites.

1666. **To maynteyne his manhoode**: see note to l. 1367.

1667. See Introduction, p. xxi.

1670. ' To you who owe money it would then be time to pay up ' ; cp. *New Test.* (Paues), *Rom.* xiii. 7, ' ȝelde ȝe to alle men ȝoure dettes : to hym þat ȝe schuleþ trybut, trybut.' Perhaps we might translate : To those of you who must, it would then be the time to pay silver ; cp. l. 1699.

1673. **copes**: the cope or long cloak was the dress peculiar to clerics ; cp. *Piers Plowman*, C. x. 209-11 (of run-away workmen),

> ' For-thi lefte thei here laboure, these lewede knaues,
> And clothed hem in copes, clerkus as hit were,
> Other on of som ordre, othere elles a prophete ',

and C. vi. 41, where Will speaks of ' thes longe clothes ' which he wore as a secular in minor orders. In B. vi. 191, the hermits cut their copes short that they might dig for Piers, and in A. iii. 138, Mede gives a cope to the bishop's commissary. In practice, however, it was not rigidly adhered to by the seculars, cp. l. 643-4, and Myrc's *Instructions to Parish Priests* (E.E.T.S. 31), ll. 43-4, 47-8:

> ' Cuttede clothes and pykede schone.
> Thy gode fame þey wole for-done . . .
> In honest clothes thow moste gon,
> Baselarde ny bawdryke were þow non.'

1683–96. A section dealing with rich wrong-doers who found hospitals for the poor by will after their death.

1683–7. We may compare *Piers Plowman*, A. viii. 20 ff. Merchants have not the full benefit of Piers's Indulgence because of the dishonesty of their commercial methods. But Heavenly Truth directs them to lay out their ill-gotten gains in building hospitals and in doing other pious works, in order that St. Michael may escort them safely to heaven.

1697–1722. A section dealing with the way wills are frustrated by the executors.

1699. Wills were proved in the bishop's registry and validated by the seal of office—that of the registry. When the fees are received the clerks throw the will into a chest and do not let it be copied (of course for a bribe). Even if a whole fifteenth is bequeathed, one receipt is given, and the executors are not supervised and do not distribute the property in their hands.

1703. An alliterative rendering of a common proverb ; cp. *Troylus*, iii. 764, ' It n'is not good a sleping hound to wake '.

Warrok : cp. *Prologue to the Tale of Beryn*, 640, ' The warrok was a-wakid ', where it is a savage dog, restrained by a clog round its neck. This suggests derivation from OF. waroquier, to girth a horse, or bind a person (see note, E.E.T.S., E.S. 105, p. 184) ; cp. *York Plays*, xxx. 525, ' That warlowe ye warrok and wraste.'

1704. A receipt shall be given to the executors, as if they had distributed the dole which they keep in their own possession. This seems to have been a common failing of medieval executors : see a Latin poem by Gower, vol. iv, p. 368, of Macaulay's edition. The *South English Legendary*, p. 430, has a story of an executor who neglected his duties to the soul of his dead cousin. The cousin incurred seven days of purgatory, and the executor went to hell. In later times we have Barclay's Fifth Eclogue, 773-6:

> ' And he which leaueth that thing for to be done
> Unto his daughter, executour, or sonne,
> Which he himself might in his life fulfill,
> He is but a foole, and hath but litle skill.'

1706. **as I do whenne I slepe** : the duty of praying for the dead when one goes to sleep, and when one wakes during the night, is laid down in ch. ii of the *Book of the Knight of La Tour Landry*, E.E.T.S. 33, p. 5, 'ye aught to praie God for the soules that ben dede, eueri day or ye slepe ; for yef ye do, the dede praiethe for you'. In the following chapter the Knight relates a story of two sisters, one of whom ' loued wel God, and praied hym atte alle tymes that she awaked for the dede'. She was consequently protected by the grateful dead in peril that befell her by night, and afterwards made a good marriage ; while her sister was disgraced and put to death.

1723-4.   See Introduction, p. xxiii.

1723-33.   A section against belief in prophecies.

1725.   Apperson, *English Proverbs*, cites *Wit Restor'd* (1658), 102, ' Straight as a rams horne is thy nose.'

1734-51.   A section on the decadence of clergy and knighthood.

1735.   **tuly** : the derivation in the Glossary was suggested by Skeat.   *O.E.D.* suggests possible derivation from ' Toulouse' on the strength of *Sir Gawain*, 77, 'Of tryed Tolouse, of Tarstapites innoghe', compared with ll. 568, 'a tule tapit', and 858, ' Tapyteȝ . . . of tuly & tars.'   But against this should be set *Cleanness*, 1108, ' alle þe toles of Tolowse', where ' Tolowse' is probably a scribal error for ' Toledo', see Sir I. Gollancz's edition, p. xvii.   Since the regular spelling ' tuly ' makes connexion with ' Tolouse' very difficult, it is more likely to be an error due to a scribe in the manuscript of *Cleanness* and *Sir Gawain*.

1737.   See note on l. 222.

1749.   **lanternes to lewed men**: cp. *Latin Poems of Walter Mapes* (Camden Society), p. 45 :

> ' Viri beatissimi, sacerdotes Dei,
> præcones altissimi, lucernæ diei.'

GLOSSARY AND INDEX OF PROPER NAMES

All line numbers not preceded by P. or a roman Passus number, refer to Part 2 (M). Vocalic *y* is treated as *i*; consonantal *y* follows *x*; *ʒ* follows *g*, except when initial, when it is treated as consonantal *y*; initial *þ* (occasionally spelt *th*) follows *t*. Verbs with prefixed *y*- not found under *i* are listed under their stems.

a-bateth, *pr.* 3 *s.* makes null and void, 1584 ; *pl.* abateth, III. 307 ; *pp.* abated, lowered, IV. 81.
abawyd, *pp.* confused, 293 ; *see Note.*
abouʒte, *adv.* round about, I. 40, II. 2, III. 107; aboute, 1567; bare abouʒte, steered crookedly, IV. 75.
a-bouue, *adv.* on high, 354; *as n.* 733 ; aboue, in Heaven, P. 34.
a-bowid, *pt. pl.* bowed, 1317.
abrayed, *pt.* 1 *s.* started, 1288 ; OE. abregdan, abrægd.
a-caunt-wise, obliquely, 915 ; OF. cant, side. *Not in O.E.D.* ; *see under* cant *sb¹.*
accordid, *pp.* agreed, 1440.
acounted, *pp.* esteemed, III. 155 ; acountid, reckoned up, III. 157.
a-countz, *pl.* financial position, 1540.
a-croke, crookedly, 784; *first example in O.E.D.* 1480.
Adam, 1228.
a-dasid, *pp.* dazzled, 715 ; *first example in O.E.D.* 1500.
aduowe, *inf.* avow, 1117 ; OF. avouer, *infl. by* Lat. advōcāre.
affendid, *pp.* offended, III. 208.
affor, *prep.* before, IV. 73 ; affore, IV. 40 ; *adv.* III. 246.
afforse, of necessity, IV. 22.
a-frountid, *pp.* insulted, 54.
agayne, *prep.* against, 515 ; in contradiction to, 1103 ; aʒeyn, against, III. 189 ; aʒeine, P. 35 ; *adv.* a[g]eyn, again, P. 29 ; ayen, 1453.
agaynes, *prep.* against, 82 ; aʒeynes, III. 10 ; *adv.* agaynes, again, 364, 819, 1211, 1265 ; *only ex. of adv. in O.E.D.* 1480.
aggreiggid, *part. adj.* made heavy, 1505 ; OF. agreger, l.Lat. *aggreviare.*

agogge, in expectation, 1590.
agoo, *pp.* gone, III. 245.
a-grete, wholesale, in profusion, 907.
agreued, *pp.* aggrieved, offended, II. 113.
a-hepe, in a crowd, 865.
alee, to leeward, towards shelter, IV. 74.
a-leehalf, on the lee side, 1253 ; *not in O.E.D.*
alie, *collect. n.* allies, confederates, III. 31.
alleigge, *inf.* give evidence, 1493.
alowe, *pr.* 1 *s.* approve, II. 69 ; *pp.* allowed, 989.
alwey, always, P. 69.
amarride, *pt. pl.* confused, P. 16.
a-masid, *part. adj.* out of one's wits, 1726.
amendes, reparation, 407.
amysse, erroneously, 680.
amonge, *adv.* at the same time, P. 57 ; among, 116, 1259.
amorwe, next morning, IV. 40.
and, if, P. 49, P. 67 ; 94, 121, 236, 1199.
anewe, *inf.* renew, III. 24.
angel, messenger, 1255.
anon, straightway, II. 126; anone to, even to, 68.
anteorist-is, *g.s.* Antichrist's, 1255.
apeire, *inf.* injure, P. 73, II. 79 ; become weaker, 1472 ; *pr. pl.* appeiren, injure, 1405 ; *pt.* 3 *s.* aperid, grew worse, I. 75 ; OF. ampeirer.
apere, *pr.* 3 *s. subj.* appear, III. 117.
aperte, *adv.* openly, IV. 36 ; aport, 812.
a-rayne, *inf.* rein, 1183 ; OF. areiner.
are, *v.* or.
areche, *inf.* reach, suffice, IV. 12.

aredy, *adv.* in readiness, II. 129.

a-rere, *inf.* retreat, 1530; *imp. s.* **arere**, return, III. 110.

arere, *adv.* backwards, 1183.

a-rete, *imp. s.* pause, 696; OF. areter; *not in O.E.D.*

[ar]ette[d], *pp.* reckoned, 1545; OF. aretter.

arith, rightly, III. 120.

Armacanes, *g s.* 496; *see Note.*

armen, *pr. pl.* harm, III. 18.

arouutyd, *part. adj.* (?) sent on his way, III. 221; OF. arouter; *see O.E.D. under* arout.

arteth, *pr. 3 s.* constrains, 1551; *cp* Lat. artāre, OF. arcté.

a-russhe, *adv.* violently, 1123; *not in O.E.D.*

a-say, *inf.* try, 105; **asay**, 850.

aschonne, *inf.* escape, II. 185.

a-serue, *inf.* deserve, 1481.

a-side, *adv.* out of the way, 781.

asketh, *v.* **axe.**

a-spie, *inf.* perceive (it), 1199.

a-square, *adv.* aloof, 1489.

assoilled, *pp.* resolved, 381.

astonyed, *part. adj.* stupefied, II. 8; **a-stonyed**, 351.

at, in, III. 25; **atte**, at the, 17, 58.

atamed, *part. adj.* tamed, III. 27.

a-tourne, *pr. 3 s. subj.* turn (? *trans.*), 1266.

atteynt, *part. adj.* convicted, 757.

attourneys, deputies, agents, 1710.

attre, poison, 53; bitterness, 1551; **pattre**, the poison, 1126; OE. āttor.

a-[t]w[art], *prep.* contrary to, 720; *dial. form of* ON. þvert, *cp.* Norw. Sw. tvert, Dan. tvært.

auctor, originator, 741.

aues, *pr. 2 s.* owest, 1201; *pt. 3 s.* **owe[d]**, IV. 89; **owed**, owned, IV. 10; *pl.* **aughten**, ought, 728; **oute**, P. 47; *impers.* **ouȝte**, it behoves, III. 173; **aughte**, II. 49, II. 130; 26, 439; **ought**, 971; **oughte**, I. 106.

aughte(n), *v.* **aues.**

Augustyn, abbeys of, houses of Austin Canons, 537, 861; **Augustines**, Austin Friars, 502.

auncetre, ancestor, 1228.

auñoyen, aged, 956.

aunsetrie, high descent, 1427.

autorisen, *pr. pl.* set up authority, 1376.

avise, opinion, III. 8

awgrym, arithmetic, IV. 53; OF. algorisme, augorime.

awilled, *pp.* willed, III. 210; OE. ā + willian.

axe, *inf.* ask, II. 34; *pr. 3 s.* **axith**, requires, II. 191; **askith**, 347; **asketh**, III. 23; provokes, 166.

ayen, **aȝeyn**, **aȝȝins**, *v.* **agayne.**

bable, *imp. s.* talk inopportunely, 291; *pr. 3 s.* **bablith**, 50; *pt. 1 s.* **bablid** on, read aloud, 308; *pl.* talked, IV. 59; **ba[b]lid**, made a confused noise, 594.

bachillier, young knight who has not yet his own banner, 260; *pl.* **bachilliers**, 792; **baccheleris**, III. 358.

bayten, *inf.* set on dogs, III. 29.

balade-wise, (in) the manner of popular songs, 1345.

bale, *n.* distress, trouble, 453; *pl.* **balys**, 94.

balkes, obstacles, barriers, 808; OE. balca, a ridge.

balle, *inf.* strike, 456.

ballid, bald, 961; barren, IV. 70.

banere, company following a certain banner, II. 66.

baneretts, knights able to lead a company of vassals under their own banners, 792.

barn(es), *v.* **børne.**

baron, Prince, 584; *pl.* **barons**, nobles, 792; **baronys**, III. 358.

barre, atte b., in court, 17, 752.

Bartholomew, 1028 (*see Note*), 1054.

bastiles, towers, 1645.

bate, *inf.* bring to an end, 1607; *pt. 3 s.* **bated**, flew down, II. 162; *aph. form of* abate.

batre, *pr. pl. subj.* batter, strike repeatedly, 183; *pt. 3 s. ind.* **baterid**, II. 152; *freq. of* bat(e), OF. batre.

battis, clubs, III. 330; **batts**, 183.

bawtid, *pt. 3 s.* drove away, II. 13; (?) ON. bauta, to beat, hunt; (?) OF. bouter, bauter, to strike, push.

be, by, P. 40, P. 80, II. 83.

bede, *n.* bidding, 358; **beede**, 995; *cp.* OE. bēodan.

beere, *n.* bear, III. 94.

beheulde, *pt. 1 s.* beheld, 902.

be-hote, *pp.* promised, IV. 91; 147.

beke, beak, 154.

belde, *inf.* grow bold, I. 113; OE. bieldan, beldan.

belefte, *pp.* b. were, dwelt, II. 30.
Belial, 568 ; *see Note.*
benche, judge's seat, IV. 69.
bene, bean, a mere trifle, III. 151 ; *pl.* benes, 903.
benefices, livings, 669.
be-nyme, *inf.* take away, P. 66 ; *pp.* bynome, 1640.
bente, *pt.* 1 *s.* turned, 946 ; *pl.* bent, III. 76 ; bente on, fastened on, IV. 72 ; *pp.* y-bente, knit, frowning, III. 214.
bereued, *pt. pl.* dispossessed, II. 137.
berlingis, little bears, followers of Warwick, III. 96.
berne, man, P. 86 ; burne, 94, 282 ; barn, 50 ; barne, 260 ; *pl.* barnes, 308, 789 ; burnes, I. 113 ; III. 192 ; burnesse, III. 241 ; OE. beorn.
besely, busily, II. 147 ; OE. bisig, bysig.
besieth, *pr.* 3 *s. reflex.* occupies, II. 147 ; *pl.* bisien, 367 ; *intrans.* are occupied, 669.
besmet, *part. adj.* (?) shaped as a besom, 561 ; OE. besma.
best, for the b., for the best advantage, for better or worse, I. 84 ; for þe beste, 712 ; atte beste, in the best way, 58.
beste, *n. coll.* stock of beasts, P. 47 ; *pl.* bestz, animals, 997.
bestiary, writer on beasts, 1054 ; l Lat. bestiarius, a hunter of wild beasts. *This sense not in O.E.D.*
bete, *inf.* amend, 453.
beten, *pr. pl.* beat, 367 ; *pp.* y-bete, 154.
beth, *pr. pl.* are, I. 66, I. 67, III. 126, III. 127.
be-þenke, think of, III. 219.
bette, *adv.* better, 1553
be-twynne, *prep.* between, II. 85 ; OE. betweonum.
beu, beautiful, III. 1 ; l.OF. beau.
bicome, *pt.* 3 *s.* went, I. 49.
bigge, *inf.* build, 1021 ; ON. byggja.
bile, bill, beak, 938.
bilieue, *n.* faith, 325, 409.
bilieue, *inf.* believe, 1562 ; *pr.* 1 *s.* 136.
billid, *part. adj.* having a beak, III. 37.
billis, *pl.*, III. 307 ; *see Note.*
bynome, *v.* be-nyme.
byrthen, burden, II. 66 ; OE. byrðen.
biside, in addition, IV. 14.

bisien, *v.* besieth.
bisynes, company, 989, 1051.
blaynes, sores, blisters, 1122 ; OE. blegen.
blames, faults, II. 174.
blernyed, blear-eyed, II. 164 ; *cp.* LG. bleer-oged ; ME. nyghe, *with prosthetic* n. ; *cp.* piggesneye.
blessid, happy, fortunate, P. 2 ; y-blessid, 94.
blethely, gladly, 995 ; OE. bliðe.
blythid, *pt.* 3 *s.* gladdened, III. 94.
blowe, *pr. pl.* snort, bluster, 1531 ; OE. blawan.
blowid, *pt. pl.* blossomed, 903 ; OE. blowan.
blussid, *pt.* 1 *s.* blushed, 239 ; OE. blyscan.
bode, *pt.* 1 *s.* remained, 946 ; boode, 584.
boy, fellow, II. 167 ; servant, 358.
boicches, *pl.* boils, 1122, 1139 ; ONF. boche.
boynard, rogue, II. 164 ; *pl.* boynardis, I. 110 ; OF. buisnard, buinard.
bolde, *pr.* 3 *s. subj.* make bold, 165 ; *pt.* 3 *s. ind.* boldid, 590 ; I. 113.
boldely, with confidence, 1210.
boltes, arrows, 269.
bomelyng, *verb. n.* humming, 1028 ; *frequent. of* boom, bum, *onomat.*
bonairely, courteously, 1317 ; OF. (de)bonnaire.
bonde-men, peasants, 789 ; ON. bondi ; l.OE. bonda, husbandman.
bondes, *pl.* bounds, limits, 268 ; OF. bodne, bone, bune.
bonet, *n.* an additional piece of canvas added to the top of a sail, IV. 72, IV. 81 ; OF. bonet.
boode, *v.* bode.
bordes, tables, 827.
bore, boar, 1531.
boru, *pr. pl.* borrow, III. 151.
borugh, town, P. 2 ; borowe, IV. 69.
Bosse, nickname for the Earl of Warwick, III. 98 ; *see Note.*
bote, *n.* help, 455, 1127 ; OE. bot.
botene, *inf.* amend, 1182 ; OE. bot +-nen.
bouche, allowance of food, 272 ; F. avoir bouche à (en) cour ; *first example in O.E.D.* 1440.
bouȝte, *pt.* 3 *s.* redeemed, P. 41.
boun, ready, III. 294 ; buune, 358 ; ON. buinn.

boures, dwellings, 1005 ; OE. būr.

bourgoys, citizen. 260 : *pl.* bourgois, 789 ; burgeis, III. 149.

bowe, *inf.* submit. 712 ; *ft.* 3 *s.* bowid. bent, IV. 79.

bowe-drawte, bowshot, III. 229 ; OE. boga + *draht ; *cf.* ON. drāttr.

brast(e`. brastyn, *v.* breste.

bred dis`, *v.* brid.

brede, breadth. P. 12 ; OE. brādu.

brede-ful, brim-full, 1048 ; OE. brerd.

breden, *inf.* spread out ; b. hem. feedryn, to spread out his plumage for them, II. 147 ; OE. brǣdan.

breden. *pr. pl.* are engendered, 987 ; OE. brēdan.

breggurdelle, loin-girdle, 1513 ; OE. *brēc-gyrdel.

breme, fierce, II. 80, III. 365 ; strong, II. 130 ; OE. brēme.

brenne, *inf.* burn. 1529 (*see Note*); *pr.* 3 *s. subj.* 187 ; *pp.* y- brent, branded, 169 *see Note* ; ON. brenna.

breris, briars, III. 75 ; 898.

breste, *inf.* break. 1127 ; *fr.* 2 *s. subj.* 1553 ; 3 *s.* brest. III. 287 ; *ft.* 3 *s. ind.* braste, III. 94 ; *pl.* brast, III. 96 : brastyn, III. 362 ; ON. bresta, OE. berstan.

brestynge, for b., for fear of breaking, IV. 79.

bribed, *pp.* enticed, 1051.

brid, bird. II. 162 ; bred, II. 152 ; bredd, II. 141 ; *pl.* breddis, III. 37 ; briddis, 154 ; OE. brid.

bringg-e`, *inf.* bring about, 1667 ; *ft.* 3 *s.* brouute, brought, II. 9 ; *pp.* III. 98.

Bristow, Bristol, P. 2.

brodid, *ft.* 3 *s.* spread, II. 141 ; OE. brād, *adj.*

bromes, broom-thickets, III. 19.

browet, broth, II. 51 ; OF. brouet.

bunne, *v.* boun.

burgeis, *v.* bourgoys.

burne(s), **burnesse**, *v.* berne.

burnisched, *pt. pl* polished, III. 76 ; *part. adj.* burnysshid, having rubbed the velvet from their antlers, 928.

busked, *ft. ft.* hastened, III. 75 ; ON. būask.

busshid, *pt. pl.* pushed, II. 39 : *pr. p.* busshinge, I. 99 ; OF. buschier, to strike.

bustusely, rudely, 50 ; *derivation*

doubtful ; cp. OF. boisteus, lame ; Norw. bausta. to act violently ; *see note on l. 911, Pearl*, ed. Sir I. Gollancz.

but, unless, III. 67, III. 115 ; 127, 197, 267, 390, 691, 913, 1394 ; only, 500 : but if, unless, I. 79, II. 3, III. 152 ; but yf, 111, 198, 1558.

cacche, *inf.* catch, III. 17. receive, III. 67 ; caicche, take, 8 ; o. no colour, make no pretence, 588 : *pr.* 3 *s.* caicchet, takes, 684; *pr.* 3 *s. subj.* caicche, come, 731 ; *pr. p.* caicching. picking up, overbearing, 164 ; NF. cachier; *cp.* cha-cheth.

caige, cage, 153 ; OF. cage, AN. *from* SWF. caige.

cam, *pt.* 3 *s.* befitted, II. 161 ; came by, befell, 422 (*first example of this sense in O.E.D.* 1523) ; *ft. pl.* come, came, I. 32, I. 92 ; *ft.* 3 *s. subj.* IV. 81.

Cambrigge. 322, 782.

Caym, Cain, 493, 498 ; *see Note.*

canon, *n.* rule, 1621.

cans, *v.* cunne.

carieth, *pr. pl.* travel. III. 302 ; *ft.* 1 *s.* caried, 554; ON. keyra, *confused with* ONF. carier.

caris, lamentations, II. 138 ; karis, troubles, I. 7.

caroigne. body, 562 ; kareyne. carrion, II. 178 (*see Note*) ; ONF. caroigne.

Carmes, Carmelites, 501 ; OF. carme.

carpe, *inf.* talk, IV. 41 ; *imp. s.* 698 ; ON. karpa.

carpinge, *verb. n.* discussion, I. 87.

caste, *n.* trick, 1154 ; *pl.* castes, I. 12 ; castis. III. 102.

caste, *inf.* devise, contrive, III. 219 ; 56, 738, 1007 ; *pr. pl.* 534 ; casten, divide, 436 : casteth hem, betake themselves, III. 132 ; *pt.* 3 *s.* caste, contrived, 347 ; *pl.* cast, IV. 24 ; *imp. s.* caste, reckon, III. 279 ; *subj. pr. pl.* caste vp, abandon, break away from, 5 ; *pp.* caste, reckoned, IV. 11 ; devised, 762 ; thrown down, 481, 1165 ; defeated, 1523 ; relegated, 816.

ca`s`ting, *verb. n.* for c. bihinde, for fear of being left behind, 266. *First example in O.E.D. from Dryden.*

Cathay-is, *g.s.* 1455.

Caton, Cato, 289 (*see Note*), 875.

cause, law-suit, III. 323; *pl.* causis, III. 318.

cautell, deceit, I. 78; III. 67; cautelle, 56; *pl.* cautelles, 689; OF. cautele.

caue, hollowed-out dwelling, 1011.

cedule, schedule, a slip of parchment appended to a document, 1734; OF. cedule, l.Lat. scedula.

certayne, *adj.* sure, 1058.

chacheth, *pr. pl.* persecute, 1721; south NF. chachier; *cp.* cacche.

chaire, professorial seat, 355.

chambris, presence-chambers, III. 126.

chanchellier, chancellor, 13; OF. chancelier, NF. cancheler.

Changwys, Jhengiz Khan, 1426, 1429, 1486; *g.s.* Changwys-is, 1414.

chapitre, chapter, general meeting of a religious body, 435.

charge, weight, I. 41, IV. 74; trouble, burden, 194, 1720; mandate, IV. 29.

chargeth, *pr.* 3 *s* regards, 82.

chaste, *inf.* correct, 355; OF. chastier.

chauncellerie, Chancellor's Court, 1608.

chaunchyth, *pr. pl.* change, III. 139; OF. changer.

cheef, *adj.* principal, I. 88.

chekonys, chickens, II. 144; OE. cicen.

chele, *n.* cold, II. 144; OE. cele.

chepe, market, III. 139.

cherè, demeanour, II. 13, III. 245; chiere, 24; OF. chere.

cheriche, *inf.* cherish, III. 203; OF. cheriss-.

cherliche, lovingly, III. 203; o[h]eerly, 939, 1305.

chese, *inf.* choose, IV. 29; *pt. pl.* chesse, I. 88; chosid, 639; *part. adj.* y-chose, 355, 704; OE. cēosan.

chesteynes, chestnuts, 900; OF. chasteine, *cp.* OE. cisten-, cystbēam.

Chester, P. 56, III. 317.

cheuallerie, the order of knighthood, 1608; OF. chevalerie.

cheualleris, knights, IV. 29.

cheuyteyns, rulers, officers of state, I. 88; OF. chevetaine.

chibolls, chives, a sort of onion, 605; OF. ciboule, NF. *chiboule.

chyders, brawlers, III. 317.

chief, *adj.* highest in rank, 13; *pl.* 39; c. of al charite, foremost in love, 704.

chiere, *v* chere.

chirche, church, P. 4; churche, 659; *g. s.* 614; OE. cyrice.

chirmed, *pt. pl.* sang, 939; OE. cirman.

c[h]o[g he, chough, jackdaw, 345.

choise, *inf.* choose, 445; OF. choisir; *first ex. in N.E.D.* 1505.

chosid, *v.* chese.

ciuile, civil law, 1619.

clappeth, *pr. pl.* chatter, 1469; *pt. pl.* clappid, IV. 89; OE. clæppan, to throb.

clapsyng, furnishing with a clasp, 1282.

clatre, *inf.* chatter, 72.

clause, sentence, P. 72, I. 83, III. 11.

cleere, *adj.* c. in þe winde, clear in the direction it is taking (*see Note*), 1552; *adv.* clearly, 380; *n.* open ground, 927; *this sense not in O.E.D.; first ex. of adj. in this use*, 1568.

cleerly, *adv.* 126, 289, 365, 939; cler[l]ie (MS. clergie), I. 83, III. 26, III. 190; clerliche, II. 191.

clepe, *inf.* call, III. 180; *pt.* 3 *s.* clepid, III. 70; *imp. pl.* clepith, 1673; *pp.* cleped, P. 4; yclepid, III. 306; OE. cleopian.

clere, *inf.* clear up, III. 366.

clergie, learning, 236, 300, 319, 635, 698, 1032.

clene, *adj.* unsullied, 1676; *adv.* entirely, 450.

clerk, learned man, I. 49.

cler[l]ie, *v.* cleerly.

cleue, *inf.* burst asunder, 562; OE. clēofan.

cleueth, *pr.* 3 *s.* clings, 1169; *pt.* 3 *s.* cleued, IV. 18; *pl.* I. 112; OE. clifian, cleofian.

clo[y]ed, *pt.* 3 *s.* lamed, III. 1c6; *see Note*.

cloos, *adj.* secret, private, 164.

clos, *n.* end, IV. 67; OF. clore, clos-, vb.

closes, *pl.* enclosures, 908; cathedral precincts, 554; OF. clos.

closeth, *pr.* 3 *s.* combines, 1037; *pr.* 3 *s. subj.* close, 3; y-closid, enclosed, 538; OF. clore, clos-.

clopid, *pt.* 3 *s.* gave clothing or livery
to, 42.
clouche, clutch, 699.
c[n]aue, serving-man, 272 ; OE.
cnafa.
cookil, corn cockle, 62 ; OE. coccul.
coy, reserved, 810.
coyffes, lawyers' caps, III. 320;
coiphes, 1141; OF. coife.
coigne, coin, 6; coyne, I. 12.
coylaige, collection of taxes, 149;
OF. cueillage, coillage ; *not in*
O.E.D ; *but cp.* cullery.
coile, *inf.* collect, choose, III. 200;
OF. coillir.
colis, *pl.* tricks, IV. 24 ; *see O.E.D.*
under cole².
colorable, fair-seeming, 286.
colour, pretence, 588 ; c. to wayve,
pretence of removing, I. 100.
combraunce, troublesome behaviour,
III. 113 ; cumbrance, 1154.
combred, *pp.* troubled, I. 78.
come, *n.* coming, IV. 71 ; OE. *cōme ;
cp. cōme, *nom. acc. sg., Ormulum,*
i. 22, &c.
come, *v.* cam.
comely, noble, 143, 962.
comers, visitors, 546.
comyne, commonalty, IV. 90 ;
[comyn], 5.
comynliche, in common, together, I.
87.
comliche, *adv.* in a seemly manner,
IV. 35.
comlynesse, seemly behaviour, III.
184.
commenche, *inf.* begin, 1485, 1552,
OF. commencier, Pic. commencher.
compte, *inf.* count, 1599 ; F. compter
(*fifteenth century*).
comsith, *pr.* 3 *s.* begins, III. 190;
pt. 3 *s.* comsid, IV. 35 ; *abbreviated*
form of commence.
comune, *n.* commonalty, 133 ; *g. pl.*
comunes, commons', IV. 18.
comunete, common people ; knyȝtis
of þe c., knights of the shire, IV.
41.
conceill, *n.* sagacity, P. 59 ; purpose,
I. 7 ; cunseil, council, 14 ; conceyll, advice, P. 84 ; *as adj.* cunseil, secret, 458.
conceill, *inf.* advise, P. 49.
conceypt, understanding, 718 ; conceipte, 103, 1304 ; conceipt,
idea, 1548 ; *cp.* conceive, *vb.* and
Lat. conceptus.

conceyued, *pt.* 3 *s.* understood, 341.
concours, haue c. to, resort to, 1245.
condicions, position, rank, 209.
congion, contemptible creature, III.
45 ; *see Note.*
congruly, harmoniously, 331 ; OF.
congru.
conyngz, rabbits, 910 ; OF. conin,
AF. coning.
conscience, joint knowledge, 14 (*as*
in Latin ; no example of this use in
O.E.D.) ; knowledge, II. 81 ; mind,
heart, III. 187 ; 457 ; conscienciou-
ness, righteousness, 493, 1387 ; of
c., in all conscience, 513.
constrewe, *inf.* explain, IV. 68;
construe, 303, 749; put a special
interpretation on, criticize, 1459.
1486 ; *pr.* 3 *s.* construeth, ex-
pounds, 289 ; *pl.* construen, 369 ;
pt. 1 *s.* construed, 240 ; *pl.* constrewed, interpreted legally, III.
327 ; *imp. s.* constrwe, explain, I.
83 ; *pr. s. subj.* constrewe, P
72.
construyng, *verb. n.* consideration,
1547.
contente, contentment, agreement,
1037 ; *first ex. in O.E.D.*, 1579.
contra, *n.* contrary, 256.
contre, country, II. 28, II. 106 ;
cuntre, district, 1560; *pl.* contres,
III. 359 ; cuntrees, 1455.
contre, *inf.* oppose, 1459.
coostz, *v.* costis.
[cope], vault, 1006 ; *pl.* copes, long
cloaks, clergy, (?) monks and friars,
1673 ; OE. *cāpe, ON. kāpa, med.
Lat. cāpa.
copie, *n.* writing, 1388, 1683.
coples, *pl.* pair of principal rafters of
a roof, 1007 ; OF. cople, a tie.
coppe, summit, 883 ; OE. copp.
corde, *inf.* agree, 1414 ; *aph. form*
of accord.
corette, *inf.* correct, P. 59.
coriouse, skilled, III. 163 ; *sup.*
curiousiste, most skilful, 1006.
coriously, exquisitely, 893 ; OF.
curius.
cornes, grains (of corn), III. 81 ; 665.
cornier, corner, cranny, 1499.
coroune, crown, 1, 3, 14 ; croune,
I. 8 ; NF. corune.
corps, body, III. 51.
cost, expense, IV. 90.
costened, *pt.* 3 *s.* cost, III. 169 ; *cp.*
ON. kostnaðr, *n.*

oostis, districts, II. 106, II. 182; **ooosts**, 436.

oote, cottage, 470; OE. cot, cote.

oothe, *pt.* 3 *s.* said, 103, 232; *pl.* quod, III. 234; *pp.* quethyn, bequeathed, 1348; y-quethe, 1704; OE. cweðan.

ootis, *pl.* coats, III. 180, III. 193.

oouchant, *adj.* quiet, humble, 810; *first ex. in O.E.D.*, 1496; *first ex. of figurative use, Dryden.*

ooude, *v.* ounne.

oouȝthe, *v.* ounne.

oountis, *pl.* accounts, III. 279, IV. 11; OF. conte, cunte.

oouraige, irritant, 1500; OF. culrage, water-pepper; *uot instanced in O.E.D. except as name of plant.*

oourid, *pt. pl.* covered, 910; *pp.* y-oourid, 893, 1592; OF. covrir.

oouryng, *verb. n.* covering, 738.

oours, movement, IV. 76; procedure, 733.

oourshidnes, oourssid, *v.* oursidnes, oursid.

oourtoys, courteous, 442; ourtoys, 810; OF. cortois, NF. curteis.

oouthe, ooupᵉ, *v.* ounne.

ooueitise, covetousness, I. 8; oueitise, 228; OF. coveitise.

oouert, concealment, shelter, 910, 1063.

[o]rao[oh]e (MS. **raoke**), rack, 560; OF. creche.

oraft, art, III. 169; 1065; orafte, IV. 76; 347; device, III. 219; (*in pejorative sense*) 457, 461; *pl.* oraftis, III. 141.

orafty, clever, 862.

orasid, *pp.* broken, I. 8, I. 70; *cf.* Sw. krasa, to crackle, OF. acraser.

oreatour, creator, 640.

oreaunoe, *n.* credit, I. 12, III. 132, IV. 17; OF. creance.

oredo, belief, 1624; *this sense not in O.E.D. till 1587.*

oreed, *pt.* 3 *s.* created, 640, 724, 1457; OF. creer.

oreasing, *pr. p.* broadening, 878; OF. creistre, creiss-.

oreste, crest, tail of a comet, 878.

orie, *n.* acclaim, 1441.

oristen, Christian, IV. 1; OE. cristen.

Oristis Ohirohe, P. 4; *see Note.*

oroftes, enclosed fields, 895, 1009.

oroke, *n.* trick, 387, 1165; *pl.* orokes, 1592; ON. krōkr, a hook.

orokk, crock, earthen pot, II. 52.

oroppe, harvest, 450; *pl.* oroppes, bunches of foliage, 1676; OE. crop, the rounded top of a herb.

oropping, *verb. n.* gathering, 1049.

orosse, 66, 483; *see Notes.*

oroupe, hind quarters, 915; OF. crope, crupe.

oulmes, stipulations, contracts, 1388; Lat. culmus, *see Ducange*; *not in O.E.D.*

oulorum, conclusion, P. 72, IV. 61; ? *corruption of* 'in saecula saeculorum'.

oumbe, coomb, a valley on the side of a hill, 878; OE. cumb; *not given in O.E.D. between 847 and 1578.*

oumbrance, *v.* combraunce.

oumforte, *inf.* strengthen, 1560.

oumpas, *n.* circle, 347; whole extent, P. 20.

oumpassid, *pp.* designed, 1011.

ounne, *inf.* learn, 319; *pr. 2 s.* oans, canst, 236; *pl.* kunne, III. 61; *pt.* 3 *s.* ooude, knew, III. 106; *pl.* oouthe, 635, 1327; ooupᵉ, could, IV. 68; *pr. 1 s. subj.* kunne, know, I. 22; 3 *s.* ounne, can, 94; *pt. 1 s.* oouȝthe, P. 49; 3 *s.* ooude, II. 18.

ounnyng, *n.* learning, knowledge, 638; kunnynge, II. 81; kunynge, III. 67.

ounnyng, *adj.* wise, 214.

ounseil, *v.* conoeill, *n.*

ountre (MS. **ountrey**), *prep.* against, 1548.

ountre, *v.* contre.

ountrefete, *inf.* imitate, 1007; OF. contrefet, *adj.*

ouringe, *verb. n.* protection, I. 95.

ouriousiste, *v.* coriouse.

oursid, *verb adj.* execrable, I. 7; oourssid, violent, 1500.

oursidnes, wickedness, III. 187; courshidnes, evil behaviour, 1154; cursidnesse, III. 113; fierceness, 1067.

ourtelle, kirtle, robe, 893; OE. cyrtel.

ourtoys, *v.* oourtoys.

ousky, *inf.* submit, 580; ON. kūgask, to be cowed into submission, *not in O.E.D. For termination, cp.* maistrie, sauere.

oustume, custom, 149, 758; oustum, toll, duty, IV. 11, IV. 16.

dagges, slashings of cloth, III. 193, *see Note.*

daies, on þe d., by daytime, III. 272.

daisshe, *pr.* 1 *s.* dash, 981 ; *cp.* Sw. daska, Da. daske.

dame, mother, III. 43, III 60.

Daniel, 1311 ; *g. s.* **Danyel-is,** 874.

date, time, 312.

datʒ, *pl.* (?) date-fruit, 648.

Dauid, 1585.

dawis, days, I. 65 ; **dawes,** 421 ; to **bringe of dawe,** to kill, 1319 ; OE. dagas, *pl.*

deabolik, wicked, inspired by the devil, III. 199 ; F. diabolique (*only ex. of this spelling in O.E.D.*).

deceipuen, *pr. pl.* deceive, 1052 ; *pr. part.* **deceipuyng,** 495 ; OF. deceiv-, *infl. by* l.ME. deceipte, *with mute* p. *This spelling not in O.E.D.*

dede, dead, 1706.

dede, *v.* do.

dede-doynge, action, IV. 31.

deede, act, outcome, 1674.

deele, part, 447 ; **dele, dole,** 1722 ; **neuere a d.,** not at all, III. 339 ; OE. dǽl.

dees, dais, 1570 ; *pl.* **des,** 647 ; OF. deis.

dees, *pl.* dice, I. 18 ; OF. de.

Degon, III. 362 (*see Note*) ; *g. pl.* **degonys,** churls', III. 351.

degre, rank, 511 ; *pl.* **degres,** III. 249.

delte, *pt.* 3 *s.* gave in charity, 1694.

delue, *inf.* dig, 977 ; *pp.* **y-doluen,** buried, 1194.

deme, *inf.* judge, I. 37 ; punish, I. 69 ; express, II. 110 ; award, III. 341 ; resolve, P. 7 ; 320, 390 ; *pr. 2 s.* **demys,** considerest, 716 ; 3 *s.* **demeth,** 466 ; *imp. s.* **deme,** judge, I. 18 ; *pp.* **ydemed,** appointed, III. 229.

demer, judge, ruler, II. 70.

departid, *pp.* divided, 4, 626, 654.

derid, *pt. pl.* troubled, II. 124 ; OE. derian.

derklich, obscurely, I. 20.

derue, strong, I. 42 ; 639 ; audacious, I. 69 ; *adv.* boldly, 1091 ; ON. djarfr.

deseueraunce, separation, II. 50.

destrued, *pt. pl.* consumed, 967 ; OF. destruire.

determyne, *inf.* put an end to, 1138.

dette, debt, I. 18, III. 148.

deue, due, 1066, 1274 ; **dewe,** rightful, III. 60 ; OF. deu, du.

deuely, duly, rightly, 511, 1219.

deuete, duty, 1476 ; AF. duete, dewete.

deupe, deep, 647 ; OE. dēop.

deuyse, device, III. 178.

diffled, *pt.* 3 *s.* defied, 334.

dignesse, pride, display, III. 128 ; OF. digne.

dyme, tenth part, IV. 15 ; OF. disme.

dineth, *v.* **dysneth.**

dyntis, *n. pl.* blows, force, I. 11.

discrecion, decision, II. 110.

discryue, *inf.* describe, explain, I. 23 ; 150, 1222 ; OF. descrivre.

dysneth, *pr.* 3 *s.* dines, 1573 ; **dineth,** gives dinner to, III. 60 ; OF. disner.

disputeson, *n.* debate, 242 ; OF. desputeisun.

dissese, discomfort, II. 71.

disware, at a loss, in despair, 1419 ; AF. *desware* = OF. eswaré, esgaré ; *see Note.*

do, *pr.* 1 *s.* cause, 411 ; **do on,** appeal to, prove by, 1010, 1222, 1743 ; *3s.* **doeth,** does, 109 ; *pl.* **doon,** 1507 ; *pt.* 3 *s.* **dude,** 1714 ; *pl.* **dede,** P. 19, III. 112 ; *pp.* **do,** I. 106.

Dobyn, III. 362 ; *see Note.*

doctourʒ, learned men, III. 289.

dollid, *part. adj.* warmed, 648.

dome, law, 1023 ; *pl.* **domes,** judgements, I. 11, III. 351 ; **d. carte,** hangman's cart, III. 137.

dome-ʒeuynge, giving of judgement, III. 329.

dooles, *n. pl.* portions, 666 ; OE. dāl.

dore-barre, a bar put across a door to secure it, 1262.

doreward, to þe d., towards the door, 842.

double, twice the ordinary size or amount, I. 57 ; 294, 647 ; divided, 1420 ; ten dublə, tenfold, I. 57.

douʒteth, *pr. pl.* fear, III. 148 ; *pp.* **y-douutid,** I. 42 ; OF. douter.

doughtful, terrible, 217 ; OF. doute + ful.

doute, fear, 1044 ; doubt, difficulty, 294 ; *pl.* **dowtes,** P. 7 ; **douʒs,** 360 ; **doutes,** 1173.

dradde, *pt.* 3 *s.* feared, I. 68 ; *pl.* IV. 93 ; **drede,** III. 339 ; OE. -drǽdan, -drēdan, *pt.* drēd.

dranes, *n. pl.* drones, 967 ; OE. dran.

draughte, drawing, 486 ; OE.* draht.

drawe, *inf.* betake itself, 692 ; *pt.*

1 *s. reflex.* drowe, 842 ; 3 *s.* drough, III. 211 ; drowe, drew, IV. 31 ; *pl.* III. 329 ; 923.

drede, *n.* fear, P. 7 ; dreede, 1262 ; dride, I. 11 ; *cp.* dradde.

droppeth, *pr.* 3 *s.* engenders, produces, 1256.

duble, *v.* double.

Duche, German, III. 193.

dude, *v.* do.

duke, leader, III. 360, III. 363.

dullisshe, somewhat dull, III. 128 ; *only ex. in O.E.D. before* 1581.

dullith, *pr.* 3 *s.* stupefies, III. 178.

dum, dumb, 756 ; OE. dumb.

dum-seede, 839 ; *see Note.*

dung-wete, dank-wet, dripping wet, 739 ; *see E.D.D.* dunk, *adj.*, *cp.* Norw. dynka, to wet.

dure, *inf.* last, III. 289 ; *pt.* 3 *s.* durid, remained, III. 233 ; *pl.* endured, 1330.

dwele, illusion, 874 ; OE. gedwela.

dwelled, *pt.* 1 *s.* remained, 842, 933.

d[wer]e, doubt, 329.

easid, *pp.* relieved, 149.

Ector, Hector, name of a hound, 917.

edder, adder, III. 22 ; OE. nǣd(d)re, nēd(d)re.

efte, again, 84 ; OE. eft.

egalite, equality, adversaries of equal rank, 1502.

egge, *inf.* urge, 1274 ; *part. adj.* eggid, inclined, 960 ; ON. eggja ; OE. ecg, *n.*

Egipte, 1326.

eye, fear, II. 9 ; OE. ege.

eildren, *v.* eldryn.

eylid, *pt.* 3 *s.* ailed, II. 46.

eyne, eyes, II. 132.

eyren, *n. pl.* eggs. III. 50 ; eire[n] (MS. heires), III. 42 ; OE. ǣgru, *pl.*

elbowis, *pl.* the lower part of the sleeve, III. 154.

elde, old age, P. 70.

eldryn, aged, 835 ; eildren, 1427 ; elderne dawis, ancient times, I. 65 ; eldryn dawes, 421 ; OE. eldra + -en.

eliche, alike, equally, I. 66 ; OE. gelīce.

elles, otherwise, 78.

endauntid, *pp.* cherished, esteemed, III. 128, III. 351 ; *see Note.*

endited, *pp.* written, I. 20, III. 63.

endurid, *v.* indure.

engendre, *inf.* produce, III. 112.

ennoye, *inf.* trouble, 1140.

entent, meaning, P. 79 ; entente, intention, purpose, II. 99 ; intent, 380, 466 ; *pl.* intentz, 461, 1420.

envien, *pr. pl.* vie with, 1374 ; OF. envier, Lat. invītāre.

eres, ears, 1238.

erie, *inf.* plough, 616 ; OE. erian.

errith, *pr.* 3 *s.* goes astray, 1502.

eschewe, *inf.* avoid, 94, 532, 1231 ; *pp.* [e]s[o]hewid, 1524.

ese, idleness, II. 46.

estate, class of people, P. 82.

euen, *adv.* exactly, P. 3 ; euene, III. 304 ; 500, 1240.

euene, *adj.* medium, 1609.

euery, each one, 1106.

euyll, hardly, IV. 52 ; euell, badly, III. 106.

fable, *inf.* talk, 145 ; *pr.* 3 *s. subj.* 41.

fables, *n. pl.* falsehoods, P. 57.

fabuler, narrator, 140 ; Lat. fabulāri.

fayne, glad, III. 97 ; desirous, 1321 ; fayn, 337.

faire, rightly, fittingly, 1277.

fairye, enchantment, 1293 ; OF. faierie.

fall, *inf.* happen, P. 27 ; falle, 1127 ; *pr.* 3 *s.* falleth, 201 ; *pl.* fallen, fail, 20 ; *pr.* 3 *s. subj.* falle, decline, 131 ; happen, 124 ; *imp. s.* f. of, withdraw, 1556 ; *pt.* 3 *s.* fell on, befel, III. 244 ; felle, was necessary, IV. 22 ; *pl.* came to pass, IV. 5 ; *pp.* fallyn, I. 81 ; falle, fallen, III. 102.

fangeth, *pr.* 3 *s.* receives, 1176 ; *pl.* fongen, 1350 ; IV. 46 ; *pt.* 1 *s.* finge, 1198 ; *pp.* y-funge, 1700 ; OE. fangen, *pp. of* fōn.

fangyng, *verb. n.* taking (bribes), 1355.

fantasie, fiction, P. 58.

fare, *n.* journey, IV. 73.

fare, *pp.* gone, II. 150.

fauȝte, *n.* lack, II. 63, II. 120 ; faute, 20 ; *pl.* fauȝtis, faults, crimes, IV. 4 ; fawtis, P. 68 ; fauutis, I. 75, III. 112.

faukyn, falcon, II. 157.

fauour, help, support, 1355.

feblen, *pr. pl.* grow weak, III. 16.

fedris, *n. pl.* feathers, II. 148, III. 52 ; OE. feðer.

feedrin, plumage, II. 147 (*see Note*) ; OE. feðer-hama.

fee-fermes, rents derived from land

held in fee-simple subject to a perpetual fixed rent, without any other services (_O.E.D._), IV. 4; AF. fee-ferme.

feele, _v._ **fele**.

feerelees, _n.pl._ marvels, 222; **ferlees**, 1737; OE. fǣrlīc, _adj._

feers, _v._ **fers**.

feet, _pp._ fetched, III. 126; OE. fetian.

feyochen, _pr. pl._ fetch, 1009; OE. fecc(e)an.

feil, _v._ **fele**.

feis, fees, 1700.

feith, loyalty, honesty, III. 198.

felawis, companions, I. 61; _see Note._

felawschepe, friendliness, I. 61; **felaship**, supporters, 1166.

fele, many, IV. 5; **feele**, 509, 950; OE. fela.

fele, _inf._ find out, P. 68; 1433; make trial, 395; **feil**, 1447; **vele**, feel, 1624; OE. fēlan.

felefold, manifold, 897; **fele-folde**, 1737.

Felice, III. 160.

fell(e), _v._ **fall**.

felle, skin, coat, III. 16; **velle**, 561; OE. fell.

felle, cruel, ruthless, 264, 864; OF. fel.

felle-whare, _collect._ furs, III. 150; OE. waru.

felliche, fiercely, II. 173.

felnesse, wisdom, shrewdness, 393; _see Note._

felon, abscess, 1124; _cp._ Lat. fel, gall.

felouns, evil-doers, III. 370; _g. pl._ **felons**, III. 102; _see Note._

fende, _pr._ 1 _s._ forbid, 1201; _aph. form of_ defende.

feoffe, _imp. s._ present, 1284; _pt._ 3 _s._ **feoffed**, put in possession, 1226; OF. fieffer, AN. feoffer.

fer, fear, IV. 65.

ferde, _pt._ 3 _s._ happened, 1293; _pl._ behaved, I. 61; went, II. 180; OE. fēran.

fere, companion, mate, III. 40; _pl._ **ferys**, 1341; OE. gefēra.

ferkid, _pt._ 1 _s._ went, 392, 622; _pl._ **ferkyd**, III, 90; OE. fercian.

ferlees, _v._ **feerelees**.

ferre, far, 41, 730.

fers, fierce, IV. 71; **feers**, 215; **fersse**, eager, 1544.

fersly, fiercely, III. 77.

fersnesse, fierceness, II. 7.

ferthe, fourth, 405.

ferthred, _pp._ advanced, 111; OE. fyrðrian.

ferthryng, _verb. n._ assistance, 107; in fourthering of, in order to help, 1425.

fetisly, becomingly, 1361; OF. feitis, fetis.

feulle, _pt._ 1 _s._ fell, 856; 3 _s. subj._ feul, 113; OE. fēoll.

fiance, confidence, 1447; OF. fiance.

fifteneth, a tax of one-fifteenth imposed on personal property, IV. 15.

figures, letters, 500; _see Note._

fyldis, fields, II. 157.

fyndist, _pr._ 2 _s._ I. 18; _pl._ **fyndyth**, provide for, IV. 51; _pt._ 3 _s._ **fonde**, found, III. 160; _pl._ II. 61.

fyne, _n._ final concord (_see Note_), III. 322; _pl._ **fynys**, fines, IV. 4.

fyne, pure, 1636.

finge, _v._ **fangeth**.

flateris, _pl._ flatterers, II. 120, III. 198; OF. flateur.

flauour, _n._ smell, 940.

flavryng, _pr. p._ smelling, 894.

fle, _inf._ flee, II. 7; _pt. pl._ **flowen**, II. 15.

fle, _inf._ fly, III. 61; OE. flēogan.

fleuble, weak, 856; [fl]eu[b]le (MS. **peuple**), 1587; OF. feuble, fleble; _adj. not in O.E.D._; _vb. in Will. Palerne_ 2660.

fleuble, _pr._ 3 _s. subj._ grow weak, 1042; OF. flebir, feblir; _cp._ **feblen**.

fleissh, flesh, III. 16; OE. flǣsc.

flite, _inf._ quarrel, 705; OE. flītan.

floter, _inf._ flutter, II. 166; OE. flotorian.

flowen, _v._ **fle**.

floxe, _n. pl._ flocks, 602.

fode, person, II. 169; 1249, 1618; _pl._ **foodis**, III. 126; **fodis**, III. 260; OE. fōda, food.

fodith, _pr._ 3 _s._ feeds, III. 52; _pt. pl._ **fodid**, II. 135; OE. fōda, _n._

foyne, beach-marten, III. 150; OF. foine.

folowe, _inf._ prosecute at law, 1618; _pp._ **folowed**, 1587; OF. folgian.

folowid, _pt. pl._ gave in baptism, 417; OE. fullwian.

foltheed, folly, II. 7; OF. folet, a fool.

fonde, _v._ **fyndist**.

fondeth, _pr._ 3 _s._ tries, 1186; _pt._ 1 _s._ fo[n]dyd, P. 50; OE. fandian.

fongen, *v.* fangeth.

foodis, *v.* fode.

fooly, foolish, 113 ; OF. ful, *adj.* + -ly.

foolie, folly, 131 ; fooly, 695 ; folie, IV. 23 ; OF. folie.

foote, foot, 1742 ; þe f. he goeth vndre, he is put into subjection, 41 ; fotte, III. 108.

for, *prep.* notwithstanding, III. 219, III. 220 ; 1511 ; for fear of, I. 39, IV. 79 ; 266, 777.

for, *conj.* because, P. 27 ; 528, 540.

forbere, *inf.* show mercy to, 476.

forckis, gallows. I. 108.

for-doth, *pr. pl.* spoil, III. 141.

forelle, covering for a book, 1586 ; OF. forrel.

for-feyturis, forfeits, fines, IV. 5.

forme, formal procedure, IV. 33.

formed, *pt.* 3 *s.* persuaded, I. 107 ; *pl.* informed, IV. 58 ; *pp.* y-fourmyd, 1553.

forne-fadres, forefathers, 1742 ; OE. foran ; *cp.* ON. for-faðir.

forth, *adv.* continuously, P. 55, III. 61 ; 1397 ; forward, III 143 ; fourth, 36, 62.

forweyned, *part. adj.* pampered, I. 27 ; OE. forwened.

forӡelde, *pr.* 3 *s. subj.* repay, 1218 ; OE. for + gieldan.

fostrith, *pr.* 3 *s.* brings up, III. 61 ; *pt. pl.* fostrid, II. 135.

fotte, *v.* foote.

foulyd, *pt.* 3 *s.* hunted wild fowl, II. 157.

founde, *inf.* try, 1133 ; funde, 1510 ; *imp. s.* 84 ; OE. fundian.

foundrith, *pr.* 3 *s.* falls, 1162 ; *pr.* 3 *s. subj.* funder, 1042 ; OF. fondrer.

fourth, *v.* forth.

fourthering, *v.* ferthryng.

frayed, *pp.* rubbed, 1586.

frayned, *v.* freyne.

frankeleyn-is, *g. s.* free-holder's, 946 ; *pl.* frankeleyns, 788 ; ALat. franc-colanus, AF. fraunclein.

fre, noble, II. 148, III. 83 ; *sup.* freyst, 1284.

freeke, man, 54, 752 ; freek, 101 ; OE. freca.

fre-holde, estate held in fee-simple, fee-tail, or for term of life (*O.E.D.*), 946 ; *first ex. in O.E.D.* 1467.

freyne, *inf.* question, 84 ; *pt.* 1 *s.*

frayned, 395 ; *pp.* 752 ; OE. fregnan.

freysh, *v.* fressh.

freyst, *v.* fre.

frelle, frail, P. 83 ; OF. fraile, frele.

freres, friars, 392, 410, 416, 424.

fressh, gaily dressed, III. 126 ; vigorous, 1280 ; freysh, 65 ; OF. freis, *m.*, fresche. *f.* ; OF. fersc.

fresshely, vigorously, IV. 73.

freted, *pt.* 3 *s.* ate, II. 127 ; OE. fretan.

frie, young fish, 897 ; *cp.* OF. frier, *var. of* froier, to spawn.

frist, *adj.* first, I. 107 ; furst, 408 ; *adv.* 143 ; frist, II. 47, III. 112 ; OE. fyrst.

fryth, wood, II. 180 ; OE. fyrhþ.

frithe, firth, II. 171 ; ON. fjorðr; *first ex. of metaph. form in O.E.D.* 1600.

frounting, *verb. n.* harsh treatment, 28 ; OF. fronter, *or aph. form of* afronting ; *this sense not in O.E.D.*

fructe, fruit, 602 ; frute, P. 58 ; OF. fruit, *infl. by* Lat. frūctus.

fruotuous, profitable, 434.

ful, thorough, true, 1149.

ful-come, *pp.* perfected (in knowledge), 848 ; *cp.* Germ. volkommen; *first example in O.E.D.* 1477.

fullfill, *inf.* fill to the full, P. 34.

fundacion, establishment, 544, 1103.

fundament, foundation, 393 ; fundement, 1192.

funde, *v.* founde.

funded, *pt.* 3 *s.* established, 1433 ; *pp.* fundid, 434 ; yffoundid, III. 265 ; OF. fonder, funder.

funder, *v.* foundrith.

fundre, *n.* founder, 494 ; OF. fonder, *v.*

furst, *v.* frist.

gaderid, *pt.* 3 *s.* collected, II. 153 ; OE. gaderian.

gadryng, *verb. n.* collection, 1412.

gaglide, *pt. pl.* cackled, III. 101 ; *onomat.* ; *cp.* mod. Icel. gagga.

gayes, ornaments, badges, II. 94 ; OF. gai, *adj.*

galle, *n.* sore, 770 ; OE. gealla.

ga[rth] (MS. gate), garden, 976 ; ON. garðr.

gaste, *part. adj.* afraid, 1543 ; OE. gæstan.

general, universal, 314.

Genesis, 1313.

gentil, noble, 1313.

gery, ever-changing, III. 131 ; *cp.* ME. gere, a fit of passion.

gettinge, *verb. n.* of g., as regards revenue, III. 242.

gye, *inf.* guide, P. 45 ; gie, III. 283 ; guye, 224 ; OF. guier.

[g]ifte (MS. 3ifte), giving, II. 96.

gile, guile, I. 12.

gylours, deceivers, I. 25 ; g[uy]leris (MS. gyuleris), III. 131.

gioure, *n.* leader, P. 29 ; guyer, 212.

gyse, fashion, III. 162, III. 212 ; *pl.* gysis, III. 192 ; OF. guise.

gyside, *pt. pl.* disguised, III. 159.

gladdest, most beautiful, 947.

glade, *inf.* rejoice, P. 40 ; OE. gladian.

glaunsyng, *verb. n.* shooting, 269 ; *cp.* OF. glacer.

glees, occasions of mirth, III. 278.

glewith, *pr. pl.* entangle, 1572 ; OF. gluer.

glymsyng, *pr. p.* glancing, 314 ; OE. *glimsian.

gloire, glory, 1163 ; OF. gloire.

glose, *n.* comment, 314 ; *also* flattery, 141, 162, 388 ; OF. glose.

glosinge, *verb. n.* flattery, IV. 38.

glowed, *pt.* 3 s. stared, glowered, 330.

go, *inf.* go on foot, II. 115 ; be reckoned, 694 ; *pr.* 3 s. goeth, takes place, 1412 ; *pr. p.* goyng vppon erthe, living, 181, 212 ; *pp.* y-gon, been distributed, II. 94.

goyng(e), *verb. n.* at þe longe g., in the end, in the long run, III. 136 ; 70, 1302 ; *see Note.*

gŏky, uneducated man, person of no importance, 1582 ; *cp.* ON. gaukr, cuckoo ; *see Note.*

gome, man, 60 ; *pl.* gomes, II. 153 ; OE. guma.

good, sufficient, III. 250 ; property, 1684, 1712 ; men of good(e), men of standing, 681, 844, 1504.

goodliche, liberally, II. 3.

goodman, man, 130 (*see Note*) ; *pl.* goodmen, householders, I. 66.

gost, mind, heart, P. 40 ; *pl.* gostis, persons, I. 25.

gouernaunce, behaviour, III. 223 ; 313 ; gouernance, good management, III. 242 ; gouerna[un]ce, III. 250.

gouuerne, *inf.* rule, 96 ; *pr.* 3 s. *subj.* gouuerne, P. 85.

gouernour, ruler, P. 45.

graffe, *inf.* graft, 1158 ; OF. grafe, *n.*

grame, *n.* evil, 726, 730 ; anger 809.

grame, *inf.* be displeased, P. 41 ; OE. grama, *n.*

grammier, grammarian, 330 ; OF. gramaire ; *not in N.E.D.*

grand mercy, thanks, 1218.

gre, degree, 1233 ; OF. gre.

grece, *n.* fat, 928.

grece, *inf.* anoint, 117.

greehonde, greyhound, II 113 ; ON. greyhundr, OE. grīghund.

greyues, *v.* grief.

grennes, *n. pl.* snares, II. 188 ; OE. grin.

grete, *pt.* 3 s. greeted, 973 ; OE. grētan, *wk.*

grett, great, P. 6, I 41 ; as *n. pl.* grette, great ones, III. 190, IV. 38.

grevance, trouble, 1160.

gr[eue], thicket, tangle of weeds, 179 ; OE. grǣfa.

grief, suffering, grievance, 134 ; *pl.* greues, I. 96, II. 65 ; greyues, IV. 38 ; griefs, sores, 117.

griefz, *n. pl.* claws, 1163 ; OF. griffe ; *first ex. in O.E.D. from* Shelley.

groyn, *n.* grumbling, 711 ; groyne, 809 ; OF. groign.

gromes, serving-men, I. 66, III. 344.

grone, *pr. pl. subj.* complain, III. 308 ; *pp.* groned, 563.

grott, trifle, whit, P. 35 ; *pl.* grotus, money, III. 82 ; grots, 134 ; M. Du. groot.

grounde, earth, P. 45 ; 1163 ; foundation II. 91 ; 1113, 1158 ; grovnd, 76 ; grovnde, cause, 1543, 1555 ; ground, 726 ; grou[n]de, II. 96.

grovnde, *inf.* establish, 1712.

groved, *pt.* 3 s. grew, 146 ; *pl.* groued, 191 ; grovid, 907 ; growed, 951.

grucche, ill-will, 269, 711.

grucchen, *inf.* grudge, P. 35 ; *pr. pl.* 1412 ; OF. groucher.

grucchinge, *verb. adj.* III. 245.

grucching[s], *n. pl.* 759.

Grumbald, 330 ; *see Note.*

guye(r), *v.* gye, gioure.

g[uy]leris, *v.* gylours.

gunne, *pt. pl.* began to, 117.

gurde, *pp.* girt, 563 ; OE. gyrdan.

gurdel, girdle, 1072 : OE. gyrdel.

gurdyng, *verb. n.* hitting, 1160, 1654 ; *derivation unknown.*

ȝe, *nom. s.* yon, I. 4; *obj.* ȝou, I. 4.
ȝere, year, II. 89; **yere-is** y[i]fte,
ǃannual present, 820.
ȝeue, *inf.* give, II. 92, III. 261; *pt.*
3 *s.* **yafe**, 422.
ȝif, if, P. 37.
ȝou, *v.* ȝe.
ȝou-self, *pron. refl.* yourself, I. 1;
emphat. ȝoure-self, II. 61.

habben, *pr. pl.* have, 8; **han**, P.
62.
hacche, *inf.* III. 44; *pr. pl.* hacchen, II. 143.
hay-nettes, nets used for catching
wild animals, 913; AF. haie;
(?) OE. hege, hedge; *see O.E.D.*;
first ex. in O.E.D. 1499.
[haynous], terrible, 1665.
halen, *pr. pl.* pull, 1568; OF. haler.
hales, tents, III. 218; OF. hale; *see
Note on* III. 216.
half, side, P. 11.
halfdell, half, III. 218; **halfdelle**,
IV. 2.
halfendele, half, 1653, 1711; OE.
þone healfan dæl.
halowid, *pp.* pursued with shouts,
III. 228; **y-hal**[ow]**id** (MS. y
haulid), 174; *cp.* OF. halloer.
halsid, *pt.* 1 *s.* greeted, 972; OE.
hālsian.
halten, *pr. pl.* hesitate, 1137; OE.
haltian.
hamward, homewards, 1179.
han, *v.* habben.
hand-m[el]le, hammer wielded by
the hand, II. 155; OF. mail; *see
Note.*
hangid, *v.* hongeth.
hansell, reward, IV. 91; OE. hand-
selen.
hantid, *pt.* 3 *s.* had resort to, fed on,
II. 178; *pp.* hauntid, 1071; F.
hanter.
happe, fortune, 123; *pl.* happes,
129; mischances, 1387.
happeth, *pr. s. impers.* happens to,
III. 22; *pr.* 3 *s. subj.* happe, comes
by chance, P. 53.
haras, stallions, III. 27; in h., at
stud, 921; OF. haraz, a stud, collection of stud-horses.
harde, ungenial, II. 134.
harmes, *n. pl.* damages, III. 332;
har[m]esse, I. 26.
hassellis, retainers, II. 25 (*see Note*);
ǃ*g. pl.* haselle, 29.

hatis, *pr.* 2 *s.* hatest, 1558.
hatte, *pr.* 3 *s.* is called, 37; *pt.* 3 *s.*
242; OE. hātan, *pass.* hātte.
hauntelere-dere, antlered deer, II.
128; OF. antoillier.
hautesse, pride, stateliness, III. 13;
F. hautesse.
he, it, I. 70; he who, III. 46.
hedid, *part. adj.* bearing horns or
antlers, 1589; **y-heedid**, 929; **y-
heedyd**, II. 4.
heed-dere, head deer, chief deer, II.
117.
heede, head, 188 (*see Note*), 1473,
1631; **heed**, III. 326; 51; head
of antlers, II. 130; *pl.* **heedes**,
heads, 1569.
heelde, *pr.* 3 *s. subj.* descend, 736;
OE. hieldan, heldan.
heere, hair, II. 188; OE. hær.
heeris, heirs, III. 100; **hoires**, 1436;
NF. heir, central F. hoir.
heeste, *v.* heste.
heyer, [h]eyere, *v.* high.
heigges, hedges, 881, 886, 919; OE.
hecg.
heipeth, *pr.* 3 *s.* heaps up, III. 42;
OE. hēap, *n.*
he-is, his, 339.
helde, *v.* holde.
hele, recovery, I. 96; prosperity, P.
75, I. 101; OE. hælu, hæl.
helid, *pp.* concealed, 415; **yhelid**,
III. 212; OE. helian.
helthe, prosperity, P. 26.
hem, them, P. 66, P. 73; **him**,. III.
286.
hende, courteous, gracious, II. 145;
OE. gehende.
hendely, courteously, 656; **hendily**,
972.
Henrri, P. 11; **Henry**, 1405; *g. s.*
Henry-is, 206.
hente, *inf.* obtain, I. 96; catch, III.
22; *pt. pl.* received, II. 43; **henten**,
III. 365; OE. hentan.
herbaige, *coll.* herbs, 606; F. her-
bage.
herborowe, *inf.* shelter, III. 217;
OE. *herebeorgian; ON. herbergja.
here, their, P. 83; **her**, P. 66, II.
151; **hir**, III. 26; [**hire**], 1437.
herkeneth to, *pr. pl.* have regard to,
seek after, III. 285.
herne, nook, corner, III. 211; OE.
hyrne.
hertis, harts, II. 4.
hertis, hearts, II. 43.

L

hertly, sincerely, zealously, 22.
heruest, autumn, II. 146, III. 44;
    harvest, I. 79.
heste, bidding, II. 58; 357; heeste,
    2; OE. hǽs.
hetith, *pr.* 3 *s.* warms, III. 42.
heulde(n), *v.* holde.
heuene[-ȝate], heaven-gate, III, 293;
    OE. geat; *see Note.*
heuy, sorrowful, III. 89; hevy, 293.
hewe. *pr.* 3 *s. subj.* strike, 1473; *pl.*
    188; *pp.* 1732.
Hicke Heuyheed, III. 66.
hye, *imp. s.* continue, prosper, 382;
    OE. hīgian.
hied, *pp.* advanced, III. 133; OE.
    hīgan, hēgan.
high, great, tall, 921; hie, III. 217;
    on h., on high, I. 108; more
    heigher, superior, 1503; as *n.*
    higher, 1578; heyer, III. 74;
    [h]eyere, II. 145; *sup.* hiest, III.
    355.
hyly, greatly, II. 117.
hille, *inf.* cover, III. 326; OE.
    *hyllan; ON. hylja.
him, *dat.* it, P. 54, III. 242; hym,
    439.
him, *v.* hem.
hyne, servant, 1189, 1209; OE.
    hīgan, *pl.*
hippe, *imp. s.* hop, 1240; OE. *hyp-
    pan; *cp.* MHG. hüpfen.
hire, *n.* payment, IV. 64; 271; hure,
    22, 1197; OE. hȳr.
hire, *inf.* hear, 596, 938; *imp. s.*
    22, 1049; *pl.* hireth, 656; OE.
    hīeran, hēran.
hirte, *n.* hurt, III. 89; OF. hurte.
his, its, 204; his . . . pat, of him
    who, 1225.
hit is, there is, 743; he is, 1213.
ho, he who, P. 85, II. 18; if any
    one, III. 123; OE. hwā.
hobbis, common fellows, I. 90;
    hobbes, 865; *by-form of* Rob
    (*O.E.D.*).
hobblid, *pp.* wandered about, II. 23;
    hoblid, III. 15.
hockerope, 1568; *not in O.E.D.*;
    see Note.
hodes, hoods, 777.
hoires, *v.* heeris.
holde, *inf.* 271; *imp. s.* 382; *pt.* 3 *s.*
    heulde, 280; *pl.* heulden, 799;
    helde, II. 48, IV. 64; *pp.* y-
    holde, III. 355.
hole, *v.* hoole.

holsum, salutary, health-giving, use-
    ful, III. 212; 102, 902; *sup.*
    holsemyst, 1209.
holsumly, with good effect, 206.
holte, wood, III. 15; *pl.* holtes, II.
    23; holtz, 886.
homelich, simply, III. 212.
homeliche, simple, II. 43.
homes, homesteads, 602.
honde, hand, P. 53, III. 116;
    ho[n]de, 1472.
hongeth, *pr.* 3 *s.* clings, 61: *pt. pl.*
    hangid, were impending, III. 318.
honour, glory, renown, III. 285.
hoole, hole, cavity, 1002.
hoole, whole, P. 26; 2; hole, 1049.
hopen, *pr. pl.* hope, III. 133.
hore, grey, hoary, 958; OE. hār.
hornes, drinking or hunting horns,
    III. 140; *see Note.*
ho-so, if any one; II. 81, IV. 61;
    who-so, 818, 850.
hovgh, how, 1; OE. hū.
hourled, *v.* hurlle.
hovs, household, 206.
hous-hennes, domestic hens, II. 143.
housholde, household goods, 271.
hovsing, habitation, 1224; houu-
    singe, building, III. 217.
houe, lawyer's coif, III. 326; OE.
    hūfe.
houyn, *inf.* brood over, II. 146; *pr.*
    3 *s.* houeth, III. 50; hangs, hovers,
    1456; *pt.* 3 *s.* houed, II. 176; 966;
    derivation unknown.
how . . . euere, however, IV. 86.
hue, she (bird), III. 50; OE. hēo.
huyst, silent, 831; ME. hust, *interj.*
hunthrid, hundred, 509.
hure, *v.* hire.
Hurlewaynis, *g. s.* I. 90; *see Note.*
hurlle, *inf.* contend, III. 27; *pr.* 3 *s.*
    hurleth, 1578; 3 *s. subj.* hurle,
    1057; *pl.* 1597 (*only ex. of this
    sense in O.E.D. is from Prompt.
    Parv.*); *pp.* hourled, assailed,
    1590; *cp.* LG. hurreln.
hurtelid, *pt. pl.* rushed, 921.

y-bounde *part. adj.* bound, III. 296.
y-canonized, *part. adj.* made authori-
    tive, 1621.
y-charchid, *pp.* ordered, III. 230;
    OF. charchier, l.Lat. carcāre.
ychid, *pt.* 3 *s.* moved, ran, 917; *see
    O.E.D. under* icchen, itch*.
ich, each, P. 72; iche, III. 108;
    OE. ylc.

ichonne, each one, II. 35, III. 268.

y-chose, *v.* chese.

y-cried, *pp.* proclaimed, 148.

y-doluen, *v.* delue.

y-douutid, *v.* douȝteth.

y-dubbid, *pp.* knighted, III. 363; OF. aduber.

yffeyned, *part. adj.* feigned, P. 58.

yffoundid, *v.* funded.

y-fourmyd, *v.* formed.

y-f[u]lled, *pp.* trampled (as cloth by the fuller), 55; OF. fuler, fouler.

y-funge, *v.* fangeth.

ygraue, *pp.* engraved, I. 40.

y-hotte, *pp.* commanded, III. 228; y-hoote, 174; *cp.* hatte.

y-ioyned, *part. adj.* enjoined, appointed to a task, 16; *aph. form of* OF. enjoindre.

y-kidde, *part. adj.* well known, 214; OE gecydd.

i-knewe, *pt. pl.* knew, I. 92.

y-lad, *v.* lede.

y-lafte, *v.* leue.

ylauȝte, *v.* lacchide.

y-lyved, *v.* leue.

yloke, *v.* looke.

ympes, saplings, 950; OE. impa.

ympne, hymn, 519; *eccl.* Lat. ymnus, ympnus; OF. ymne, ympne.

y-murid, *part. adj.* imprisoned, 1195; F. murer.

increceth, *pr.* 3 *s.* makes prosperous, 610.

incumbreth, *pr.* 3 *s.* hampers, entangles, 66.

indure, *inf.* be able, 472; *pr. pl.* induren, bear, 742; *pt. pl.* endurid, remained, P. 22.

ynned, *pp.* lodged, III. 135; 1062; OE. innian.

ynnere, further in, III. 195.

ynowe, *adj.* enough, II. 27; *adv.* y-now, IV. 84; OE. genōge, *pl.*

in-sight, knowledge, 746.

intachid, *part. adj.* fastened, 1735; ? *variant of* attached.

intent(z), *v.* entent.

intre, *inf.* enter, 1242.

intremitte, *inf.* introduce themselves, meddle, 559; OF. entremetre, *infl. by* Lat. intermittere.

y-pighte, *v.* picche.

y-pynned, *pp.* fledged, II. 148; OF. penne, *n.*

y-plumed, *v.* plewme.

ypouudride, *part. adj.* sprinkled, I. 46.

y-quethe, *v.* cothe.

y-runne, *v.* renne.

y-seye, *v.* se.

y-shourid, *pp.* rained down, 760; *first ex. in O.E.D.* 1573; *first figurative use in Shakespeare.*

y-sibbe, related, 1247; OE. gesibb; *cp.* sibbe.

y-soupid, *pp.* supped, IV. 55; y-s[o]pid, 549; OF. soper, souper.

issues, *n. pl.* profits from fines, IV. 8.

y-twyght, *pp.* jerked, 420; OE. *twiccan, *cp.* LG. twikken.

yuell, evil, II. 40.

y-wedid, *part. adj.* clothed, 957; *not in O.E.D.*; *cp.* un-wēded, Lindisfarne Matt. xxii. 11.

i-wis, certainly, 701; OE. gewis.

yworewid, *v.* wirwe.

y-wounde, *part. adj.* wrapped, III. 215.

iablid, *pt.* 3 *s.* gabbled, 346; *variant of* jabber; *first ex. in O.E.D.* 1570.

jaces, fringes, ribbons, III. 131; *apparently a variant of* jess, a strap of leather or silk confining the leg of a hawk; OF. jes.

Iacobynes, Dominicans, 503.

Ieometrie, geometry, 346.

jette, fashion, III. 159; iette, 375; [i]ette (MS. yette), 311; OF. jet.

jewis, punishment, III. 341; OF. juise.

Ihesus, *g. s.* 514.

icygned, *pp.* joined together, 514.

ioynour, joiner, carpenter, 346.

Ioseph, 1313.

Iudas, *g. s.* 503.

iuges, judges, magistrates, 16.

iustice, *n. pl.* judges, 16.

iust[es] (MS. iustice), jousts, 514; OF. juste.

kayseris, emperours, I. 85; ON. keisari.

kareyne, *v.* caroigne.

karis, *v.* caris.

kempe, man, 1221; OE. cempa; *see Note.*

kenetta, small hunting-dogs, 927; ONF. kennet, OF. chienet.

kenne, *pr. pl.* hatch out, III. 51 (*the only ex. of this sense in O.E.D.*); OE. cennan.

kenneth, *imp. pl.* teach, 1c68.
kepe, *n.* heed, IV. 61 ; 912.
kepe, *inf.* hold, III. 93 ; 562 ; protect, 738 ; *pr. pl.* kepeth, keep, III. 138 ; *pt.* 3 *s.* kepte, II. 167 ; *pp.* I. 76.
kerne, *inf.* form seed, 67 ; OE. *cyrnan. cp.* Norw. kyrna.
keuere, *inf.* regain health, III. 17.
keuereth, *pr.* 3 *s.* covers, III. 51.
kew-kaw, corruption, venality, III. 299 ; *see Note.*
kynde, nature, II. 4 ; kinde, 962, 1675 ; kynde, class, I. 91 ; of k., natural, III. 53.
kynde, natural, III. 55, III. 70, IV. 76.
kindely, natural, 1458 ; *adv.* thoroughly, 109, 1065.
kindenes, kinship, natural affection, 640.
kynne, kin, I. 90 ; what kynnes, what kind of, II. 19 ; 100 ; no k., no kind of, 256.
kisshyng, *verb. n.* kissing, touching, 915 ; OE. cyssan.
[kitte] (MS. light), light woman, 1357 ; *first ex. in O.E.D.* 1577 ; *but cp. P. Plowman,* C. viii. 304.
knotte, carved ornament, 3.
knowes, *pr.* 2 *s.* 85 ; *pt. pl.* knewe, understood, III. 323.
knowlache, knowledge, 733 ; *cp.* OE. cnaw læcung.
kow, cow, III. 262.
kunne, *v.* cunne.
kun(n)ynge, *v.* cunnyng.
kuyttis, kites, II. 158 ; OE. cyta.

[l]ab[b]ing (MS. babling), *verb. n.* chattering, 1483.
laboreth, *pr.* 3 *s.* travels, 1580.
lacchide, *pt. pl.* took, I. 72 ; lau3te, II. 159 ; *pp.* ylau3te, II. 173, III. 336 ; laught, 533, 1168 ; OE. læccan.
lacke, *pr. pl.* are lacking in, 6 ; *pt. pl.* lacked, were lacking, I. 55.
ladde, fellow, III. 146.
ladde, *v.* lede.
lafte, *v.* leue.
lay, *pt.* 3 *s.* l. to, pertained to, 361.
laikid, *pt. pl.* played, 919 ; ON. leika.
land-is ende, 1397.
langage, P. 43 ; OF. langage.
lappe, fold of a garment, 250.

large, liberal, II. 2 ; *adv.* fully, 870 ; freely, 1184.
lasse, *adj.* less, 158, 1334.
laste, burden, heavy cargo, IV. 74 ; OE. hlæst.
Latyne, 744.
laudate, ignoramus, 637 (*see Note*) ; lesson of l., lauds, 1359 ; *not in O.E.D.*
laught, (y)lau3te, *v.* lacchide.
launde, lawn, open space among woods, 930 ; OF. lande, launde.
lawelesse, lawlessly, I. 2.
lede, man, II. 49 ; leode, III. 255 ; lude, 1310 ; *pl.* leodis, II. 2 ; ludes, 115 ; OE. lēod.
lede, *inf.* lead, conduct, 1374 ; ledyn, III. 175 ; *pt.* 3 *s.* ladde, III. 57 ; *pl.* I. 68 ; *pp.* y-lad, 135 ; lad, 419.
leef, dear, I. 4 ; *sup.* leuest, II. 156 ; *comp. adj.* levir, rather, 805 ; leuer, 1519 ; *sup.* leueste, most especially, P. 65 ; OE. lēof.
leef, page, P. 37 ; *pl.* lyfe[s], 384 ; OE. lēaf.
leesinge, ? broadening, extending, III. 158 ; OF. lese, breadth ; *cp.* Fr. laize, largeur d'une étoffe, *Dict. Acad.* ; *not in O.E.D.*
lefte, *v.* leue.
legiance, allegiance, I. 24 ; legaunce, II. 104 ; OF. legiance.
ley3ttone, garden, 978 ; OE. lēah-tūn, *lēac-tūn, an enclosure for leeks.
leyne, ? estate held as a benefice, II. 136 ; OE. læn ; *not in O.E.D. between 1000 and 1844.* Or scribal error for 'lyene', lien.
lele, loyal, II. 83 ; OF. leel.
lelly, faithfully, II. 57.
lemes, limbs, II. 156.
lemmans, mistresses, 1351.
lendys, loins, III. 59 ; OE. lendenu.
lendith, *pr. pl.* dwell, 108 ; OE. lendan.
lene, *inf.* l. to, support oneself by, II. 62 ; *pr.* 3 *s.* leneth, leans, is partial, 1625.
lene, *adj.* lean, III. 59.
lente, *pt. pl* gave out, III. 330.
leode, leodis, *v.* lede.
lere, *inf.* teach, II. 18 ; *pp.* lerid, instructed, 636 ; OE. læran.
lerne, *inf.* learn, 621 ; *imp. pl.* lerneth, I. 9 ; *pp.* lerned, instructed, P. 43.

lese, establishment of hounds, II.
114; OF. lesse ; *see Note*.

lese, *inf.* lose, III. 309.

lesing, *verb. n.* lie, 423, 1444; *pl.*
lesingz, 419, 1402 ; OE. lēasung.

leste, least, 1652.

leste, unless, 581.

lete, *inf.* shed, I. 31 ; *pr. pl.* letith
lyghte, think lightly, III. 284;
imp. lete sle him, have him slain,
III. 234.

lette, *inf.* desist, II. 86; hinder, 748;
pt. pl. II. 60; *pr. s. subj.* III. 115 ;
pt. s. letted, II. 3 ; *pp.* y-lettid,
761 ; OE. lettan.

lettrure, learning, 1352, 1358 ; OF.
lettreure.

leue, *inf.* cease, 618, 1090 ; allow,
611 ; *pt.* 3 *s.* lefte, forsook, 811;
lafte, left, 969; *pl.* III. 80 ; *imp.*
s. leue, 83; 2 *s. subj.* cease, 1557 ;
pl. leave, III. 1 ; *pp.* y-lafte, IV.
21.

leue, *inf.* believe, I. 93, III. 179;
1511 ; *pr.* 2 *s.* leves, 680; 3 *s.*
leueth, III. 117 ; *pt.* 1 *s.* lyeued,
531 ; *imp. s.* lyve, 1030 ; *pr.* 2 *s.*
subj. lieue, 1202 ; *pp.* leued, III.
143 ; y-lyved, 59 ; lyeued, 36.

leue, *inf.* live, III. 25, III. 266 ; lyve,
1749 ; *pt.* 3 *s. subj.* leued, III.
290 ; *pp.* leuyd, living, II. 83 ;
see Note.

leued, *pp.* made weak, III. 59 ; OE.
gelēfed.

leued, levde, *v.* lewde.

leuel, an instrument for indicating
the horizontal, 348.

leuerey, giving of badges, II. 2 ;
leuere, delivery, III. 330 ; livery,
II. 26 ; lyuraye, 803.

leues, *n. pl.* leaves, II. 186.

leuynge, *verb. n.* faith, II. 83.

levir, leuer, leuest(e), *v.* leef.

lewde, unlearned, II. 53, III. 267 ;
1362 ; worthless, foolish, III. 146,
III. 326 ; lewed, 637, 1749; back-
ward, dull, 620 ; leued, unlearned,
12 ; levde, unchaste, 1357.

lewte, loyalty, I. 44, III. 117 ; AF.
lewte, OF. leaute.

liage, *v.* liege.

librarie, collection of books, 1626.

licke, *inf.* ? lick up, make profit, 441.

lickyng, *verb. n.* infringing (on),
I 27.

lyden[e], language, 1030 ; OE. lēo-
den.

Lydfford, III. 145 ; *see Note*.

liege, subject, II. 49 ; liage, P. 25 ;
pl. liegis, II. 20; OF. lige, liege.

lien, *pr. pl.* tell lies, 1352 ; lyen,
510.

lieue, lyeued, *v.* leue.

lifes, *n. pl.* lives, 205.

lyfe[z], *v.* leef.

lyff-daies, days of one's life, III. 175.

lyfflode, food, III. 253 ; lyuelode,
1177 ; OE. liflād.

lifte, *pt.* 1 *s.* lifted, 889 ; *pp.* ylyfte,
carried away, I. 4.

liggen, *pr. pl.* lie, lodge, 1356 ; *pr.*
2 *s. subj.* ligge, be overthrown,
1557.

light, frivolous, III. 123.

lyghte, *pt.* 3 *s.* came, II. 172.

lyghtlich, easily, I. 4 ; lyghtliche,
III. 117; lightly, 59, 761; quickly,
827 ; lygh[t]liche, III. 336.

lygnees, *v.* lyne.

like, *inf.* be pleasing to, 1616; *pt.*
3 *s.* likyde, III. 158 ; *pt.* 3 *s. subj.*
liked, P. 64 ; *pr. p.* lykynge,
liking, II. 56.

likerous, pleasant, 128, 1177 ; AF.
*likerous, OF. lecheros ; *cp.* ONF.
liquerie.

lykynge, *verb. n.* at l., to one's
pleasure, III. 25.

lille for lalle, tit for tat, 1357 ; OE.
læl wið læle = livorem pro livore,
Ex. xxi. 25.

lymed, *part. adj.* smeared with bird-
lime, II. 186.

limitacions, districts allotted to
separate friars, 438.

limitour, friar licensed to beg in a
certain district, 440.

lynage, tribe, II. 179; OF. linage.

lynche, unploughed strip between
fields, 857 ; OE. hlinc.

lyne, plumb-line, 348 ; *pl.* lynes,
snares made of cord, 1161 ; lygnees,
lineages, 1745.

list, *pr. impers.* it pleases, P. 37 ;
lustiþ, III. 38 ; luste, 340 ; liste,
II. 18; *subj. pr.* II. 71 ; *pers. pr.*
3 *s.* luste, desires, 748 ; *pt. pl.* list,
II. 62 ; OE. lystan, lust, *n.*

lite, *n.* little, P. 25, III. 183, IV.
62 ; l. and a lite, little by little,
1677 ; *adj.* [lite] 662 ; OE. lȳt,
ON. lītt.

lithe, *inf.* relieve, 857 ; OE. līðe,
mild.

lither, evil, 969, 1069 ; OE. lȳðre.

lyve, *v.* leue.
lyuelode, *v.* lyflode.
lyuraye, *v.* leuerey.
loby, clothing, II. 170; *see Note.*
loeth, troublesome, 184; l. of, averse
to, 46.
loyally, faithfully, 136.
loigge, dwelling, 1241; *pl.* loigges,
845, 1021; OF. loge, loige.
loiggeth, *pr.* 3 *s.* dwells, 187; *pp.*
loigged, sheltered, 901.
loising, *verb. n.* losing, 1177; OE.
losian, *vb.*
loke, *inf.* take measures, III. 31;
study, P. 37; *pt.* 1 *s.* lokid, 845;
3 *s.* lokide, III. 255; *pp.* loked,
361.
Lollards, *g.pl.* 417 : *see Note.*
lolle, *inf.* hang, 419.
londe, vppon l., in the country, II.
143; lond-is lawe, law of the
land, 751.
London, 1356.
longe, *adv.* long, 211.
longith, *pr.* 3 *s.* pertains, II. 67, III.
43; longeth, 219; *pt.* 3 *s.* longid,
II. 172; IV. 76.
looke, *pp.* locked, closely bound, 803;
yloke, I. 44; OE. lūcan, gelocen.
loos, fame, report, 1508, 1557, 1580;
OF. los.
looste, *v.* lust.
lordis, *g. pl.* of lords, II. 30; lorden,
1356; lordyns, II. 60.
lordschepe, domain, II. 172; lordship, 1328; sovereignty, 1627.
lore, doctrine, P. 63; 76.
lorell, rogue, II. 170; lorel, 1302;
pl. lorelles, 1391; OE. loren, lost.
losers, destroyers, 1362.
lotebies, paramours, 1351; *cp.* ME.
lot(i)en, OE. *lotian, to lurk.
lothe, *n.* harm, 1511.
lourid, *pt.pl.* frowned, I. 72; *pr.* 3 *s.*
subj. lovre, 83.
loute, *inf.* bow, 1328; OE. lūtan.
loue, *inf.* praise, 406; OE. lofian.
loued, *pt.* 3 *s.* loved, P. 12.
loue-dayes, agreements made by
friendly settlement, 1145.
lowe, *inf.* humiliate, 1519; *pt.* 3 *s.*
louyd, II. 179; *pp.* III. 310.
lucas, ?'luck-ace', luckless person,
775; ace, the lowest throw at dice.
Lucifer, 1157.
lude(s), *v.* lede.
luggid, *pp.* worried, baited, II. 173;
y-luggyd, III. 336.

lurker, skulker, III. 57.
lust, desire, III. 175; looste, 128;
pl. lustus, I. 30; lusts, P. 82.
luste, lustip, *v.* list.
lusty, pleasing, P. 63; 901, 905.

maces, clubs, III. 268.
maddid, *pt.* 3 *s.* bewildered, I. 63;
pl. II. 132.
mafflid, *pt. pl.* mumbled, IV. 63; *cp.*
early mod. Du. maffelen.
maij, May, 1644 (2).
mayntenance, wrongfully aiding and
abetting litigation, III. 312; 27,
485; mayntennance, 1566.
maisons deu, hospitals, 1687.
maiste, *pr.* 2 *s.* mayst, III. 62; mays,
1278, 1471; 3 *s.* may, 1644 (1);
pl. moun, III. 166; mowe, II.
133; 47; *pt.* 3 *s.* my3th, P. 6; *pr.*
2 *s. subj.* mowe, 86.
maistrie, *inf.* master, overcome, 882;
OF. maistrier.
[make], *n.* mate, 337.
make vp, *inf.* put together, 1278;
pp. y-made, 206.
malaperte, impudent one, III. 237;
OF. malapert, the reverse of 'apert',
frank, open. *In English sense is*
improperly bold; *see O.E.D.*
male, bag, 825; OF. male.
malgre, *v.* maul-gre.
man, servant, 1254; *g. pl.* men,
men's, 461, 541, 1332.
manachyd, *pt.* 3 *s.* menaced, 579;
pp. manaced, III. 337; OF. mane-
cier, manechier; AF. manasser.
manasshing, *verb. n.* threatening,
485.
mangier, manger, 560.
manhoode, dignity, 1666.
maniere, custom, 819; for þe manere, in accordance with custom,
IV. 44.
mansions, houses, 887, 1004.
man-sleer, murderer, 1301.
Marche, IV. 7; *see Note.*
marches, bordering countries, 1422;
this sense not in O.E.D.
Marie, 454, 672, 1089.
marrid, *pt.* 3 *s.* troubled, 350.
mase, *n.* on þe m., in confusion,
1731 : *pl.* mases, deceits, 1252.
matall, metal, II. 155.
mates, companions, 673.
maul-gre, in spite of, 1525; malgre
his chekes, notwithstanding his
resistance, 1300.

me, *pron.* one, 72 ; OE. man.
mede, *n.* reward, II. 84 ; 87.
medlers of, those busied with, III. 335.
medues, meadows, 887.
meen, *v.* mene.
meyny, company, 47 ; meeyne, 158; mene, III. 224; OF. meyne.
meyneteyne, *pr. pl.* support in litigation, III. 311; *pp.* menteyne[d], III. 354.
meyntenour, 'maintainer', II. 78 ; *pl.* meyntenour3, III. 268.
melis, meals, III. 313.
melle, *inf.* speak, 344, 526, 674 ; *pt.* 3 *s. subj.* mellid, 287 ; OE. meðlan.
mellen, *pr. pl.* concern themselves, 429, 1411 ; OF. meller.
mellid, *pt.* 3 *s.* beat, II. 155 ; *cp.* OF. mail, mal, a hammer.
memoire, memorial, commemoration, 630.
men, *v.* man.
mende, *inf.* amend, P. 38 ; 92 ; *pr.* 3 *s.* mendeth, benefits, 1695.
mendis, *n.* amends, I. 59, III. 354; *aph. form of* amends.
mene, *n.* medium, II. 139; meen, 618.
m[en]e, *adj.* mean, poor, 1503.
mene, *v.* meyny.
menest, *pr.* 2 *s.* meanest, III. 65 ; menys, 91 ; 3 *s.* meneth, 161; *pp.* ment, intended, 544.
Menours, Minorites, Franciscans, 504.
mensshid, *pp.* honoured, 774 ; OE. menniscu, *n. Not in O.E.D., except in Northern form* mense.
menteyne[d], *v.* meyneteyne.
meri, happy, II. 139 ; *comp.* myrier, 849.
meritable, meritorious, 207.
merke, *inf.* provide with badges, II. 20, II. 56 ; strike, III. 268 ; *pt.* 1 *s.* merkid, observed, 315 ; *pl.* merkyd, II. 42 (*see Note*) ; OA. gemercian.
Merlyn, 1724 ; *see Note.*
meruaille, *pr.* 1 *s.* marvel, 233 ; *impers.* merueilith, II. 1.
messaigier, envoy, ambassador, 1138; OF. messagier.
messe, dish, 834 ; OF. mes.
mesurable, moderate, reasonable, 1244.
mesure, moderation, II. 139.

mete, dinner-time, 687.
mete, *inf.* measure, III. 172.
mette, *pt.* 1 *s.* dreamed, 871; 3 *s.* 1315; *pt. pl. subj.* 1394; OE. mætan.
meukest, *v.* muke.
meuve, *inf.* move, P. 32; meve, bring forward, I. 84 ; *pt.* 1 *s.* moeued, 326 ; moeuyd, 396 ; moevid, 557; 3 *s.* meved, moved, IV. 37; *pl.* brought forward, III. 321 ; moued, I. 103 ; *pr.* 2 *s. subj.* moeue, 676; *pr. p.* mevinge, moving, III. 108 ; *pp.* meved, III. 2 ; OF. muev-, *strong stem of* moveir.
mevynge, *verb. n.* inducement, II. 55.
miche, *v.* muche.
myddwardis, middle, P. 67.
my3tffull, powerful, II. 95, III 237.
my3th, *v.* maiste.
mynde, intellect, 634 ; judgement, 1709.
myndelees, stupid, 716.
mynged, *pt. pl.* spoke of, I. 103 ; OE. myngian.
mynne, *inf.* remind, 285; *pr.* 3 *s. subj.* [mynne], 166 ; ON. minna.
myrier, *v.* meri.
mysdo, *inf.* do evil, III. 188 ; *pt. pl.* mysdede, I. 59.
myserule, *n.* misrule, IV. 3.
myssecheff, misfortune, P. 22 ; myssheff, I. 111 ; mischief, 166.
mistike, deep, mysterious, 1089.
mystirmen, *pl.* these m., men of this kind, III. 335; OF. mestier, occupation.
myter, mitre, bishop's head-dress, 579.
mo, more, II. 27, III. 130; þe mo, the majority, IV. 86 ; 678.
moche, *v.* muche.
moeue(d), *v.* meuve.
molde, earth, III. 9 ; 363, 1206.
momeling, *verb. n.* babbling, 233.
momeling, *pr. p.* muttering, 595.
moneth, month. 198.
mony, money, IV. 37.
monside, *pt. pl.* cursed, III. 105 ; *pp.* monsyd, 504; *aph. form of* amanse, I.OE. amānsian.
moore, *v.* more.
moppe, fool, 620 ; *pl.* moppis, III. 276 ; *cp.* MSw. mopa, to befool.
morder, murder, I. 77; morthir,

III. 103; mourdre, 732; OE. morðor.

more, *n.* root, 1117, 1655; moore, 731; OE. more.

more, greater, 158.

morwe. morning, III. 172.

mos, *pr.* 2 *s.* must, 678, 1249, 1273; *pt.* 3 *s.* moste, 317; *pr.* 3 *s. subj.* mote, may, 211.

mose, moss, 1644.

mote, hill, 932; castle, 1244, 1259; OF.mote, mound, castle-hill,castle.

mote, discussion, 278, 1138; OE. mōt.

mote, *v.* mos.

mote-halle, council chamber, 484.

motyng, *verb. n.* litigation, 1566; OE. mōtung.

Moubray, IV. 7; *see Note.*

mouche, *v.* muche.

moulde, top of head, crown, 1117; OE. molda *or* molde; *see Note.*

moun, *v.* maiste.

mourdre, *v.* morder.

moustre, *inf.* show, 1411; OF. moustrer.

moued, *v.* meuve.

mowe, *v.* maiste.

mowtynge, *verb. n.* shedding of antlers, II. 12; OE. *mūtian, to exchange.

muche, great, 1254; miche, much, I. 21; mouche, 424; *as n.* moche, II. 139; *adv.* P. 16; OE. mycel.

muke, gentle, 1273; *sup.* meukest, 1031; ON. mjūkr.

mukely, meekly, 92.

mukyn, *inf.* humble, 1516; *cp.* Norw. Sw. mjūkna.

mulden, *pr. pl.* knead, 464; OF. modle, mould.

mvmme, *inf.* behave as Mum, keep silence in a person's favour, 819; *pr.* 3 *s.* mvmmeth, 818; *pp.* y-mummyd, forcibly silenced, III. 337.

mwse, *inf.* meditate, I. 21.

nadde, *pt.* 3 *s. subj.* had not, I. 77.

nale, atte n., at the ale, 1390.

namely, especially, 1200.

nape, *pr.* 3 *s. subj.* hit (on the nape of the neck), 1061.

nedeth, *pr.* 3 *s.* is needful, 470.

ney, near, 971, *comp.* nere, III. 231; 971; neer, 866; *adj.* nyre, 302; *sup.* nest, I. 51; next, 1200.

neyed, *v.* nyeth.

nempne, *inf.* mention, I. 51, II. 6; 909; *pp.* y-nempnyd, 520; nemp-nyd, 1186; nempned, appointed, III. 231; OE. nemnan.

nere, near, 1561; ON. nær; *see also under* ney.

nere, never, 10; ner noþer, neither, 559; ner ... ner, neither ... nor, 344; OE. næfre.

nest, *v.* ney.

nether, nor, 259.

newe, of þe n., afresh, III. 161; 84.

newith, *pr.* 3 *s.* is renewed, 611; *pl.* neweth, P. 66; *pt. pl.* newed, IV. 6; *pp.* I. 7; *pr. pl. subj.* newe, renew, 1595.

next, *v.* ney.

nyce, foolish, 247; *comp.* nycier, 237.

nycete,foolishness, 311, 375; nicete, 650; nysete, III. 144.

Nicholas, 387; *see Note.*

nyeth, *pr.* 3 *s.* approaches, III. 39; *pt.* 1 *s.* neyed, 971; 3 *s.* nyhed, III. 231.

nymeth, *imp. pl.* take, 611.

nyne-folde tyme, nine times, 237.

nyre, *v.* ney.

nys, is not, P. 42.

nyst, *v.* witte.

Noe-is, *g. s.* 1235.

noye, *inf.* give trouble, 1492; *pr.* 3 *s.* noyeth, troubles, 1208.

noyes, *n. pl.* troubles, P. 66.

noyous, harmful, 74, 375.

nolde, *v.* wolt.

nolle, head, I. 20, III. 46, III. 66; 1061; *pl.* nollis, III. 128; OE. hnoll.

nones, for þe n., on purpose, 305, 398.

nonsuyte[s], stoppage or withdrawal of suits, 1595.

noon, *adj.* no, 235; *adv.* non, III. 195.

not, smooth, close-cropped, III. 46; OE. hnot.

not, *v.* witte.

notable, worthy of note, 1295.

note, nut, 866.

note, note, voice, III. 73; *pl.* nots, 1029.

noteth, *pr.* 3 *s.* marks, IV. 54.

noþer (with ne), nor... either, P. 74, IV. 12; nother, 157.

no þinge, not at all, III. 11.

nouellerie, novelty, 1208; OF. novellerie.

nownagis, payments due to the king, when an estate fell to a minor, IV. 6; AF. nounage, OF. nonage.

of, *adv.* off, 188, 1556.

of, concerning, P. 9, P. 32, II. 2; from, II. 13; 57, 204; in, II. 184; by, III. 151; arising from, III. 13; for, II. 45; III. 350; 98; of þe same, in the same way, P. 14.

oygnons, onions, 606; F. oignon.

oyle, for o., by means of flattery, 247; *pl.* oyles, holde vp o., to flatter, 271, 831; beringe vppon oilles, flattering, III. 186 (*see Note*).

on, one, II. 42; in oone, in agreement, 90.

on, *adv.* alone, III. 9; oon, 80; oone, 1003; al oon, 830.

on, in, II. 190, III. 15, III. 97; 337, 699, 894, 951, 1194, 1290, 1430, 1513; by, II. 118; on his dayes, for his time of life, 965.

ony, any, P. 76.

oones, once, 83; of o., 152 (*see Note*); at ones, at one sweep, I. 92.

or, *conj.* before, II. 57, III. 117, III. 306, IV. 81, IV. 85; are, 1517, 1557; OE. ǣr, ON. ār.

Orleance, 323; *see Note*.

ornements, accessories, furniture, 659.

oþer, others, III. 158; 16; o. half wintre, one and a half years, 1347, 1409; non other, nothing else, 577.

oþer, or, P. 37; OE. oðð̄e.

oþer-while, sometimes, P. 70; 1365.

ought, anything, 642; oute, III. 342; out, IV. 37.

oute, *v.* aues, ought.

outher, either, 747; OE. ōhwæðer.

ouere euen, the night before, IV. 55.

ouere grewe, *pt. pl.* surpassed, III. 344.

ouere-loked, *pt. pl.* despised, II. 35.

ouer-lepe, *inf.* pass by, 1234.

ouer-sette, *pp.* oppressed, 1524.

ouere-waoche, late hours, III. 282.

ouer-woxe, *pp.* overgrown, 177; OE. weaxan.

owed, *v.* aues.

owen, own, III. 69.

Oxenford, 323.

page, household officer, 34.

pay, satisfaction, 1296.

pale, fence, 930.

pallette, head-piece, III. 325; OF. palet.

panne, skull, head, III. 63; *pl.* pannes, I. 55, III. 325; OE. panne.

panteris, *n. pl.* snares, II. 187; OF. panter.

papegeay, parrot, 152; OF. papegai, AF. papeiaye; *cp.* ONF. gai, Cent. F. geai = jay.

paragals, peers, I. 71; OF. paregal.

parceit, perception, P. 17; *cp.* OF. perceveir, perceiv-.

parcelle, portion, 444, 1365.

parcelle-mele, *n.*, in p., into portions, 437.

pare, *n.* peel, 522; OF. parer, *vb.*

parfitely, fully, 538; OF. parfet.

parle, *inf.* speak officially, IV. 48; *pt.* 3 *s.* parlid, 811; *pl.* 152.

parlement, council, IV. 14, IV. 25.

parroishens, parishioners, 1380.

parroisshe, *collect.* parishioners, 1360; OF. paroisse.

partie, *adj.* two-faced, 530.

partie, *n. pl.* parts, 611.

partninge, *verb. n.* sharing, I. 71; *cp.* partner, *var.* of parcener, OF. parcener.

passe, *inf.* surpass, III. 34; 238; *pr.* 3 *s.* p[as]sith, III. 111; *pt.* 1 *s.* passid, paced, P. 1; 3 *s.* surpassed, P. 17; *imp. s.* passe, penetrate, 1514; *pr. p.* passinge, surpassing, II. 108; *pp.* y-passid, paced, II. 24.

passion, suffering, P. 23; Miracle of the Passion, 721.

pasture, food, III. 14.

pasture, *inf.* feed, 1368.

peere, pear, P. 73; pere, 522; peyre, 443; OE. pere.

peeris, *n. pl.* peers, I. 44; 155; peeres, 742; peris, 793; peres, 1135.

peesith, *v.* pese.

peyne, penalty, I. 39.

peynte, *part. adj.* adorned, embroidered, III. 196.

peynt[ur]e (MS. preynte), colouring, 61; OF. peinture.

peyre, *v.* peere.

peyren, *pr. pl.* injure, 1603; *aph. form of* appair, OF. ampairer.

penanche, penance, 491; OPicard, penanche.

peniles, penniless one, III. 196; *adv.*

penylees, being unbribed, 1584; *no ex. of adverbial use in O.E.D.*

pens-lac, lack of money, III. 142.

perceipues, *pr.* 2 *s.* perceivest, 719; *cp.* deceipuen; *this spelling not in O E.D.*

pere, *v.* peere.

peres, peris, *v* peeris.

perillous, to be feared, 702.

Pernell, III. 156; Pernelle, 1360; *see Notes.*

personages, parsonages of secular clergy, 536; personagz, 860.

persones, incumbents of livings, 1354. 1372.

perte, *adv.* as p , as openly as possible, IV 88.

pese, *inf.* pacify, keep in peace, 1607; *pr.* 3 *s.* peesith, 1012; OF. paiser.

pesinge. *verb. n.* joining together, III. 168.

pete, pity, P. 23, I. 17.

peuple, people, 1, 13, 224.

Phisic, natural science, 334.

picche, *inf.* place for sale; p. and paye, pay ready money, 1598; *pp.* pight, laid, II. 187; y-pighte, founded, 541.

pies, magpies, II. 192; piez, 152.

piking, *verb. n.* picking out, taking, 565.

pikis, staves, III. 232.

Pilat, 721.

pille, *inf.* steal, 444; *pp.* piled, plundered, 1491; OE. *pilian, peolian.

pillynge, *verb. n.* robbery, I. 13.

pillourz, plunderers III. 303.

pynen, *pr. pl.* suffer, 764; *pp.* y-pyned, tortured, 168; OE. pīnian.

pynnyd. *pp.* fastened up, II. 165.

pipoudris, *adj.* as wayfarers, III. 319; F. pied-poudreux; *see Note.*

pirith, *pr.* 3 *s.* peers, III. 48; *cp.* LG. pīren.

pithy, vigorous, 964.

pitte, burrow, 912; *this sense not in O.E.D.*

playnte, complaint, suit, 811.

plaisance, complaisance, 389.

plaisant, agreeable, 1296.

plaise, *imp. s.* be agreeable, 257.

plantz, outgrowth, fruit, 703.

plede, *inf.* sue, 1582.

pledyng, *verb. n.* lawsuits, 1368.

plete, *inf.* plead, I. 60, III. 349; *pt. pl.* pletid, III. 328; OF. plaitier.

plewme, *inf.* pull, II. 163; *pp.* y-plumed, plucked, 153.

plytis, pleats, III. 156; AF. plit, NF. *pleit = OF. ploit.

plomayle, plumage, II. 32; OF. plumail.

pluralite, holding of more than one benefice by the same person, 555, 1372; *pl.* pluralites, benefices so held, 860.

poynte, *n.* condition, III. 34; to þe poynt, exactly, 1333; F. à point.

poynteth, *pr.* 3 *s.* points out, 1174.

poyse, motto, 1344; OF. poesie.

poysie-wise, manner of the posy of a ring, 497.

pol, head, II. 163.

polaille, poultry, 603; OF. polaille.

polaxis, pole-axes, I. 17; pollaxis, III. 328.

polle, pool, 1514; OE. pōl, pull.

[poperyng], *pr.p.* trotting, 1373.

pore, *v.* pure.

portier, porter, 550; OF. portier.

pouaire, power, 1323; AF. pouair; OF. poeir, pooir.

poundage, subsidy on imports and exports, IV. 14.

pourchas, acquirement of property, 1368.

poure, *pr.* 3 *s. subj.* pore, P. 71; ? OE. *pūrian.

pourpoos, *n.* of p., intended, 1333.

pouraile, the poor, 1380; *gen.* purraile-is, II. 165; OF. povraille.

pourete, poverty, 550.

practike, *n.* practice, 389.

pray, *n.* prey, II. 163; manner of hunting, III. 23.

prebendiers, holders of prebends, 1372; OF. prebendier; *first ex. in O.E.D.* 1556.

prece, *n.* crowd, multitude, 119, 786; putte in prees, to exert oneself, 267; OF. presse.

prece, *inf.* urge one's way, 706; preece, 1658; *pr.* 3 *s.* precyth, III. 47; OF. presser.

preche, *inf.* declare, 1360; exhort, 598.

prechement, preaching, 1104; OF. prechement.

preied, *pp.* entreated, III. 350.

preiere, prayer, P. 1; request, IV. 14.

preifis, *n. pl.* experiences, P. 17; OF. prueve.

preynte, *n*. impress, 61; **prynte**, device, II. 108; OF. priente, preinte.

preyntid, *pp*. marked, written, 1344; *cp*. OF. empreinter.

preysinge, *verb. n*. appraising, I. 17.

prelat, ecclesiastical dignitary of high rank, head of a religious house, 624; *pl*. **prelatz**, 538.

prentise, apprentice; **p. of courte**, barrister of less than 16 years' standing, III. 350; *pl*. **prentys**, 18.

preson, prison, III. 271; OF. preson.

preson. *inf*. imprison, III. 303.

pressonere, jailer, 1251; med.Lat. præsonerius.

prest, ready, 1014; OF. prest.

pretiest, cleverest, 991.

preue, *v*. **pryved**.

preuy, proved, strong, III. 325; lusty, III. 14; manifest, III. 111; **priuy**, II. 108; **pryue**, valuable, 1344; **pryvy**, 1055; *see Note on* II. 108.

preuy, *v*. **priuy**.

preuyly, openly, II. 175 (?) I. 52; *see Note on* II. 108

preuyly, **preuylich(e)**, *v*. **priuyly**.

price, *v* **pris**.

prien, *pr. pl*. seek, III. 306.

prikkyth, *pr*. 3 *s*. spurs, III. 14.; *pt*. 3 *s*. **prickid**, II. 122.

prime, early, III. 34.

prime-saute, spirited, 922; *see Note*.

principal, ruler, 764, 1012; *pl*. 1424.

principaly, more especially, 173.

prynte, *v*. **preynte**.

pris, value, I. 36; **price**, honour, 684; OF. pris.

prisely, nobly, 555.

prisiest, most excellent, 18.

pryved, *pt*. 1 *s*. proved, 719; *pr*. 3 *s*. *subj*. **preue**, test, P. 71; OF. prover, pruev-.

pryuete, secrecy, 1399.

priuy, confidential, 684; **pryvy**, 1658; **pryuy**, 185; **p. to**, participating in, 742; **preuy**, secret, II. 192, IV. 25; **priuy**, 415; **pryuy**, 688.

priuy, **pryue**, *v*. **preuy**.

priuyly, secretly, 155; **pryuely**, 952; **pryuyly**, 1424, 1698; **preuy-ly**, P. 71; **preuyliche**, II. 122, II. 187; **preuylich**, III. 48.

pr[o]ffit, profit, III. 167; **prophete**, IV. 10, IV. 48.

propirte, nature, III. 38; **propriete**, 990, 993.

proprid, *pp*. set aside, appointed, 1132; **y-properid**, 1041; OF. proprier.

proute, proud, 1603; *sup*. **pruttist**, 684; lOE. prūt.

pulled, *pt. pl*. plucked, II. 126; *pp*. **y-pullid**, 153.

pulter, rags, II. 165; *see Note*.

pure, very, III. 4; 52; **pore**, II. 32.

purraile-is, *v*. **pouraile**.

puruyours, purveyors, IV. 13.

quayer, quire, small book, 1348; OF. quaier.

quarellis, *v*. **querele**.

quarter, division, 1012.

queyntid, *pt*. 1 *s*. acquainted, 556; OF. queinte, *adj*.; *cp*. OF. cointier.

quelle, *pr*. 3 *s. subj*. destroy, 1044.

queme, *inf*. please, III. 176; OE. cwēman.

quenche, *inf*. oppress, III. 327.

quentise, device, badge, II. 107; elegance, III. 176; OF. quentise, cointise.

querele, objection, 633; *pl*. **querellz**, accusations, 1207; **quarellis**, III. 327; OF. querele.

quethyn, *v*. **cothe**.

quyk, quickly, 633.

quyke, *inf*. revive, 190; OE. cwician.

quynzieme, fifteenth, 1704.

quyre, choir, 399, 556.

quitance, release from debt, 1207; **quita[nce]**, receipt, 1704; *pl*. **quitances**, 1348.

quite, *inf*. pay, 87, 190, 1207; *pr. pl*. **quiten**, requite, 1086; OF. quiter.

quod, *v*. **cothe**.

radde, *v*. **reede**.

rafte, *pp*. taken away, I. 6; OE. rēafian.

raggeman rolle, document, 1565; *see Note*.

Ragenelle, 1565; *see Note*.

ray, array, clothing, III. 123, III. 221; **raye**, 644; *aph. form of* OF. arei; *cp*. OF. roi, ? AF. *rei.

rayed, *pp*. dressed, III. 120.

rancour, bitterness, III. 185.

rancune, anger, 729, 1123; OF. rancune; *not in O.É.D*.

rapely, quickly, P. 13; ON. hrapa-liga.

rascaille, *collect. n*. rabble, 210;

rascaile, young lean deer, II. 119;
rasskayle, II. 129; raskall, II.
137, II. 140; OF. rascaille.
rathe, eager, earnest, 40; *comp. adv.*
rather, sooner, 1125; OE. hraðe,
adv.
raughte, *pt.* 1 *s.* went, 553; *pl.* 911;
OE. ræcan.
raundon, a r., swiftly, 911; OF. a
randon; *cp.* reclayme.
raveyn, violence, II. 159; F. ravine.
realles, royal representatives, nobles,
III. 301; *g. pl.* I. 91; OF. real.
realte, royal state, I. 53.
reason(s), *v.* reson.
reccheles, reckless, III. 209; rechelees, 1635.
recchith, *pr. pl.* care, III. 120; *pl.*
subj. reeche, take heed, 19; OE.
reccan.
reclayme, *n.* a r., at the call, II.
182; OF. a reclaim; *see Note.*
rede, *n.* counsel, P. 48; reede, III.
123.
rede, red, 770.
redeles, redeless, without counsel, I.
1; redelees, 553; reedelees, 843.
redely, promptly, P. 54.
redelles, *n. pl.* riddles, 416; OE.
rǣdels.
reden, *v.* rood.
reede, *inf.* read, 303; interpret, 416,
516; counsel, 729; rede, III. 258;
pr. 1 *s.* 255; 3 *s.* redeth, 550; *pt.*
1 *s.* radde, read, 315; 3 *s.* reed,
III. 119; *imp. pl.* redeth, P. 54.
reeuell, merry-making, IV. 20; OF.
revel.
reffourmed, *pp.* reformed, P. 21.
reffresshe, *inf.* strengthen, P. 32;
1366.
galie, royal prerogative, 1128;
OF. regalie, administration for the
king of the revenues of vacant
ecclesiastical benefices.
rehershing, *pres. p.* recounting, 210,
1211; rehershyng, 299: *pp.* rehersid, II. 98.
reyne, rain, 1456.
religion, *collect.* the religious orders,
553, 1364.
remeveth, *pr. pl.* travel, III. 301.
[rend], *part adj.* torn up, II. 140.
renke, man, II. 31; 1211; *pl.* renkes,
1635; ON. rekkr, OE. rinc.
renne, *inf.* run, II. 58; *pr. pl.* renneth ouere, oppress, III. 303 (*not*
in O.E.D.); *pt. pl.* ronne, ran,

II. 5; runne, 926; *pr. p.* rennynge
ouere, oppressing. III. 185; rennyng, at racing speed, 1396; *pp.*
y-runne in riches, grown rich,
1686; ON. renna, OE. rinnan.
rent, revenue, IV. 12, IV. 20; rente,
547, 646; *pl.* rentis, II. 159.
reot, *v.* riott.
repeute, *inf.* consider, P. 19; F.
reputer.
repreff, reproach, disgrace, P. 56.
repreue, *inf.* reprove, III. 197.
rere, *inf.* raise up, 1015.
reremys, bats, III. 272; OE. hrere-
mūs.
resceyte, *n.* receiving, II. 98.
reson, argument, P. 56, II. 31, IV.
70; reason, 745, 1548; *pl.* reasons,
40, 299.
rest, peace, I. 6.
reste, *inf.* cease from action, 1496.
restore, *pr.* 1 *s.* make restoration,
return, come back to my subject,
III. 1.
reule, maxim, II. 69; revle, 314;
religious order, 516; rewle, order,
government, III. 119; reuylle,
664; OE. reule.
reule, *inf.* rule, 225; rewle, behave,
III. 272.
reuylle, ? revelry, 664.
reuyng, *verb. n.* plundering, 1153.
rewarde, *n.* regard, 89; ONF. reward, OF. reg(u)ard.
rewe, *n.* row, company, 807, 1366;
pl. rewis, P. 54; OE. ræw.
reweth, *imp. pl.* have pity, I. 1.
rewme, realm, P. 74; OF. reaume.
rewthe, pity, P. 21.
riall, magnificent, III, 123; *as n.*
rial, noble, III. 340; OF. rial.
Richard, P. 9, III. 110, III. 338,
IV. 3; R. þe redeles, I. 1.
ryff, *adv.* numerously, II. 5.
ryffled, *pt. pl.* plundered, I. 16.
riffleris, plunderers, III. 197.
rigge, back, III. 287; OE. hrycg.
right, rightly, 1725; rith, very, P.
16.
riȝtyn, *inf.* redress, P. 13; righte,
1015.
riott, revelry, I. 6; reot, IV. 20.
ripe, *pr.* 3 *s. subj.* ripen, 62; OE.
rīpian.
rith, justice, II. 137; *pl.* rithis, rights,
III. 269.
rithffully, rightfully, P. 48.
robis, robes of honour, official posi-

tion, II. 159; **robes**, 97, 288; men of position, 1497; *transferred senses not in O.E.D.*

rode, rood, P. 56.

roff, roof, covering, III. 248.

royaulme, kingdom, 146; **royaume**, 225; OF. roialme, roiaume.

romansid, *pt. pl.* related, 146; Norm. romancer = racouter (Godefroy).

rome, *imp. s.* wander, 696.

ronne, *v.* **renne**.

roobuc, roebuck, 926.

rood, *pt.* 3 *s.* rode, III. 361; *pl.* **reden**, I. 53.

roote, *pr.* 3 *s. subj.* take root, 729; *pp.* **rotid**, rooted, established, 1366.

rorid, *pt. pl.* roared, complained, II. 119.

rosse, *pt.* 3 *s.* rose, P. 13.

rotus, *n. pl.* roots, II. 140.

rou3te, rout, III. 99; *pl.* **routus**, I. 16; OF. route.

runne, *v.* **renne**.

sad, serious, III. 201; 963; dull, IV. 66.

sadly, heavily, 870.

saff, safe, P. 81.

sage, wise man, 305, 354, 769, 954; *pl.* **sages**, III. 257; *gen. pl.* III. 8.

saides, *v.* **seye**.

saye, *pr.* 2 *s. subj.* try, 1313; *imp. s.* **seye**, 1713 (2); *aph. form of* OF. asaier.

saise, *inf.* seize, 250; **sese**, establish, 1437; *pr.* 3 *s.* **sesith**, seizes, III. 49; *pr.* 3 *s. subj.* **seese**, 1265; OF. saisir.

sallere, salary, IV. 46; **salaire**, 1176; OF. salaire, AF. salarie.

Salomon, 1212; *g. s.* **Salomon-is**, 304.

salue, ointment, 317.

salue, *inf.* anoint; **salwyn**, 847.

saluelees, without salve, 1130.

sauce, a piquant accompaniment, 473.

sauf, except, 831.

saufconduyt, safe-conduct, 586.

[S]aunder þe seruiselees, 44.

sauere, *inf.* be agreeable to, 200; *pr. pl.* take pleasure, 202; enjoy, P. 55; *pr. pl. subj.* **sauery of**, apprehend, 1309; OF. savourer.

sauynge, in default of, III. 8.

sawe, speech, 71, 202; *pl.* **sawis**, P. 8, III. 201; **sawys**, 1250.

scant, *inf.* be scarce, 1056; ON. skamt, *neut. adj.*

scantly, barely, 405.

scathe, *n.* damage, 73.

schappe, *n,* shape, fashion. III. 213.

schenshepe, disgracing, III. 259; *cp.* **shente**.

schew, *n.,* here s. lost, gained nothing by appearing, IV. 56.

schewe, *inf.* appear, IV. 30; *pt.* 1 *s.* shewed, put forward my case, 328; *pl.* schewed, appeared, IV. 56.

schire-kny3tis, knights of the shire, IV. 32.

schoppe, *inf.* chop, III. 230.

schore, score, II. 42; lOE. scoru, ON. skor.

sc[h]or[n] (MS. **scort**), scorn, III. 194 (*see Note*); **scorne**, 73; OF. escarn, escharn.

schorned, *pt. pl.* scorned, III. 236.

schrapid, *pt.* 3 *s.* scratched the ground, III. 58; OE. scrapian.

schreuys, sheriffs, IV. 28; OE. scīrgerēfa.

schrewe, wretch, rascal, III. 58; 1254.

schrewed, *v.* **shrewed**.

schroff, refuse, such as cinders and light wood, used for burning, II. 154; *cp.* OE. sceorf = scurf.

schroup, ? rubbish, II. 154; *cp.* scrub, shrub; OE. scrybb.

sclaundre, *n.* slander, 73; OF. esclandre.

scole, school, university faculty, 324, 1065; *pl.* **scoles**, 1233.

scripture, writing, 369.

scorowe, scroll, 1489; OF. escroue.

se, throne, I. 86; 1430; **see**, III. 352; 1003; OF. se.

se, *imp. pl.* se ... ouere, peruse, P. 55; *pp.* **seye**, seen, 175; **y-seye**, 38; seie, III. 292 (2).

sechith, *v.* **siche**.

seel, *n.* seal, sealed document, 817.

seely, holy, 410; OE. gesǣlig.

seelyng, *verb. n.* sealing, 649.

seemes, *n. pl.* seams, III. 166.

seese, *v.* **saise**.

segge-is, *g. s.* man's, 71; OE. secg.

seye, *inf.* say, 1713 (1); *pt.* 2 *s.* **saides**, 234.

seie, seyo, *v.* **saye, se**.

se[in]tis, girdles, III. 140; OF. ceint.

sekirly, assuredly, IV. 92; *cp.* **siker**.

selcoupe, marvellous, P. 5; **silde-couthe**, 746; *as n. pl.* **silde-couthes**, marvels, 873; OE. seldan + cūþ.

selde, seldom, III. 58 ; seilde, 38 ;
silde, 151, 592 ; OE. seldan.

semblable, comparable, 1501.

semblant, seeming, demeanour, 963.

semble, *n.* company, IV. 85 ; AF.
semblé, OF. assemblee.

sembled, *pt. pl.* assembled, P. 19.

semely, goodly, 354.

semeth, *pr. s. impers.* becomes, 220.

semyd, *part. adj.* seamed, 427.

s[end]e, *pp.* sent, 589

Seneca, 305 (*see Note*), 1212.

sentence, saying, 519 ; judgement,
653 ; substance, gist, 1283.

serche, *inf.* examine, probe, 1338 ;
pp. y-serchid, 771.

ser[gi]auntis, barristers, III. 349 ;
sergeantz, 17 ; officers whose duty
is to arrest offenders, 250.

serue þere-after, *inf.* act accordingly, 625 ; *pr. pl. subj.* 202 ; seruen,
win, 235 ; *pt.* 3 *s. subj.* seruyd
of noon other, was of no other
use, 98 ; *pp.* seruyd, served,
244.

serue, *inf.* deserve, 1217 ; *pr.* 2 *s.*
serues, 75 ; *pt. pl.* seruid, II. 28 ;
serued, IV. 59 ; *pp.* serued, II.
185 ; *aph. form of* OF. deservir.

seruice, employment, III. 257.

seruiselees, out of work, 44 ; *this
sense not in O.E.D.*

seruitute, servitude, 1422 ; OF. ser-
vitute.

sese, *v.* saise.

[s]ete, *n.* seat, III. 49.

sett, *inf.* fix, III. 166 ; sette, assume,
1307 ; lay out, II. 45 ; *pr. pl.*
settith, III. 140 ; setten to taske,
enjoin as study, 508 ; *pt.* 3 *s.* sette
shorte, held in low estimation,
343 ; *pp.* y-sette, 1546 ; sette,
appointed, 1413.

seure, *pr. pl.* assure, 1702 ; *aph. form
of* OF. aseurer.

seurely, assuredly, 766 ; infallibly,
1339.

shadue, *n.* shadow, 1110.

shadued, *pt. pl.* shaded, 918.

shal, *pr.* 2 *s.* shalt, 1401 ; *pl.* shullen,
owe, 1670 ; *pt.* 1 *s.* shulde, ought,
P. 77 ; 2 *s.* shuldes, shouldst, 79 ;
pr. 3 *s. subj.* sholle, III. 28.

shame, *n.* s. thenke, be ashamed,
199.

shapeth, *pr.* 3 *s.* takes measures,
1693 ; *pl.* shape þaym, take their
way, 1019.

sharpely, quickly, 737, 760 ; sharply,
837.

shente, *pt. pl.* spoiled, II. 51 ; *pp.*
shent, punished, 433 ; y-shent,
169 ; OE. scendan.

sheutyng, *pr. p.* shooting, 1403 ; OE.
scēotan.

sheue, *pr. pl.* shove, 1567 ; OE.
scēofan, scūfan.

shewe(d), *v.* schewe.

shynant, shining, 1316.

shyne, glimpse, 829 (*see Note*), 1384 ;
OE. scēne, scīene, *adj.*

shire-men, representatives of the
shires, 1131.

sholle, *v.* shal.

shonde, *n.* disgrace, 747 ; OE. scand,
scond.

shony, *inf.* shun, 161 ; OE. scunian.

shophister, sophist, 342 ; OF. so-
phistre.

shrewed, wicked, 93, 1189 ; schrewed, III. 20.

shulde(s), shullen, *v.* shal.

shuldrid, *pt. pl.* jostled, 824.

sibbe, akin, III. 30 ; OE. sibb ; *cp.*
y-sibbe.

siche, *inf.* seek, 370, 1098, 1143 ;
sike, 1328 ; *pr. pl.* sechith, 250 ;
pt. pl. souȝte, probed, I. 45 ; *pp.*
sought, 771 ; souȝte, besought,
III. 349 ; OE. sēcan.

sicour, *v.* siker.

side, broad, extensive, II. 51, III.
170, IV. 28 ; OE. sīd.

syde-herne, sequestered corner, 1260 ;
cp herne.

side-wayes, by-ways, crooked paths,
370, 1143.

sidis, parties, P. 8.

Sidrac, 304 (*see Note*), 1212.

siege, *n.* seat, 359, 596 ; OF. siege.

signes, badges, II. 21.

sike, sick, 564, 1381.

sike, *v.* siche.

siker, trusty, 97 ; sicour, 1175 ; OE.
sicor.

silde, *v.* selde.

silde-couthe(s), *v.* selcouþe.

sille, *inf.* sell, 1521 ; OE. sellan,
syllan.

Symond, IV. 55 (*see Note*) ; *g. s.*
Symon-is, 508.

simple, foolish, 105.

siphre, cipher, naught, IV. 53.

sir, lord, I. 86 ; *pl.* siris, I. 104.

sises, assizes, 1567 ; OF. sise.

sith, since, 955 ; OE. siðð̄an.

sittinge, sitting-time, III. 39.

skathed, *pt.* 3 *s.* injured, II. 105.

skylle, reason, II. 105; **skile**, 1056; *pl.* **skiles**, 405.

slaueyn, mantle, III. 236; OF. esclavine; cp. sclavus, a Slav or a slave.

sle, *inf.* slay, III. 234; 182.

slidre, unstably, 675; OE. slidor, *adj.*

slygh, clever, 182.

slode, *pt.pl.* trailed, III. 234.

smaicche, *inf.* taste, 7; OE. smæccan.

smote, *pt.* 3 *s.* penetrated, 941.

so, provided that, P. 44, III. 148; **so þat**, 586.

sodeynly, suddenly, P. 5.

soeth, truth, 283; [svth], 1336; **her sothes**, the truth about themselves, II. 151 (*see Note*).

softe, *pr.* 1 *s.* soften, alleviate, 1338.

soleyne, sullen, IV. 66; *as n.* **soleyn**, a solitary person, 830.

solue, *inf.* pay, 1670; *pp.* y-soluid, 1699; *first ex. of this use in O.E.D.* 1558.

solue, *inf.* sol-fa, practise singing the scale, 1147; *see Note.*

sonde, dispensation, P. 35; *pl.* **sondis**, messages, IV. 28; OE. sand, sond.

sone, straightway, III. 161.

soon, son, 366, 1111.

soope, *pp.* sipped, 1050; OE. sūpan.

sore, bitter, unwelcome, P. 8.

sorowe, trouble, I. 113, II. 185; 169; **s. on** (*emphatic negative*), 617 (*see Note*), 829.

sothes, *v.* soethe.

sothe-sigger, truth-teller, 38; *pl.* **sothe-siggers**, 235.

sought, sou3te, *v.* siche.

sovke, *inf.* suck, 1020; *pt.* 3 *s.* sowkid, consumed, IV. 9.

soulde, *n.* pay, 17, 1176; OF. soulde.

soule, single, I. 62; OF. soul.

sounen, *pr. pl.* tend, 88; OF. soner, suner.

sourdid, *pt. pl.* arose, P. 5; OF. sourdre.

soutelly, subtly, 1384.

soutille, *inf.* argue subtly, 370; OF. soutillier; *cp.* **subtilite**.

souurayn, master, 32, 1541; *pl.* **souurayns**, nobles, rulers, 791, 931, 1131, 1435; **souereynes**, IV. 32; *g. pl.* III. 8.

souuraynete, position of authority, 1250.

sowers, sewers, III. 165.

sowkid, *v.* sovke.

spareth, *pr.pl.* avoid, III. 37.

speciales, mistresses, 1379.

spede, advancement, 163.

spede, *inf.* prosper, 86.

spekys, *pr.* 2 *s.* speakest to, 91.

sperelees, without a sting, 1033; *not in O.E.D.*

spicerie, *coll.* spices, *perhaps* department of the king's spicery, III. 273; bribery, 479 (*this sense not in O.E.D.*).

spices, *n. pl.* bribes, 507, 691 (*this sense not in O.E.D.*).

spie, *inf.* espy, 242, 333.

spille, *inf.* perish, 1121; OE. spillan.

spirith, *pr.* 3 *s.* inspires. 1229; OF. spirer; *this sense not in O.E.D.*

spiritual, ecclesiastical, 1100.

spitous, malevolent, 507; *aph. form of* OF. despitos.

spones, *n. pl.* splinters, 1474; OE. spōn.

spores, *n. pl.* spurs, 482.

sports, pastimes, 1291.

spracke, brisk, 507; *first ex. in O.E.D.*, 1747.

spurnyng, *verb. n.* spurning, kicking, 1190 (*cp.* l. 1185).

squyre, *n.* square, 348; OF. esquire.

squyers, squires, 1489.

stable, *inf.* make firm, 226; stand firm, III. 249; *pr.* 3 *s.* **stablithe**, I. 10; *pt.* 3 *s.* **stablid**, established, 1431.

stall, *v.* steleth.

stalworth, stalwart, sturdy, 965; OE. stælwierðe.

stappen, *pr. pl.* go, 1193; OE. stœppan.

stare, *inf.* glare, III. 189; *pt.* 1 *s.* starid, 351.

statt, state, position, III. 174.

status, statutes, 1593: OF. statut.

stedis, horses, III. 21.

steeris, oxen, III. 251.

steleth, *pr. pl.* steal, III. 21; **stele**, 1506; *pt.* 3 *s.* **stall**, II. 164; *pl.* **stelen**, II. 120.

sturede, sterid, *v.* stireth.

steriers, inciters, 1569; *cp.* stireth.

styff, strong, III. 104; **stif**, stubborn, III. 134; *sup.* **styuest**, 1569; OE. stif.

styffe, *pr. pl.* grow strong, III. 54.

stynte, *inf.* cease, 322; *pt.pl.* stynted, II. 125.

stireth, *pr. pl.* act, III. 121; stiren, 1507; *pt.* 3 *s.* stirid, excited, I. 114; *pl.* brought forward, 409; sterede, acted, III. 269; *pr.* 3 *s. subj.* stire, utter, 755; *pt. pl.* sterid hem, bestirred themselves, IV. 80.

stonyed, *pt. pl.* amazed, confused, II. 125; *part. adj.* stonyd, 578; *aph. form of* OF. estoner.

stont, *pr.* 3 *s.* stands, 755.

store, capital, reserve of goods, III. 177; 1507.

stouttely, vigorously, I. 114.

straite, *adv.* hardly, 1518.

strake, a reef in a sail, IV. 80; *cp.* OE. streccan.

strattely, strictly, 1641; OF. estreit.

streicchen, *pr.pl.* pull, 1571; OE. streccan.

strie, *inf.* destroy, III. 269; strue, 1593; *pr.* 3 *s.* stroyeth, III. 134; *pl.* strien, 1506; *pt.* 3 *s.* stried, II. 26; stroied, II. 104; *aph. form of* OF. estruire.

striked, *pp.* struck, taken in, IV. 80.

strivyng, contention, 1506.

strouters, strutters, swaggerers, blusterers. III 269; OE. strūtian.

strouutynge, swaggering, III. 121, III. 134; stroutynge, III. 177; stroutyng, 1193.

strue, *v.* strie.

studieth, *pr. pl.* exercise themselves, III. 121.

stuffure, stuff, household materials, 1507; OF. estoffure, AF. (e)stuffure.

subtilite, cunning, 1053; OF. soutilite, *inf. by* Lat. subtilitas; *cp.* soutille.

suffrance, patience, 713.

suget, obedient, P. 77; OF. suget.

sum-dell, *n.* some part, P. 55; *adv.* sumdele, somewhat, 715; OE. sum + dǽl.

[svth], *v.* soethe.

swerdis, swords, III 328.

swetter, *adv.* more pleasantly, 1368.

sweuene, dream, 1288; OE. swefn.

swiche, such, III. 126, IV. 29.

swymmers, water birds, III. 86.

swynke, *n.* labour, 1084.

swythe, forthwith, III. 60; OE. swǐðe.

tabart, tunic, 196; OF. tabart.

tabre, tabor, I. 58.

tachid, *pp.* fastened, 1747; *aph. form of* OF. atachier.

taicches, vices, 93, 969; OF. teche, taiche.

ta[y]l (MS. tale), conclusion, 1470.

take, *inf.* accept, P. 79; grant, II. 92; *pr.* 3 *s.* 1261; *imp.pl.* 612; *pt.* 3 *s.* toke, took up, 815; *pp.* ytake forth, advanced, III. 143; y-take fourth, 36; *first ex. of this phrase in fig. sense in* O.E.D., 1530.

tallage, an arbitrary feudal tax levied upon the towns and crown demesnes, I. 15; OF. taillage.

tarre, *inf.* vex, 195; OE. *terwan, tergan.

taske, *inf.* tax, 1600; ONF. tasque, *n. metath. form of* Lat. taxa.

techet, *pr.* 3 *s.* teaches, 1224.

teere, *inf.* tear, 184.

tel(l)de, *v.* tolde.

temperate, suitable, 1025; Lat. temperāre, to mix in due proportion.

temporal, secular, 785, 1099.

tempre, *inf.* control, III. 278; *pp.* temprid, harmonized, 90; controlled, III. 202; amisse t., out of harmony, 178, 295; ytemprid, blended, I. 19.

tende, *inf.* listen, hear, 460, 996; *pr. pl.* tendeth, attend, 1079; *aph. form of* OF. atendre, entendre.

teneth, *pr.* 3 *s.* harms, 1470; *pr. 3 s. subj.* tene, 1205; *pp.* tenyd, III. 79; 171; OE. tēonian.

tente, intention, purpose, II. 92, II. 97; 74, 90, 1465; *aph. form of* OF. atente, entente.

teryng, *verb. n.* tearing, 777.

terme, duration, 205; *pl.* termes, words, 304; in t., in formal speech, 48.

terrene, earthly, 339; AF. terrene.

testament[s], *n. pl.* wills, 1697.

texte, exact words, 160.

Tibourne, 420.

tideth, *pr. impers.* happens, 1205; OE. tīdan.

tidewel, good fortune, 205; *not in* O.E.D.

til, to, 80; ON. til.

tiliers, husbandmen, I. 54.

tyllinge, *verb. n.* tillage, III. 247; OE. tilian.

tymbre, *n.* building material, 1008.

tymbre, *pr.* 3 *s. subj.* build, 9.

tyme, in t., seasonably, 49 ; **in his t.**, for his time of life, 964.

ty[n]ed, *pt.* 3 *s.* lost, III. 81 ; ON. tyna.

titil, mark over a letter, 499 (*see Note*) ; [t]it[l]e, division, section, 1697.

tituleris, tattlers, tale-tellers, IV. 57 ; *see Note on* 499.

to, toward, against, III. 342 ; **to be,** for being, III. 173.

toyes, trifles, foolish tales, 120 ; *first ex. of this sense in O.E.D.*, 1542.

toille, *inf.* contend at law, 1540 ; toylle, 1558; *pp.* toylid, harassed, 1591 ; AF. toiler, to dispute ; OF. toillier, to stir up.

toke, *v.* take.

tolde, *pt.* 1 *s.* spoke of, III. 36 ; tellde, told, III. 68 ; 3 *s.* telde, II. 151.

tolle, toll, proportion exacted, 1361.

tolle, *inf.* exact a charge. 1615 ; *pt.* 3 *s.* tolled, taxed, III. 81 ; *pp.* tollid, taken toll of, 666.

toppe, hair of head, 48 ; head, 191.

topte saile, topsail, IV. 72.

toquen, token, 487.

tornement, reversal, 67 ; OF. tornement; *not in O.E.D.*

to-teereth, *pr. pl.* tear out, 48.

totid, *pt.* 1 *s.* peeped, 885 ; OE. tōtian.

touche, subject of conversation, 339 ; *cp.* F. être a la touche de quelqu'un, être de son usage familier (Godefroy).

towarde, *adj.* promising, 95.

trade, *pt.* 1 *s.* trod, 801.

traylid, *part. adj.* covered in a trailing pattern, I. 47 ; y-traylid, 892.

traison, treason, 753.

traueile, *inf.* labour, P. 51 ; *pr. pl.* trauaillen, 388 ; trauelyn, 985 ; *pp.* traueilid, III. 202.

travers, *n.* traversing, a formal denial in legal pleading of some one fact alleged by the other side, 295, 815.

trauerssid, *pp.* opposed, contradicted, 57.

treete, *inf.* negotiate, 1710.

trendith, *imp. pl.* turn, twist, 1672 ; OE. trendan.

tresour, *n.* treasure, P. 46.

trespas, *n.* wrong, 1540 ; misdemeanour not amounting to treason or felony, 753.

treste, *n.* trust (? = tressed, twisted) I. 47.

tretis, treatise, P. 51.

trevly, truly, 460.

triacle, sovereign remedy, II. 151 ; OF. triacle.

trien, *inf.* judge, II. 85; trie, III. 332.

tristi, trusty, II. 103.

tristith, *imp. pl.* trust, III. 247 ; trostip, l. 102 ; *cp.* treste.

trouble, *adj.* confused, 1392 ; F. trouble.

troupe, loyalty, P. 79 ; trouthe, question of truth, II. 85.

trusse, *inf.* pack up, be off, III. 228 ; 174.

tuoke, *pr.* 3 *s. subj.* pull, 196 ; *cp.* MLG. tucken.

tuly, red, 1735 ; ? OF. tieule, tilecoloured.

turmentours, *g. s.* tormentor's, III. 118 ; *see Note.*

twiggis, rods, III. 79.

twynned, *pt. pl.* separated, III. 243 ; 277.

twynte, *n.* jot, III. 81 ; 339, 985 ; *cp.* MDu. twint.

þache, the ache, 741.

þaleys, the alleys, 953.

þan, then, III. 130.

þanger, the anger, 1126.

þassise, the assize, customary standard, 565.

þat, that which, III. 292 (2) ; 133, 1066 (2) ; to whom, P. 77 ; him that, 1525 ; for that which, IV. 13 ; to those that, 1330 ; þat ... in, in which, P. 58, III. 2 ; ynne, I. 111 ; þat ... he, who, 103 ; that ... þat, he ... who, III. 116 ; þat ... to, to whom, P. 77 ; þat ... þaire, whose, 504.

þattre, *v.* attre.

þees, these, 501 ; *cp.* thus.

þende, the end, 45, 1544.

þenke(th), *v.* thyn[o_hith.

þenne, than, 1519 ; thenne, 253, 486, 1522.

þegre, the bitter, 1657 ; OF. aigre.

þer, where, P. 1 ; ther, I. 87 ; þere, 188 ; when, 763.

þer-after, accordingly, P. 45.

þestres, the divisions, rooms, 1225 ; OF. estre, condition.

thewed, *part. adj.* mannered, natured, 1301 ; OE. þēaw, custom.

þicke, frequently, 510.

þilke, that same, III. 146 ; OE. ilca.

thyn[o]hith, *pr. impers.* seems, III.

wattis, *n. pl.* people, IV. 49; *used especially in phrase* great wats; *see* O.E.D.

waxe, *v.* wexe, woxe.

wecchis, *v.* wacche.

wedde, *inf.* wager, P. 43; 122; *pp.* y-weddid, pledged, 104; OE. weddian.

weddis, *n. pl.* pledges, III. 309; OE. wedd.

wede, clothing, III. 118.

wedir, weather, storm, II. 131; wedre, 1024; OE. weder.

wedir-side, windward side, IV. 77.

welden, *inf.* obtain, IV. 52; *pr.* 3 *s.* weldeth, rules, 23; OE. *gewieldan, geweldan.

well, weal, prosperity, III. 298; welle, III. 291; OE. wela.

well-doynge, right behaviour, II. 110.

welth, worldly goods, III. 288; welthe, prosperity, 124.

wendith, *imp. pl.* turn, 1672.

wenys, *pr.* 2 *s.* thinkest, 233.

weping watre, tears, 288.

werche, *v.* wyrchen.

werchinge, *v.* wirching.

werk, work, II. 68; *pl.* werkis, P. 87.

werre, *n.* war, I. 15, IV. 50.

werre, *inf.* fight, III. 28; *pt.* 3 *s.* werrid, P. 10.

wessh, *v.* waisshe.

wete, *v.* witte.

wexe, wax, III. 274; 610; wex, IV. 26; waxe, sealing, 25; OE. weax.

wexe, *v.* woxe.

whane, when, I. 86; OE. hwanne.

what, *rel. pron.* that, 615.

what-so, whatever, 307; [what]-so, 610.

whedir, whether, P. 28.

wher-by, by what means, I. 10.

where : *pt. pl.* were, P. 15, II. 128.

where-so, wherever, II. 180, II. 189.

while, *n.* wheel, III. 130; whele, 203; OE hwēol.

while, *adj.* former, III. 363; OE. hwīl, *n.*

whinge, *v.* wynge.

who-so, *v.* ho-so.

whom, *dat. sg. neut.* what, III. 65; OE. hwām.

wy, man, 284; *pl.* wies, 306; OE. wiga.

wickett, gate, III. 233; ONF. wiket, OF. guichet.

wyde, flowing, III. 127.

wifes, wives, 512.

wike, wyke-is, *v.* woke.

wile, craft, 1081; *pl.* wyles, deceits, I. 3; prehist. Scand. *wihl, ON. vēl.

wyle, *conj.* while, P. 10.

willes, *pr.* 2 *s.* desirest, 678; *pl.* willeth, 37; OE. willian.

wylffulnesse, self-will, P. 52.

willfull, purposed, I. 5.

willis, *n. pl.* desires, I. 27.

wilne, *inf.* desire, II. 55; w. to woo, desire woe for, III. 30; *pr.* 1 *s.* wilne, desire to know, III. 64; 2 *s.* wilnest, wishest, 255; OE. wilnian.

wyman, woman, 1386; OE. wīfmann.

wynge, power of flight, II. 149; vndre whinge, under wing, quiet, 154.

wynke, *n.* sleep, 869, 1289.

wynne, *inf.* make his way, 1257; *pt.* 1 *s.* wanne, obtained, 301.

wyntre, *pl.* years, 11; winter, 683.

wyrchen, *pr. pl.* make, 1048; worchen, work, III. 316; 980; *pt. pl.* wroute, I. 43; wrou3th, II. 192; *pr.* 3 *s. subj.* werche, P. 44; *pl.* wirche, 203; OE. wyrcan.

wirching, *verb. n.* working, 991; werchinge, I. 105, III. 114.

wyre, perplexity, 296; wire, 316; ME. were; ?ONF. were, werre.

wirwe, *inf.* destroy, 1075; *pr. pl.* wyrwen, 979; *pp.* yworewid, III. 72; OE. wyrgan.

wise, *inf.* instruct, 307, 1094; OE. wīsian.

wisliche, wisely, I. 74.

wissely, surely, 468; OE. wislīce.

wissen, *inf.* teach, P. 31; wisse, 159; *pr.* 1 *s.* 78; OE. wissian.

wite, *n* blame, 735; OE. wīte.

wyte[t]h, *imp. pl.* blame, I. 80; wytteth, I. 80; OE. wītan.

with, at the hands of, from, 1750; in the case of, III. 288.

withynne, *prep.* w. hymself, by his own resources, 1415; *first ex. in* O.E.D., 1518.

witholde, *pp.* supported, 528.

without, *prep.* outside, III. 238.

withseye, *pr.* 1 *s.* oppose, 245.

witt, wisdom, P. 69, III. 286; witte, 301; *pl.* wittes, understanding, 553.

witte, *inf.* know, II. 55; wyttyn,

The manufacturer's authorised representative in the EU for product
safety is Oxford University Press España S.A. of El Parque Empresarial
San Fernando de Henares, Avenida de Castilla, 2 - 28830 Madrid
(www.oup.es/en or product.safety@oup.com). OUP España S.A. also acts
as importer into Spain of products made by the manufacturer.
Printed and bound by CPI Group (UK) Ltd, Croydon, CR0 4YY
05/05/2026
02102998-0003